DATE DUE

MY 12 '98	JY 1 6 '99		
OC 27 '98	JE ~ 7 '10		
NO 13 '98	DE 1 '10		
	DE 1 2 '11		
AP 8 '99			
OC 15 '99			
MR 1 4 '00			
AG 7 '00			
JE 1 7 '02			
NO 2 0 '02			
OC 21			
MR 27 '04			
MY 31 '05			
JE 7 '06			
FE 1 '08			
OC 13 '08			

DEMCO 38-296

SIMPLIFY, SIMPLIFY

SIMPLIFY, SIMPLIFY

And Other Quotations from
HENRY DAVID THOREAU

K. P. Van Anglen

Columbia University Press
New York

Columbia University Press

Publishers since 1893

New York   Chichester, West Sussex

Copyright © 1996 Columbia University Press

ata

enry David Thoreau /

1. Thoreau, Henry David, 1817–1862—Quotations. 2. Quotations,
American. I. Van Anglen, Kevin P. II. Title.

PS3042.V3 1996

818'.302–dc20   95–47962

⊗

Casebound editions of Columbia University Press books are printed on
permanent and durable acid-free paper.

Printed in the United States of America

c 10 9 8 7 6 5 4 3 2 1

CONTENTS

$\mathcal{A}$CKNOWLEDGMENTS

I want first of all to thank Dr. Elizabeth Hall Witherell, Editor-in-Chief of the Princeton Edition of *The Writings of Henry D. Thoreau*, for her help in the early planning of this collection. I am also indebted to Professors James Engell, Alan Heimert, John Hildebidle, William L. Howarth, John Mahoney, Joel Myerson, and Joel Porte for their advice and continuing interest; to the staffs of the Widener and Child Memorial Libraries at Harvard University, and the O'Neill Library at Boston College for their courtesy and professionalism; to Dr. Stephen Szaraz for the provision of research material; and to the administration of Pope John XXIII National Seminary for its support. I am grateful as well to my editor and copy editor at Columbia University Press, James Raimes and Ivan Farkas, without whose hard work and patience I could never have completed this volume. Finally, among my many debts of a more personal nature, let me mention two. The first is to my parents, whose love and encouragement mean so much. They remain my best teachers. The second is to Professor Sarah Mace. If, as Thoreau says, true friends "do not live in harmony merely, . . . but in melody," then ours has been a single line, deep and strong now, for many years. For that I am immensely grateful.

K. P. Van Anglen
Weston, Massachusetts

$\mathcal{A}$ NOTE ON THE TEXT

The contents of this volume form part of a larger body of quotations selected from the writings of Henry David Thoreau for the CD-ROM version of *The Columbia World of Quotations*. They include the most significant quotations found either in the works Thoreau prepared for publication during his lifetime or in his personal correspondence. (The CD-ROM version includes other important quotations from Thoreau's works and letters, as well as quotations from his *Journal*). The source text for both the quotations printed here and those included on the CD-ROM is the most recent complete edition of Thoreau's works: *The Writings of Henry David Thoreau* (Boston and New York: Houghton Mifflin Company, 1906). Where necessary, obvious printer's errors in the Houghton Mifflin edition have been silently corrected (when possible, in consultation with the still unfinished Princeton University Press edition of *The Writings of Henry D. Thoreau*). In addition, unless they were clearly intended by Thoreau to help convey substantive meaning, peculiarities of spelling, punctuation, capitalization, etc., in the Houghton Mifflin edition have been silently regularized to conform to modern American publishing practice. No attempt has been made to annotate the quotations, unless doing so was necessary in order to make them comprehensible for the reader.

Introduction

Henry David Thoreau (1817–1862) is one of the most frequently quoted American authors. His best-known work, *Walden* (1854), alone contains scores of passages that have become famous. Even on individual subjects (like that of how life ought to be lived), it yields such familiar citations as the warning that we must "simplify, simplify" in order to live with integrity (p. 159); the rueful observation that "the mass of men lead lives of quiet desperation" (p. 97); and Thoreau's declaration that "if a man does not keep pace with his companions, perhaps it is because he hears a different drummer. Let him step to the music which he hears, however measured or far away" (p. 85). The same is true of Thoreau's other writings and correspondence. Whether it be his impassioned comparison, in "A Plea for Captain John Brown" (1859), of Brown's execution for leading the slave revolt at Harper's Ferry to the crucifixion of Christ; or his revision in "Civil Disobedience" (1849) of the old maxim that "that government is best which governs least," to "that government is best which governs not at all" (p. 71), his sharply pointed views on politics, society, and individual rights have become well known to generations of English-speaking readers, from nineteenth-century English Fabians and Mahatma Gandhi to Martin Luther King, Jr., and the antiwar activists of the 1960s. Similarly, for well over a century nature lovers, environmentalists, and ordinary concerned citizens have looked both to longer works such as *Walden*, *The Maine Woods* (1864), and *Cape Cod* (1855–1865), and to the shorter natural history essays in order to cite Thoreau's observations on nature, and humanity's relationship to nature, in support of causes ranging from the foundation of the National Parks system to the ecology movement. Even Thoreau's less well-known writings and correspondence have yielded passages now familiar to many: like his 1850 letter (pp. 67–8) recounting the death of the American Transcendentalist and feminist, Margaret Fuller (a chilling description of shipwreck and drowning that has inspired—and sometimes enraged—writers from Nathaniel Hawthorne to the present).

Thoreau has become so much a part of the consciousness of the English-speaking peoples largely because of who he was, what he believed, and how he wrote. For one thing, he possessed an extraordinary breadth of intellectual interests, a characteristic that allowed him to speak to a broad spectrum of readers on a variety of issues. In strictly literary terms alone, for example, Thoreau's range was unusual (even in comparison with such well-read contemporaries as Fuller, Emerson, and Melville). A student at Harvard of Latin, Greek, French, Italian, and German, in later life he continued to read widely in all these languages, easily becoming the most distinguished Transcendentalist critic and translator of the Classics, and an able interpreter of modern European literature as well. The evidence of this engagement is obvious in his quotations, which contain frequent allusions to or citations of classical and modern European texts, alongside perceptive commentaries on authors such as Homer, Æschylus, Virgil, Dante, and Goethe. Similarly, Thoreau had a lifelong interest in English literature that manifested itself not only in early essays on John Milton and Thomas Carlyle (and in an abortive attempt in the early 1840s to create his own anthology of English poetry), but also in the allusive and learned quality of his writings. The quotations gathered together in this volume represent this rich literary texture; for in them Thoreau insightfully (and quotably) engaged the whole English literary tradition, from Chaucer and Shakespeare to such nineteenth-century figures as Wordsworth, Coleridge, and Sir Walter Scott. In much the same way, his razor-sharp comments on American contemporaries like Emerson, Fuller, Hawthorne, and Whitman are of an equally high quality, and have proven just as interesting to students of American literature.

More recently, Thoreau's writings have become popular because they also reflect his study of non-Western literatures and cultures. Indeed, in the decade and a half after his 1837 graduation from Harvard, he arguably became the most appreciative American scholar of his day of Asian religions and literatures: publishing articles about, translating excerpts from, and commenting upon Confucius, Menu, Buddha, and the Sanskrit scriptures. At the same time, because of his personal need for a more contemplative spirituality, he came to have religious attitudes and employ meditational techniques akin to those found in Hinduism and Zen Buddhism. When combined with his extraordinary range of reading in travel literature and his often devastating comments on Christianity—most famously in the "Sunday" Chapter of his first book, *A Week on the Concord and Merrimack Rivers* (1849)—his interest in Asia has given Thoreau a unique influence on the history and growth of alternative religions in America.

As this suggests, Thoreau has proven immensely influential as a philosopher and religious thinker as well. This is in part because of the content of his philosophical thought, and the fact that it intersects so much with his thinking on nature. For in reacting against the rationalism and empiricism of the eighteenth century, Thoreau (like many another romantic writer) sought to restore a sense of unity and of the spiritual to the universe. He found a philosophy that seemed to do both these things in the Transcendentalism of his older Concord neighbor, Ralph Waldo Emerson, since Emerson (in the idealist tradition of Plato, Kant, and Coleridge) believed (as their fellow Transcendentalist, George Ripley, put it) "in an order of truths which transcends the sphere of the external sense," and "in the supremacy of mind over matter." By his mid-twenties, therefore, Thoreau affirmed the existence of an order of reality known not passively by means of empirical experience, but actively by means of the intuitive faculty within the consciousness that Kant called "Reason." He also believed that this faculty was the source (in Orestes Brownson's words) both of "all our ideas of the Absolute, the Supersensible, and all the internal facts which are purely intellectual, . . . and which cannot be derived through sensation from external nature;" and of our insight into the unity of things in their spiritual dimension: of the world as One when seen from the Transcendental angle of vision.

This philosophical position—which defends an essentially religious and monistic view of reality in the face of the dualism, skepticism, materialism, and atheism to which empiricism seemed (after Hume) to lead—informs many of Thoreau's best-known descriptions of nature, including several of the most famous passages in *Walden* (e.g., his measurement of the height and depth and breadth of the Pond; p. 183). It is also the chief source of his immense influence on succeeding generations. For inspired by his Transcendentalism, his nature writing—whether it be his descriptions of individual species like the fox in "Natural History of Massachusetts" (1842) or the loon in *Walden* (pp. 64 and 99–100, respectively); his accounts of specific activities (like going huckleberrying); or the more famous descriptions of Walden itself—is a passionate, personal declaration of faith in the regenerative powers of nature on the human soul. And so, to readers ever since, the Thoreau who lived at Walden and "sauntered" across the landscape, seeing the natural world as a place of renewal (a sacred ground whereupon, as in both *Walden* and *A Week*, we may reverse Adam's Fall and return to Eden), has been a writer who expresses their own belief in a nature resonant with spiritual and mythic potential. (Not to mention their faith that, by living such a life as he led, in touch with nature, one may come into contact with a higher power and "Higher Laws").

Yet beginning in at least the early 1840s, Thoreau also differed with his fellow Transcendentalists in his insistence on attending first to the phenomena of the material world known through sense experience, before then moving on to Reason's intuitions of what Emerson called "the Over-soul." This is why even so Transcendentalist a passage as the "Railway Cut" episode in the "Spring" chapter of *Walden* (in which the veil of the empirical is rent, and Thoreau is transported back to the moment of Creation in Eden, which he realizes is present before him too, here and now, in Concord), dwells at length first on the gritty but beautiful pattern and flow—the physical sight—of the sand as it is heated by the sun, and flows down the railway embankment at the start of the natural year (pp. 145–6). Later, after he had reflected in *The Maine Woods* on his experience atop Mount Ktaadn of the alienness and lack of spirit in material nature (pp. 90–2), his writings took on a more empirical, scientific, and descriptive cast. It is no exaggeration to say, in fact, that after about 1850, Thoreau began to lose hope in the possibility of knowing the Transcendental through nature directly. He took refuge instead in a new, more empirically orientated attitude toward the natural world, one that he hoped at least would help him explore the nature of his existence in the world as a conscious but material being, both different and yet unseparated from the rest of creation.

As one might expect, this loss of faith in romantic nature has not (until recently) proven as popular with readers as Thoreau's earlier Transcendentalism. But it does help explain the different tenor of the last ten or twelve years of his life, a period during which he gradually ceased seeking "the Spirit itself which resides in the wood" (p. 64), and turned instead toward extensive scientific collecting for Louis Aggasiz at Harvard; the composition of *The Maine Woods, Cape Cod*, the highly empirical volumes of his later *Journal*, and his only recently published study of "Fruits and Seeds"; and reading Darwin. Moreover, this later (in many respects, both original and intellectually courageous) mode of thought has not been entirely without distinguished admirers: including poets like William Carlos Williams (who invoked this side of Thoreau in *Paterson*); and philosophers, from William James in the nineteenth century (who along with the other Harvard Pragmatists represents the next stage in New England's retreat from Transcendentalism) to Stanley Cavell today (for whom Thoreau is a philosophical predecessor of such twentieth-century giants as Martin Heidegger).

Certainly few doubt the courage (intellectual or otherwise), deep spiritual commitment, and high seriousness of Thoreau's political and social writings, particularly in the years after Walden. Indeed, these characteristics are among the chief reasons why his reputation during the twentieth century as a moral and social critic has been so high. To be sure, as readers of his quotations will quickly note, much of what he has to say about human destiny and human nature; independence, conformity, and self-reliance; integrity, morality, and truthfulness; and human relationships (from friendship and hostility to love, marriage, and sex) is, of course, of inherent interest too. Likewise, he is also worth reading for his views *per se* about human institutions and activities, including armies, courts, jails, and schools; war, trade, and farming. But the thing that gives these opinions much of their currency is the fact that in them one finds the same passionate high-mindedness and love of truth, the same hope for the achievement of human regeneration through contact with "Higher Laws," as in his meditations on nature.

This is all the more true because, even when Thoreau began to question his faith in the Transcendentalist vision of nature, he never lost his belief in the redemptive quality of a life lived with integrity and independence. If anything, in fact, his trust in such a life grew all the stronger during the 1840s and 1850s, as he confronted the main evils of his day: slavery, industrialization, dehumanization, and greed. In the face of increasing doubt and opposition, on these and more specific political, moral, and social topics (like the Mexican-American War, the Compromise of 1850 and the Fugitive Slave Act, capitalism and economic depression, factories, prejudice, and immigration), he increasingly drew upon his New England heritage of resistance to tyranny to speak with the spiritual force and certainty of an Old Testament prophet or a seventeenth-century puritan preacher—yet one who always emphasized the primacy of individual moral insight.

One sign of this full commitment of his very self to the cause of truth is the way Thoreau (like Gandhi and Martin Luther King, Jr., later on) struggled with questions of political morality and his own personal responsibility as the Civil War approached. In the early stages of his coming to terms with the "darkness visible" of *antebellum* America, in "Civil Disobedience" (1849) and "Slavery in Massachusetts" (1854), he was merely antinomian: merely a defender of the individual's right (and his own right) to deny society's claims of authority passively in the name of adherence to "Higher Laws." Later, though, as he came to feel the evils of his day (especially slavery) more strongly, and to work against them more actively, Thoreau's stance changed; now, as in his orations on behalf of John Brown, he felt the need for more militant, even bloody action in order to assert the right in a civilization gone wrong. And so, once more drawing on his puritan heritage, Thoreau made Brown into a saviour and a general—Christ and Oliver Cromwell combined (pp. 14–7)—a hero who claimed (as Thoreau himself claims by the tone of his rhetoric) not the right to dissent, but the right to do and to command.

These qualities of integrity and personal engagement also help explain the persistent interest in Henry David Thoreau as a local writer as well. Here, too, readers have frequently felt drawn to his sketches of friends and acquaintances, events in local history, specific facts, or locations along the way on account of their intrinsic merit as descriptions. In particular, the way he fully realizes the person, thing, or scene before him, yet connects it to the deeper moral or spiritual issues it evokes has made this aspect of his writing popular. (Prominent examples among the quotations gathered in this volume include his many comments on Alex Therien and Joe Polis, his Indian guides in Maine; the Hannah Dustan and Lovewell's Fight incidents in *A Week*; and—not always to his credit—his passages about women, Irish immigrants, and charitable institutions). Yet readers have also frequently found these descriptions interesting because of Thoreau's palpable presence, his commitment of his self to them in both their specific and general dimensions. Whether it be as local historian and yet historian-general to the universe, student of human nature but Concord neighbor and friend, or enemy of capitalism (though manager of a pencil-factory), here as in his nature writing, typically it is the whole Thoreau we get: all of him, in full intellectual action, whatever his mood or purpose. This should not be surprising, for, in this way, Thoreau's prose merely reflects his ever-popular Transcendentalist beliefs in two ways. First, by linking the particular to the universal, Thoreau simply seeks to reproduce that deeper identity found in nature— open to inspection by Reason—between multeity and unity: the individual with its type, and the type with the "Over-soul" (the source of all individuals and types). Second, the fact that he does this even in some of his briefest quotations suggests that Thoreau implicitly lays claim to possession of what Coleridge called the imagination's "esemplastic" power (its ability to uncover moments of disclosure in which the One makes its presence felt amidst the flow of the many). Indeed, as a presence fully engaged in the scenes and persons before him, he becomes the link by which the many relate to the One. This role marks him as a "Poet" in the Emersonian sense: one who can connect the quotidian with the eternal; the fate of a fugitive slave and the moral destiny of a nation; a single Maine Indian with universal human nature and history; the flow of wet sand to the act of Creation; huckleberries with heaven. And so, like the Christ of Christian theology, Thoreau's prose arrestingly proclaims that he is "very God and very man," eternal and now, transcendent and incarnate—an embodiment of the Transcendentalist view both of the nature of reality and the literary vocation.

The Transcendentalism that informs Thoreau's prose helps explain some of the popularity of his works in other ways as well. For instance, on the broadest scale his writings rather famously fail to achieve what the New England Transcendentalists (in common with many other romantics) called "organic form" (i.e., an aesthetic structure that parallels nature's own unity). One token of this is the clumsy, digressive organization of his longer works, which are only loosely held together by artificial cyclical or linear tropes (like "the week" it supposedly took the Thoreau brothers to travel up the Concord and Merrimack Rivers or "the year" into which Thoreau fits his two years' sojourn at Walden). Yet such is not the case with Thoreau's prose at the level of the sentence or the phrase (or even sometimes the paragraph). On the contrary, at that level—the length of a typical quotation—he is something of master of organic form. Not only (as we have seen) does he generally successfully mirror nature by linking the specific to the universal through the mediating presence of his committed self, he also strives for—and often attains—both a density of utterance and an esemplastic ability to bridge polarities that bespeak the operations of a Transcendentalist soul "at white heat."

While this may not be entirely evident in some of his later, less "Transcendentalist" works (like *Cape Cod* or "Fruits and Seeds"), the result elsewhere is a prose that little resembles the fairly formal, balanced, neo-classical, rationally persuasive rhetoric still largely taught at Harvard in Thoreau's day. It is, instead, a style that tries to be true to the strictest standards of description, yet being either aphoristic or prophetic in its forceful concision and insightful compression. For by such a style, Thoreau deliberately betokens his adherence to the Transcendentalist belief that the Poet (whether sage, prophet, or man-of-letters) speaks with gnomic or scriptural voice when in access to truth. Even the quotations found on a single page of *Walden* illustrates the degree to which Thoreau (an author fascinated with the oracles, prophecies, and "ethnical scriptures" of many nations) had committed himself to this view (and so strove to create maxims and aphorisms): "Old deeds for old people, and new deeds for new" (p. 123); and "One may almost doubt if the wisest man has learned anything of absolute value by living" (p. 97). Similarly, Thoreau's passages on John Brown and slavery illustrate his tendency to take up the Poet's prophetic mantle and manifest "true pulpit power" with Jeremiah-like scorn for the evils of his day.

Allied to Thoreau's aphorism and scripturalism is his esemplastic striving after paradox, irony, and the unification of opposites (what the rhetoricians call *discordia concors*), something that also helps explain his quotable impact on English-speaking readers. Wherever this impulse manifests itself, it helps Thoreau claim to have fulfilled the Transcendentalist writer's chief commission: to unite the many to the One, thereby opening up a higher truth. In one place, it may help him reveal the spiritual bankruptcy of modern life (and of an America divided sectionally over slavery) in the ironically disjunctive connection of technological means to social ends ("We are in great haste to construct a magnetic telegraph from Maine to Texas; but Maine and Texas, it may be, have nothing important to communicate;" see p. 39); in another, it may uncomfortably aid his connection of the individual to Higher Laws by paradoxically pointing to the essential evil—deeper even than that of the wars they fight—behind all armies ("It is impossible to give the soldier a good education without making him a deserter. His natural foe is the government that drills him;" p. 163). And most ironic of all, in the series of quotations that emerge from the description of the shipwreck early in *Cape Cod* it may even enable Thoreau to bridge the seemingly discordant dualisms he found there (of land and sea, nature and civilization, life and death, hope and despair, light and darkness, discovery and ignorance, Old World and New, earliest discoverer and latest immigrant) in one grand, liminal expression of authorial despair at the possibility of ever again achieving just such an esemplastic imaginative link between the flotsam and jetsam tossed out of the shipwreck of life, and the One that binds them (and us) all.

Indeed, as all this may suggest, Thoreau's quotations as a whole have weight in our culture precisely because they emanate in manner and matter from a life fully and thoughtfully lived in engagement with its experience, yet in the hope of something more. Though he was born in Concord, Massachusetts, in an America only just emerging from the old, natural, premodern, village world, Henry David Thoreau speaks to us today through his quotations because his life reflects our own challenges, hopes, and experience as late moderns increasingly bewildered by the fracturing pace of change. Whether as naturalist or literary critic, abolitionist or observer of human folly, philosopher or captain of a huckleberry party, he reminds us that the antidote to displacement is to travel far in Concord, and the answer to disunity is ever to fix one's sights on the economy of truth. In London or Los Angeles, Boston or even Bombay, now as then, the advice exemplified by his life and contained in his writings remains startlingly relevant still: to understand the complexities of our existence, merely "Simplify, simplify."

SOURCES

EDITIONS:

The Writings of Henry David Thoreau. 12 Volumes. Boston and New York: Houghton Mifflin, 1906. The most recent and complete edition of Thoreau's collected works.

The Writings of Henry D. Thoreau. Princeton: Princeton University Press, 1971 - . The following volumes in this ongoing scholarly edition have been published: *Walden,* ed. J. Lyndon Shanley (1971); *The Maine Woods,* ed. Joseph J. Moldenhauer (1972); *Reform Papers,* ed. Wendell Glick (1973); *Early Essays and Miscellanies,* ed. Joseph J. Moldenhauer et al. (1975); *A Week on the Concord and Merrimack Rivers,* ed. Carl F. Hovde et al. (1980); *Translations,* ed. K. P. Van Anglen (1986); *Cape Cod,* ed. Joseph J. Molden-hauer (1988); and 5 volumes (to date) of the *Journal,* gen. eds. John C. Broderick and Robert Sattelmeyer (1981 -).

Faith in a Seed: The Dispersion of Seeds and Other Late Natural History Writings, ed. Bradley P. Dean. Washington, D.C. and Covelo, CA: Island Press / Shearwater Books, 1993. Publishes the extensive "Fruits and Seeds" writings of Thoreau's last years for the first time.

BIOGRAPHIES:

Borst, Raymond R. *A Thoreau Log: A Documentary Life of Henry David Thoreau, 1817–1862.* New York: G. K. Hall, 1992. An invaluable resource for serious students of Thoreau's life.

Canby, Henry Seidel. *Thoreau.* Boston: Houghton Mifflin, 1939. A still useful and readable older life of the author.

Harding, Walter. *The Days of Henry Thoreau.* Revised Edition. Princeton: Princeton University Press, 1992. Perhaps the best introduction to Thoreau's life and work.

Lebeaux, Richard. *Thoreau's Seasons.* Amherst: University of Massachusetts Press, 1984. Along with the next-named volume, the second part of an ongoing psychobiography of Thoreau.

–. *Young Man Thoreau.* Amherst: University of Massachusetts Press, 1977. The first volume in Lebeaux's psychobiography.

Richardson, Robert D., Jr. *Henry David Thoreau: A Life of the Mind.* Berkeley: University of California Press, 1986. An impressive intellectual biography focusing on Thoreau's reading and its impact on his writing and thought.

Schneider, Richard J. *Henry David Thoreau*. Boston: Twayne, 1987. A good short biography aimed at the general reader.

REFERENCE WORKS:

Harding, Walter and Michael Meyer. *A New Thoreau Handbook*. New York: New York University Press, 1980. A summary of Thoreau's life and works and the scholarship they have attracted.

Myerson, Joel, ed. *The Cambridge Companion to Henry David Thoreau*. Cambridge, England: Cambridge University Press, 1995. A guide to the author's life, thought, works, and later influence by a panel of distinguished Thoreau scholars.

Sattelmeyer, Robert. Thoreau's Reading: *A Study in Intellectual History, with a Bibliographical Catalogue*. Princeton: Princeton University Press, 1988. A bibliography of Thoreau's reading and sources, with a good introduction.

CRITICISM:

Adams, Stephen and Donald Ross, Jr. *Revising Mythologies: The Composition of Thoreau's Major Works*. Charlottesville: University of Virginia, 1988. Particularly helpful in understanding Thoreau's intellectual habits as a writer.

Buell, Lawrence. *Literary Transcendentalism: Style and Vision in the American Renaissance*. Ithaca: Cornell University Press, 1973. An excellent general literary and historical treatment of the New England Transcendentalists, including Thoreau.

–. *New England Literary Culture: From Revolution through Renaissance*. Cambridge, England: Cambridge University Press, 1986. An account of late eighteenth and early nineteenth-century New England literature, with several important chapters dealing with Thoreau.

–. *The Environmental Imagination: Thoreau, Nature Writing, and the Formation of American Culture*. Cambridge, MA: Harvard University Press, 1995. Discusses Thoreau and American nature writing, ecology, publishing history, and natural science: both as to how he influenced them, and as to how his own reception and reputation have been shaped by these and other cultural forces.

Cavell, Stanley. *The Senses of Walden*. Expanded Edition. San Francisco: North Point Press, 1981. A difficult but important philosophical and linguistic reading of Walden, to which the author has added related essays on Ralph Waldo Emerson.

Christie, John Aldrich. *Thoreau as World Traveler*. New York: Columbia University Press, 1955. A comprehensive study of Thoreau's reading in works of geography, exploration, and travel; especially relevant to his interest in non-western cultures.

Christy, Arthur. *The Orient in American Transcendentalism: A Study of Emerson, Thoreau, and Alcott*. New York: Columbia University Press, 1932. For many years the standard account of Thoreau and the religions and literatures of the East.

Fink, Steven. *Prophet in the Marketplace: Thoreau's Development as a Professional Writer*. Princeton: Princeton University Press, 1992. Drawing in part on the research of the Princeton Thoreau Edition and earlier scholars, this volume impressively details Thoreau's career as a writer in the context of the antebellum literary marketplace.

Garber, Frederick. *Thoreau's Fable of Inscribing*. Princeton: Princeton University Press, 1991. An analysis of Thoreau as a writer on and observer of nature from a twentieth-century philosophical perspective. Particularly important with regard to works like The Maine Woods and the Journal.

—. *Thoreau's Redemptive Imagination*. New York: New York University Press, 1977. A good account of Thoreau as a romantic writer.

Hildebidle, John. Thoreau: *A Naturalist's Liberty*. Cambridge, MA: Harvard University Press, 1983. A fine treatment of Thoreau as a scientist ad natural historian in comparison with figures like Charles Darwin.

Howarth, William L. *The Book of Concord: Thoreau's Life as a Writer*. New York: Viking, 1982. A readable and intelligent account of Thoreau both as public author and as keeper of a journal.

Krutch, Joseph Wood. *Henry David Thoreau*. New York: William Sloane, 1948. A famous appreciation of Thoreau by a fellow naturalist.

Matthiessen, F. O. *American Renaissance: Art and Expression in the Age of Emerson and Whitman*. New York: Oxford University Press, 1941. The now classic study of Thoreau and the other authors of antebellum New York and New England.

McIntosh, James. *Thoreau as Romantic Naturalist: His Shifting Stance Toward Nature*. Ithaca: Cornell University Press, 1974. A good treatment of Thoreau as romantic observer of nature.

Meyer, Michael. *Several More Lives to Live: Thoreau's Political Reputation in America*. Westport, CT: Greenwood, 1977. As its title indicates, a study of Thoreau's influence on American politics from his own day to the 1960's.

Neufeldt, Leonard N. *The Economist: Henry Thoreau and Enterprise*. New York: Oxford University Press, 1989. A persuasive treatment of labor, economy, and related themes central to Walden in particular.

Paul, Sherman. *The Shores of America: Thoreau's Inward Exploration.* Urbana: University of Illinois Press, 1958. Still the best general literary critical survey of Thoreau's life and art.

Peck, H. Daniel. *Thoreau's Morning Work: Memory and Perception in "A Week on the Concord and Merrimack Rivers," the "Journal," and "Walden."* New Haven: Yale University Press, 1990. An instructive comparison of 'Thoreau's published writings and his Journal.

Porte, Joel. *Emerson and Thoreau: Transcendentalists in Conflict.* Middletown: Wesleyan University Press, 1965. The Thoreau half of this book ably characterizes his life long philosophical struggle to reconcile idealism and empiricism.

Sayre, Robert F. *Thoreau and the American Indian.* Princeton: Princeton University Press, 1977. Although some of its readings of specific Thoreau texts are dubious, this is the best account to date of Thoreau's interest in and involvement with Native Americans.

Seybold, Ethel. *Thoreau: The Quest and the Classics.* New Haven: Yale University Press, 1951. An excellent survey of Thoreau's interest in the writers of classical antiquity; see also the introduction to the Translations volume in the Princeton Edition.

Shanley, J. Lyndon, *The Making of "Walden."* Chicago: University of Chicago Press, 1957. Though somewhat out of date, still the basic study of the composition history of Thoreau's most famous book.

Stoller, Leo. *After "Walden": Thoreau's Changing Views on Economic Man.* Stanford: Stanford University Press, 1957. The first treatment of Thoreau's later years.

Versluis, Arthur. *American Transcendentalism and Asian Religions.* New York: Oxford University Press, 1993. Effectively updates Christy's account of Thoreau's interest in Asia and Asian beliefs.

$\mathcal{A}$CTION

Let him see that he does only what belongs to himself and to the hour.

"Civil Disobedience," originally published as "Resistance to Civil Government" (1849), in *The Writings of Henry David Thoreau*, vol. 4, p. 381, Houghton Mifflin (1906).

See also MORALITY

We must heap up a great pile of doing, for a small diameter of being.

Letter, December 19, 1853, to Harrison Blake, in *The Writings of Henry David Thoreau*, vol. 6, p. 221, Houghton Mifflin (1906).

See also EXISTENCE

From exertion come wisdom and purity; from sloth ignorance and sensuality.

Walden (1854), in *The Writings of Henry David Thoreau*, vol. 2, p. 244, Houghton Mifflin (1906).

See also WISDOM

To act collectively is according to the spirit of our institutions.

Walden (1854), in *The Writings of Henry David Thoreau*, vol. 2, p. 122, Houghton Mifflin (1906).

See also INDEPENDENCE

$\mathcal{A}$FRICAN-AMERICANS

The Ethiopian cannot change his skin nor the leopard his spots.

Letter, November 14, 1847, to Ralph Waldo Emerson, in *The Writings of Henry David Thoreau*, vol. 6, p. 140, Houghton Mifflin (1906).

$\mathcal{A}$LCOTT, *AMOS BRONSON*

He has no venture in the present.

Walden (1854), in *The Writings of Henry David Thoreau,* vol. 2, p. 296, Houghton Mifflin (1906).

He is perhaps the sanest man and has the fewest crotchets of any I chance to know; the same yesterday and to-morrow. Of yore we had sauntered and talked, and effectually put the world behind us; for he was pledged to no institution in it, freeborn, *ingenuus.* Whichever way we turned, it seemed that the heavens and the earth had met together, since he enhanced the beauty of the landscape. A blue-robed man, whose fittest roof is the overarching sky which reflects his serenity. I do not see how he can ever die; Nature cannot spare him.

Walden (1854), in *The Writings of Henry David Thoreau,* vol. 2, pp. 296–297, Houghton Mifflin (1906).

I think that he must be the man of the most faith of any alive.

Walden (1854), in *The Writings of Henry David Thoreau,* vol. 2, p. 296, Houghton Mifflin (1906).

$\mathcal{A}$MBITION

The heavens are as deep as our aspirations are high.

Letter, May 2, 1848, to Harrison Blake, in *The Writings of Henry David Thoreau,* vol. 6, p. 166, Houghton Mifflin (1906).

$\mathcal{A}$MERICA AND AMERICANS

I am reminded by my journey how exceedingly new this country still is. You have only to travel for a few days into the interior and back parts even of many of the old States, to come to that very America which the Northmen, and Cabot, and Gosnold, and Smith, and Raleigh visited.

"Ktaadn" (1848) in *The Maine Woods* (1864), in *The Writings of Henry David Thoreau,* vol. 3, p. 90, Houghton Mifflin (1906).

See also RALEIGH, SIR WALTER

If Columbus was the first to discover the islands, Americus Vespucius and Cabot, and the Puritans, and we their descendants, have discovered only the shores of America.

"Ktaadn" (1848) in *The Maine Woods* (1864), in *The Writings of Henry David Thoreau*, vol. 3, p. 90, Houghton Mifflin (1906).

See also COLUMBUS, CHRISTOPHER

We have advanced by leaps to the Pacific, and left many a lesser Oregon and California unexplored behind us.

"Ktaadn" (1848) in *The Maine Woods* (1864), in *The Writings of Henry David Thoreau*, vol. 3, p. 91, Houghton Mifflin (1906).

There is something strangely modern about him. He is very easily turned into English.

A Week on the Concord and Merrimack Rivers (1849), in *The Writings of Henry David Thoreau*, vol. 1, p. 239, Houghton Mifflin (1906).

Along with his contemporaries, Thoreau mistook a much later Hellenistic collection known as the *Anacreontea* for the poetry of Anacreon.

$\mathcal{A}$NTS

One day when I went out to my wood-pile, or rather my pile of stumps, I observed two large ants, the one red, the other much larger, nearly half an inch long, and black, fiercely contending with one another. Having once got hold they never let go, but struggled and wrestled and rolled on the chips incessantly. Looking farther, I was surprised to find that the chips were covered with such combatants, that it was not a *duellum*, but a *bellum*, a war between two races of ants, the red always pitted against the black, and frequently two red ones to one black. The legions of these Myrmidons covered all the hills and vales in my wood-yard, and the ground was already strewn with the dead and dying, both red and black. It was the only battle which I have ever witnessed, the only battle-field I ever trod while the battle was raging. . . . On every side they were engaged in deadly combat, yet without any noise that I could hear, and human soldiers never fought so resolutely.

Walden (1854), in *The Writings of Henry David Thoreau*, vol. 2, pp. 253–254, Houghton Mifflin (1906).

See also WAR

$\mathcal{A}$PPLES AND APPLE TREES

Apples, these I mean, unspeakably fair,—apples not of Discord, but of Concord!

"Wild Apples" (1862), in *The Writings of Henry David Thoreau*, vol. 5, p. 314, Houghton Mifflin (1906).

Thoreau here alludes to the Judgment of Paris in Greek mythology and its consequences, in the process making a pun on the name of his native town.

Here on this rugged and woody hillside has grown an apple tree, not planted by man, no relic of a former orchard, but a natural growth, like the pines and oaks. Most fruits which we prize and use depend entirely on our care. . . . But the apple emulates man's independence and enterprise. It is not simply carried, as I have said, but, like him, to some extent, it has migrated to this New World, and is even, here and there, making its way amid the aboriginal trees; just as the ox and dog and horse sometimes run wild and maintain themselves. Even the sourest and crabbedest apple, growing in the most unfavorable position, suggests such thoughts as these, it is so noble a fruit.

"Wild Apples" (1862), in *The Writings of Henry David Thoreau*, vol. 5, pp. 300–301, Houghton Mifflin (1906).

It is remarkable how closely the history of the apple tree is connected with that of man.

"Wild Apples" (1862), in *The Writings of Henry David Thoreau*, vol. 5, p. 290, Houghton Mifflin (1906).

See also EVOLUTION

Nevertheless, *our* wild apple is wild only like myself, perchance, who belong not to the aboriginal race here, but have strayed into the woods from the cultivated stock. Wilder still, as I have said, there grows elsewhere in this country a native and aboriginal crab-apple, *Malus coronaria*, "whose nature has not yet been modified by cultivation." . . . But though these are indigenous, like the Indians, I doubt whether they are any hardier than those backwoodsmen among the apple trees, which, though descended from cultivated stocks, plant themselves in distant fields and forests, where the soil is favorable to them. I know of no trees which have more difficulties to contend with, and which more sturdily resist their foes. These are the ones whose story we have to tell.

"Wild Apples" (1862), in *The Writings of Henry David Thoreau*, vol. 5, pp. 301–303, Houghton Mifflin (1906).

See also WILDNESS

The apple tree has been celebrated by the Hebrews, Greeks, Romans, and Scandinavians. Some have thought that the first human pair were tempted by its fruit. Goddesses are fabled to have contended for it, dragons were set to watch it, and heroes were employed to pluck it.

"Wild Apples" (1862), in *The Writings of Henry David Thoreau*, vol. 5, p. 291, Houghton Mifflin (1906). See also MYTHOLOGY

The cultivated apple tree was first introduced into this country by the earliest settlers, and is thought to do as well or better here than anywhere else. Probably some of the varieties which are now cultivated were first introduced into Britain by the Romans. Pliny, adopting the distinction of Theophrastus, says, "Of trees there are some which are altogether wild (*sylvestres*), some more civilized (*urbaniores*)." Theophrastus includes the apple among the last; and, indeed, it is in this sense the most civilized of all trees. It is as harmless as a dove, as beautiful as a rose, and as valuable as flocks and herds. It has been longer cultivated than any other, and so is more humanized; and who knows but, like the dog, it will at length be no longer traceable to its wild original? It migrates with man, like the dog and horse and cow: first, perchance, from Greece to Italy, thence to England, thence to America; and our Western emigrant is still marching steadily toward the setting sun with the seeds of the apple in his pocket, or perhaps a few young trees strapped to his load. . . . For when man migrates, he carries with him not only his birds, quadrupeds, insects, vegetables, and his very sward, but his orchard also.

"Wild Apples" (1862), in *The Writings of Henry David Thoreau*, vol. 5, pp. 292–293, Houghton Mifflin (1906).

Thoreau here draws on the contemporary belief in a historical *translatio imperii* ("transfer of empire") and *translatio studii* ("transfer of the arts") from the Old World to the New.

The era of the Wild Apple will soon be past. It is a fruit which will probably become extinct in New England. . . . Since the temperance reform and the general introduction of grafted fruit, no native apple trees, such as I see everywhere in deserted pastures, and where the woods have grown up around them, are set out. I fear that he who walks over these fields a century hence will not know the pleasure of knocking off wild apples. Ah, poor man, there are many pleasures which he will not know! . . . Now that they have grafted trees, and pay a price for them, they collect them into a play by their houses, and fence them in,—and the end of it all will be that we shall be compelled to look for our apples in a barrel.

"Wild Apples" (1862), in *The Writings of Henry David Thoreau*, vol. 5, p. 321, Houghton Mifflin (1906).

Thoreau follows this lament with a long biblical quotation from the prophet Joel, thus denoting that this, the final passage in "Wild Apples," is a jeremiad-like denunciation of the decline of New England.

See also PROGRESS

$\mathcal{A}$RCHITECTURE

The sight of one of these frontier houses, built of these great logs, whose inhabitants have unflinchingly maintained their ground many summers and winters in the wilderness, reminds me of famous forts, like Ticonderoga or Crown Point, which have sustained memorable sieges.

"Chesuncook" (1858) in *The Maine Woods* (1864), in *The Writings of Henry David Thoreau*, vol. 3, p. 144, Houghton Mifflin (1906).

See also NATURE VERSUS CIVILIZATION

Where the citizen uses a mere sliver or board, the pioneer uses the whole trunk of a tree.

"Chesuncook" (1858) in *The Maine Woods* (1864), in *The Writings of Henry David Thoreau*, vol. 3, p. 139, Houghton Mifflin (1906).

Thoreau refers to a log cabin in the Maine woods.

See also PIONEERS

$\mathcal{A}$RT

The material was pure, and his art was pure; how could the result be other than wonderful?

Walden (1854), in *The Writings of Henry David Thoreau*, vol. 2, p. 360, Houghton Mifflin (1906).

See also "THE ARTIST OF KOUROO"

"THE ARTIST OF KOUROO"

There was an artist in the city of Kouroo who was disposed to strive after perfection. One day it came into his mind to make a staff. Having considered that in an imperfect work time is an ingredient, but into a perfect work time does not enter, he said to himself, It shall be perfect in all respects, though I should do nothing else in my life.

Walden (1854), in *The Writings of Henry David Thoreau*, vol. 2, p. 359, Houghton Mifflin (1906).

AUTHORS

A modern author would have died in infancy in a ruder age.

A Week on the Concord and Merrimack Rivers (1849), in *The Writings of Henry David Thoreau*, vol. 1, p. 402, Houghton Mifflin (1906).

AUTOBIOGRAPHY

I should not talk so much about myself if there were anybody else whom I knew as well.

Walden (1854), in *The Writings of Henry David Thoreau*, vol. 2, p. 4, Houghton Mifflin (1906).

In most books, the *I*, or first person, is omitted; in this it will be retained; that, in respect to egotism, is the main difference.

Walden (1854), in *The Writings of Henry David Thoreau*, vol. 2, p. 3, Houghton Mifflin (1906).

See also WALDEN, WRITING OF

We commonly do not remember that it is, after all, always the first person that is speaking.

Walden (1854), in *The Writings of Henry David Thoreau*, vol. 2, pp. 3–4, Houghton Mifflin (1906).

$\mathcal{A}$UTUMN

Most persons visit the seaside in warm weather, when fogs are frequent, and the atmosphere is wont to be thick, and the charm of the sea is to some extent lost. But I suspect that the fall is the best season, for then the atmosphere is more transparent, and it is a greater pleasure to look out over the sea. The clear and bracing air, and the storms of autumn and winter even, are necessary in order that we may get the impression which the sea is calculated to make. In October, when the weather is not intolerably cold, and the landscape wears its autumnal tints, such as, methinks, only a Cape Cod landscape ever wears, especially if you have a storm during your stay,—that I am convinced is the best time to visit this shore.

Cape Cod (1855–1865), in *The Writings of Henry David Thoreau*, vol. 4, p. 272, Houghton Mifflin (1906).

See also CAPE COD, LANDSCAPE OF

$\mathcal{B}$EACHGRASS

In Dwight's "Travels in New England" it is stated that the inhabitants of Truro were formerly regularly warned under the authority of law in the month of April yearly, to plant beach-grass, as elsewhere they are warned to repair the highways. . . . In this way, for instance, they built up again that part of the Cape between Truro and Provincetown where the sea broke over in the last century. . . . Thus Cape Cod is anchored to the heavens, as it were, by a myriad little cables of beach-grass, and, if they should fail, would become a total wreck, and ere long go to the bottom.

Cape Cod (1855–1865), in *The Writings of Henry David Thoreau*, vol. 4, pp. 207–209, Houghton Mifflin (1906).

See also CAPE COD, LANDSCAPE OF

$\mathcal{B}$EANS

I was determined to know beans.

Walden (1854), in *The Writings of Henry David Thoreau*, vol. 2, p. 178, Houghton Mifflin (1906).

Mine was, as it were, the connecting link between wild and cultivated fields; as some states are civilized, and others half-civilized, and others savage or barbarous, so my field was, though not in a bad sense, a half-cultivated field. They were beans cheerfully returning to their wild and primitive state that I cultivated, and my hoe played the *Ranz des Vaches* for them.

Walden (1854), in *The Writings of Henry David Thoreau*, vol. 2, p. 174, Houghton Mifflin (1906).

See also GARDENS AND GARDENING

*B*EDS

As it was cold, I collected quite a pile of wood and lay down on a board against the side of the building, not having any blanket to cover me, with my head to the fire, that I might look after it, which is not the Indian rule. But as it grew colder towards midnight, I at length encased myself completely in boards, managing even to put a board on top of me, with a large stone on it, to keep it down, and so slept comfortably. I was reminded, it is true, of the Irish children, who inquired what their neighbors did who had no door to put over them in winter nights as they had; but I am convinced that there was nothing very strange in the inquiry. Those who have never tried it can have no idea how far a door, which keeps the single blanket down, may go toward making one comfortable.

A Week on the Concord and Merrimack Rivers (1849), in *The Writings of Henry David Thoreau*, vol. 1, p. 196, Houghton Mifflin (1906).

*B*ERMUDA

The Bermudas are said to have been discovered by a Spanish ship of that name which was wrecked on them. . . . Yet at the very first planting of them with some sixty persons, in 1612, the first governor, the same year, "built and laid the foundation of eight or nine forts." To be ready, one would say, to entertain the first ship's company that should be *next* shipwrecked on to them.

Cape Cod (1855–1865), in *The Writings of Henry David Thoreau*, vol. 4, p. 266, Houghton Mifflin (1906).

BIBLE, THE

It is remarkable that, notwithstanding the universal favor with which the New Testament is outwardly received, and even the bigotry with which it is defended, there is no hospitality shown to, there is no appreciation of, the order of truth with which it deals. I know of no book that has so few readers. There is none so truly strange, and heretical, and unpopular. To Christians, no less than Greeks and Jews, it is foolishness and a stumbling-block.

A Week on the Concord and Merrimack Rivers (1849), in The Writings of Henry David Thoreau, vol. 1, p. 73, Houghton Mifflin (1906).

There are, indeed, severe things in it which no man should read aloud more than once. "Seek first the kingdom of heaven." "Lay not up for yourselves treasures on earth." "If thou wilt be perfect, go and sell what thou hast, and give to the poor, and thou shalt have treasure in heaven." "For what is a man profited, if he shall gain the whole world, and lose his own soul? Or what shall a man give in exchange for his soul?" Think of this, Yankees! "Verily, I say unto you, if ye have faith as a grain of mustard seed, ye shall say unto this mountain, Remove hence to yonder place, and it shall remove; and nothing shall be impossible to you." Think of re-peating these things to a New England audience! thirdly, fourthly, fif-teenthly, till there are three barrels of sermons! who, without cant, can read them aloud? Who, without cant, can hear them, and not go out of the meeting-house? They never *were* read, they never *were* heard. Let but one of these sentences be rightly read, from any pulpit in the land, and there would not be left one stone of that meeting-house upon another.

A Week on the Concord and Merrimack Rivers (1849), in The Writings of Henry David Thoreau, vol. 1, pp. 73–74, Houghton Mifflin (1906).

BILLERICA, MASSACHUSETTS

When we were opposite to the middle of Billerica, the fields on either hand had a soft and cultivated English aspect, the village spire being seen over the copses which skirt the river, and sometimes an orchard straggled down to the water-side, though, generally, our course this forenoon was the wildest part of our voyage. It seemed that men led a quiet and very civil life there. The inhabitants were plainly cultivators of the earth, and lived under an organized political government. The schoolhouse stood with a meek aspect, entreating a long truce to war and savage life.

A Week on the Concord and Merrimack Rivers (1849), in The Writings of Henry David Thoreau, vol. 1, pp. 53–54, Houghton Mifflin (1906).

See also FARMERS AND FARMING

BIOGRAPHY

The fact which interests us most is the life of the naturalist. The purest science is still biographical.

A Week on the Concord and Merrimack Rivers (1849), in The Writings of Henry David Thoreau, vol. 1, p. 387, Houghton Mifflin (1906).

See also SCIENTISTS AND SCIENCE

BIRDS

Sitting in that dusky wilderness, under that dark mountain, by the bright river which was full of reflected light, still I heard the wood thrush sing, as if no higher civilization could be attained. By this time the night was upon us.

"The Allegash and East Branch" (1864) in The Maine Woods (1864), in The Writings of Henry David Thoreau, vol. 3, pp. 302–303, Houghton Mifflin (1906).

See also WILDERNESS

BITTERNS

As we shoved away from this rocky coast, before sunrise, the smaller bittern, the genius of the shore, was moping along its edge, or stood probing the mud for its food, with ever an eye on us, though so demurely at work, or else he ran along over the wet stones like a wrecker in his storm-coat, looking out for wrecks of snails and cockles. Now away he goes, with a limping flight, uncertain where he will alight, until a rod of clear sand amid the alders invites his feet; and now our steady approach compels him to seek a new retreat. It is a bird of the oldest Thalesian school, and no doubt believes in the priority of water to the other elements; the relic of a twilight antediluvian age which yet inhabits these bright American waters with us Yankees. There is something venerable in this melancholy and contemplative race of birds, which may have trodden the earth while it was yet in a slimy and imperfect state. Perchance their tracks, too, are still visible on the stones.

A Week on the Concord and Merrimack Rivers (1849), in The Writings of Henry David Thoreau, vol. 1, pp. 249–250, Houghton Mifflin (1906).

One wonders if, by its patient study by rocks and sandy capes, it has wrested the whole of her secret from Nature yet. What a rich experience it must have gained, standing on one leg and looking out from its dull eye so long on sunshine and rain, moon and stars! What could it tell of stagnant pools and reeds and dank night-fogs! It would be worth the while to look closely into the eye which has been open and seeing at such hours, and in such solitudes its dull, yellowish, greenish eye. Methinks my own soul must be a bright invisible green.

A Week on the Concord and Merrimack Rivers (1849), in The Writings of Henry David Thoreau, vol. 1, p. 250, Houghton Mifflin (1906).

Blessings

Truly, our greatest blessings are very cheap.

"Thomas Carlyle and His Works" (1847), in The Writings of Henry David Thoreau, vol. 4, p. 355, Houghton Mifflin (1906).

See also CARLYLE, THOMAS

Boatmen

The news spread like wildfire among us youths, when formerly, once in a year or two, one of these boats came up the Concord River, and was seen stealing mysteriously through the meadows and past the village. It came and departed as silently as a cloud, without noise or dust, and was witnessed by few. One summer day this huge traveler might be seen moored at some meadow's wharf, and another summer day it was not there. Where precisely it came from, or who these men were who knew the rocks and soundings better than we who bathed there, we could never tell. We knew some river's bay only, but they took rivers from end to end.

They were a sort of fabulous rivermen to us. It was inconceivable by what sort of mediation any mere landsman could hold communication with them. Would they heave to, to gratify his wishes? No, it was favor enough to know faintly of their destination, or the time of their possible return.

A Week on the Concord and Merrimack Rivers (1849), in The Writings of Henry David Thoreau, vol. 1, pp. 222–223, Houghton Mifflin (1906).

See also SHIPS AND BOATS

BODY, THE

I stand in awe of my body, this matter to which I am bound has become so strange to me. I fear not spirits, ghosts, of which I am one,—that my body might,—but I fear bodies, I tremble to meet them. What is this Titan that has possession of me? Talk of mysteries! Think of our life in nature,— daily to be shown matter, to come in contact with it,—rocks, trees, wind on our cheeks! the solid earth! the actual world! the common sense! Contact! Contact! Who are we? where are we?

"Ktaadn" (1848) in The Maine Woods (1864), in The Writings of Henry David Thoreau, vol. 3, pp. 78–79, Houghton Mifflin (1906).

See also EXISTENCE

BOOKS

Books can only reveal us to ourselves, and as often as they do us this service we lay them aside.

Letter, April 26, 1857, to B.B. Wiley, in The Writings of Henry David Thoreau, vol. 6, pp. 300–301, Houghton Mifflin (1906).

See also KNOWLEDGE

It is remarkable, but on the whole, perhaps, not to be lamented, that the world is so unkind to a new book. Any distinguished traveler who comes to our shores is likely to get more dinners and speeches of welcome than he can well dispose of, but the best books, if noticed at all, meet with coldness and suspicion, or, what is worse, gratuitous, off-hand criticism.

"Thomas Carlyle and His Works" (1847), in The Writings of Henry David Thoreau, vol. 4, p. 321, Houghton Mifflin (1906).

See also CRITICISM, LITERARY

Books are the treasured wealth of the world and the fit inheritance of generations and nations.

Walden (1854), in *The Writings of Henry David Thoreau*, vol. 2, p. 114, Houghton Mifflin (1906).

It is not all books that are as dull as their readers.

Walden (1854), in *The Writings of Henry David Thoreau*, vol. 2, p. 119, Houghton Mifflin (1906).

See also READING

The book exists for us, perchance, which will explain our miracles and reveal new ones.

Walden (1854), in *The Writings of Henry David Thoreau*, vol. 2, p. 120, Houghton Mifflin (1906).

At least let us have healthy books.

A Week on the Concord and Merrimack Rivers (1849), in *The Writings of Henry David Thoreau*, vol. 1, p. 101, Houghton Mifflin (1906).

*B*RAVERY

Everywhere "good men" sound a retreat, and the word has gone forth to fall back on innocence. Fall forward rather on to whatever there is there.

A Week on the Concord and Merrimack Rivers (1849), in *The Writings of Henry David Thoreau*, vol. 1, p. 78, Houghton Mifflin (1906).

See also PROGRESS

We have need to be as sturdy pioneers still as Miles Standish, or Church, or Lovewell. We are to follow on another trail, it is true, but one as convenient for ambushes. What if the Indians are exterminated, are not savages as grim prowling about the clearings today?

A Week on the Concord and Merrimack Rivers (1849), in *The Writings of Henry David Thoreau*, vol. 1, p. 124, Houghton Mifflin (1906).

See also INTEGRITY

*B*ROWN, *JOHN*

Editors persevered for a good while in saying that Brown was crazy; but at last they said only that it was "a crazy scheme," and the only evidence brought to prove it was that it cost him his life. I have no doubt that if he had gone with five thousand men, liberated a thousand slaves, killed a hundred or two slaveholders, and had as many more killed on his own side, but not lost his own life, these same editors would have called it by a more respectable name. Yet he has been far more successful than that. He has liberated many thousands of slaves, both North and South. They seem to have known nothing about living or dying for a principle. They all called him crazy then; who calls him crazy now?

"The Last Days of John Brown" (1860), in *The Writings of Henry David Thoreau*, vol. 4, pp. 445–446, Houghton Mifflin (1906).

See also HEROES AND HEROISM

Of all the men who were said to be my contemporaries, it seemed to me that John Brown was the only one who *had not died.*

"The Last Days of John Brown" (1860), in *The Writings of Henry David Thoreau*, vol. 4, p. 449, Houghton Mifflin (1906).

See also DEATH

We soon saw, as he saw, that he was not to be pardoned or rescued by men. That would have been to disarm him, to restore to him a material weapon, a Sharp's rifle, when he had taken up the sword of the spirit,— the sword with which he has really won his greatest and most memorable victories. Now he has not laid aside the sword of the spirit, for he is pure spirit himself, and his sword is pure spirit also.

"The Last Days of John Brown" (1860), in *The Writings of Henry David Thoreau*, vol. 4, pp. 448–449, Houghton Mifflin (1906).

A man of rare common sense and directness of speech, as of action; a transcendentalist above all, a man of ideas and principles,—that was what distinguished him.

"A Plea for Captain John Brown" (1859), in *The Writings of Henry David Thoreau*, vol. 4, p. 413, Houghton Mifflin (1906).

See also TRANSCENDENTALISM

He could not have been tried by a jury of his peers, because his peers did not exist.

"A Plea for Captain John Brown" (1859), in *The Writings of Henry David Thoreau*, vol. 4, p. 425, Houghton Mifflin (1906).

He did not go to the college called Harvard, good old Alma Mater as she is. He was not fed on the pap that is there furnished. . . . But he went to the great university of the West, where he sedulously pursued the study of Liberty, for which he had early betrayed a fondness, and having taken many degrees, he finally commenced the public practice of Humanity in Kansas, as you all know. Such were his *humanities,* and not any study of grammar. He would have left a Greek accent slanting the wrong way, and righted up a falling man.

"A Plea for Captain John Brown" (1859), in *The Writings of Henry David Thoreau,* vol. 4, p. 411, Houghton Mifflin (1906).

See also LIBERTY

He was one of that class of whom we hear a great deal, but, for the most part, see nothing at all,—the Puritans. It would be in vain to kill him. He died lately in the time of Cromwell, but he reappeared here. Why should he not? Some of the Puritan stock are said to have come over and settled in New England. They were a class that did something else than celebrate their forefathers' day, and eat parched corn in remembrance of that time. They were neither Democrats nor Republicans, but men of simple habits, straightforward, prayerful; not thinking much of rulers who did not fear God, not making many compromises, nor seeking after available candidates.

"A Plea for Captain John Brown" (1859), in *The Writings of Henry David Thoreau,* vol. 4, p. 412, Houghton Mifflin (1906).

I am here to plead his cause with you. I plead not for his life, but for his character,—his immortal life; and so it becomes your cause wholly, and is not his in the least. Some eighteen hundred years ago Christ was crucified; this morning, perchance, Captain Brown was hung. These are two ends of a chain which is not without its links. He is not Old Brown any longer; he is an angel of light.

I see now that it was necessary that the bravest and humanest man in all the country should be hung. Perhaps he saw it himself. I *almost fear* that I may yet hear of his deliverance, doubting if a prolonged life, if *any* life, can do as much good as his death.

"Misguided!" "Garrulous!" "Insane!" "Vindictive!" So ye write in your easy-chairs, and thus he wounded responds from the floor of the armory, clear as a cloudless sky, true as the voice of nature is: "No man sent me here; it was my own prompting and that of my Maker. I acknowledge no master in human form."

"A Plea for Captain John Brown" (1859), in *The Writings of Henry David Thoreau,* vol. 4, pp. 438–439, Houghton Mifflin (1906).

See also HARPER'S FERRY, WEST VIRGINIA, JOHN BROWN'S RAID

I should say that he was an old-fashioned man in his respect for the Constitution, and his faith in the permanence of this Union. Slavery he deemed to be wholly opposed to these, and he was its determined foe.

"A Plea for Captain John Brown" (1859), in *The Writings of Henry David Thoreau*, vol. 4, pp. 410–411, Houghton Mifflin (1906).

See also SLAVERY

No man in America has ever stood up so persistently and effectively for the dignity of human nature, knowing himself for a man, and the equal of any and all governments. In that sense he was the most American of us all.

"A Plea for Captain John Brown" (1859), in *The Writings of Henry David Thoreau*, vol. 4, p. 425, Houghton Mifflin (1906).

See also INDEPENDENCE

Think of him,—of his rare qualities!—such a man as it takes ages to make, and ages to understand; no mock hero, nor the representative of any party. A man such as the sun may not rise upon again in this benighted land. To whose making went the costliest material, the finest adamant; sent to be the redeemer of those in captivity; and the only use to which you can put him is to hang him at the end of a rope! You who pretend to care for Christ crucified, consider what you are about to do to him who offered himself to be the saviour of four millions of men.

"A Plea for Captain John Brown" (1859), in *The Writings of Henry David Thoreau*, vol. 4, p. 437, Houghton Mifflin (1906).

See also HEROES AND HEROISM

When some one remarked that, with the addition of a chaplain, it would have been a perfect Cromwellian troop, he observed that he would have been glad to add a chaplain to the list, if he could have found one who could fill that office worthily. It is easy enough to find one for the United States Army. I believe that he had prayers in his camp morning and evening, nevertheless.

"A Plea for Captain John Brown" (1859), in *The Writings of Henry David Thoreau*, vol. 4, p. 413, Houghton Mifflin (1906).

Thoreau here refers to John Brown's "company [of abolitionist guerillas] in Kansas."

You don't know your testament when you see it.

"A Plea for Captain John Brown" (1859), in *The Writings of Henry David Thoreau*, vol. 4, p. 439, Houghton Mifflin (1906).

₿UDDHA

I know that some will have hard thoughts of me, when they hear their Christ named beside my Buddha, yet I am sure that I am willing they should love their Christ more than my Buddha, for the love is the main thing, and I like him too.

> *A Week on the Concord and Merrimack Rivers* (1849), in *The Writings of Henry David Thoreau*, vol. 1, p. 68, Houghton Mifflin (1906).
>
> See also JESUS CHRIST

₿UNYAN, JOHN

I think that *Pilgrim's Progress* is the best sermon which has been preached from this text; almost all other sermons that I have heard, or heard of, have been but poor imitations of this.

> *A Week on the Concord and Merrimack Rivers* (1849), in *The Writings of Henry David Thoreau*, vol. 1, p. 72, Houghton Mifflin (1906).
>
> See also BIBLE, THE

CANADA AND CANADIANS

When we returned . . . a Province man was betraying his greenness to the Yankees by his questions. Why Province money won't pass here at par, when States' money is good at Fredericton,—though this, perhaps, was sensible enough. From what I saw then, it appears that the Province man was now the only real Jonathan, or raw country bumpkin, left so far behind by his enterprising neighbors that he did n't know enough to put a question to them. No people can long continue provincial in character who have the propensity for politics and whittling, and rapid traveling, which the Yankees have, and who are leaving the mother country behind in the variety of their notions and inventions. The possession and exercise of practical talent merely are a sure and rapid means of intellectual culture and independence.

"Ktaadn" (1848) in *The Maine Woods* (1864), in *The Writings of Henry David Thoreau*, vol. 3, p. 16, Houghton Mifflin (1906).

Thoreau's use of "Jonathan" is double edged here, as it was under this name, meaning "son of John" (i.e., "John Bull"—England), that the United States was then personified.

I fear that I have not got much to say about Canada, not having seen much; what I got by going to Canada was a cold.

"A Yankee in Canada" (1853), in *The Writings of Henry David Thoreau*, vol. 5, p. 3, Houghton Mifflin (1906).

The soldier here, as everywhere in Canada, appeared to be put forward, and by his best foot. They were in the proportion of the soldiers to the laborers in an African ant-hill. . . . On every prominent ledge you could see England's hands holding the Canadas, and I judged from the redness of her knuckles that she would soon have to let go.

"A Yankee in Canada" (1853), in *The Writings of Henry David Thoreau*, vol. 5, p. 16, Houghton Mifflin (1906).

Thoreau's plural ("the Canadas") refers to the two main provinces of early nineteenth-century British North America: Upper and Lower Canada (roughly, modern-day Ontario and Quebec).

See also COLONIALISM

This universal exhibition in Canada of the tools and sinews of war reminded me of the keeper of a menagerie showing his animals' claws. It was the English leopard showing his claws.

"A Yankee in Canada" (1853), in *The Writings of Henry David Thoreau*, vol. 5, p. 79, Houghton Mifflin (1906).

See also COLONIALISM

Why should Canada, wild and unsettled as it is, impress us as an older country than the States, unless because her institutions are old? All things appeared to contend there, as I have implied, with a certain rust of antiquity, such as forms on old armor and iron guns,—the rust of conventions and formalities. It is said that the metallic roofs of Montreal and Quebec keep sound and bright for forty years in some cases. But if the rust was not on the tinned roofs and spires, it was on the inhabitants and their institutions.

"A Yankee in Canada" (1853), in *The Writings of Henry David Thoreau*, vol. 5, pp. 80–81, Houghton Mifflin (1906).

See also UNITED STATES

CANOES

He had previously complimented me on my paddling, saying that I paddled "just like anybody," giving me an Indian name which meant "great paddler."

"The Allegash and East Branch" (1864) in *The Maine Woods* (1864), in *The Writings of Henry David Thoreau*, vol. 3, p. 325, Houghton Mifflin (1906).

See also POLIS, JOE

CAPE COD

The time must come when this coast will be a place of resort for those New-Englanders who really wish to visit the seaside. At present it is wholly unknown to the fashionable world, and probably it will never be agreeable to them. If it is merely a ten-pin alley, or a circular railway, or an ocean of mint-julep, that the visitor is in search of,—if he thinks more of the wine than the brine, as I suspect some do at Newport,—I trust that for a long time he will be disappointed here. But this shore will never more be more attractive than it is now. Such beaches as are fashionable are here made and unmade in a day, I may almost say, by the sea shifting its sands. Lynn and Nantasket! this bare and bended arm it is that makes the bay in which they lie so snugly. What are springs and waterfalls? Here is the spring of springs, the waterfall of waterfalls. A storm in the fall or winter is the time to visit it; a lighthouse or fisherman's hut, the true hotel. A man may stand there and put all America behind him.

Cape Cod (1855–1865), in *The Writings of Henry David Thoreau*, vol. 4, pp. 272–273, Houghton Mifflin (1906).

We went to see the ocean, and that is probably the best place of all our coast to go to. If you go by water, you may experience what it is to leave and to approach these shores; you may see the stormy petrel by the way, *thalassodroma*, running over the sea, and if the weather is but a little thick, may lose sight of the land in mid-passage. I do not know where there is another beach in the Atlantic States, attached to the mainland, so long, and at the same time so straight, and completely uninterrupted by creeks or coves or fresh-water rivers and marshes.

Cape Cod (1855–1865), in *The Writings of Henry David Thoreau*, vol. 4, pp. 269–270, Houghton Mifflin (1906).

CAPE COD, INHABITANTS OF

So we took leave of Cape Cod and its inhabitants. We liked the manners of the last, what little we saw of them, very much. They were particularly downright and good-humored. The old people appeared remarkably well preserved, as if by the saltness of the atmosphere, and after having once mistaken, we could never be certain whether we were talking to a coeval of our grandparents, or to one of our own age. They are said to be more purely the descendants of the Pilgrims than the inhabitants of any other part of the State. We were told that "sometimes, when the court comes together at Barnstable, they have not a single criminal to try, and the jail is shut up." It was "to let" when we were there. Until quite recently there was no regular lawyer below Orleans. Who, then, will complain of a few regular man-eating sharks along the Back Side?

Cape Cod (1855–1865), in *The Writings of Henry David Thoreau*, vol. 4, pp. 257–258, Houghton Mifflin (1906).

CAPE COD, LANDSCAPE OF

All accounts agree in affirming that this part of the Cape was comparatively well wooded a century ago. But notwithstanding the great changes which have taken place in these respects, I cannot but think that we must make some allowance for the greenness of the Pilgrims in these matters, which caused them to see green. We do not believe that the trees were large or the soil was deep here. Their account may be true particularly, but it is generally false. They saw literally, as well as figuratively, but one side of the Cape.

Cape Cod (1855–1865), in *The Writings of Henry David Thoreau*, vol. 4, pp. 254–255, Houghton Mifflin (1906).

See also PILGRIMS, NEW ENGLAND

Here in Wellfleet, this pure sand plateau, known to sailors as the Tablelands of Eastham, on account of its appearance, as seen from the ocean ... stretched away northward from the southern boundary of the town, without a particle of vegetation,—as level almost as a table,—for two and a half or three miles, or as far as the eye could reach; slightly rising towards the ocean, then stooping to the beach, by as steep a slope as sand could lie on, and as regular as a military engineer could desire. It was like the escarped rampart of a stupendous fortress, whose glacis was the beach, and whose champaign the ocean. From its surface we overlooked the greater part of the Cape. In short, we were traversing a desert, with the view of an autumnal landscape of extraordinary brilliancy, a sort of Promised Land, on the one hand, and the ocean on the other. Yet, though the prospect was so extensive, and the country for the most part destitute of trees, a house was rarely visible,—we never saw one from the beach,— and the solitude was that of the ocean and the desert combined. A thousand men could not have seriously interrupted it, but would have been lost in the vastness of the scenery as their footsteps in the sand.

Cape Cod (1855–1865), in The Writings of Henry David Thoreau, vol. 4, pp. 62–63, Houghton Mifflin (1906).

Notwithstanding the universal barrenness, and the contiguity of the desert, I never saw an autumnal landscape so beautifully painted as this was. It was like the richest rug imaginable spread over an uneven surface; no damask nor velvet, nor Tyrian dye or stuffs, nor the work of any loom, could ever match it. There was the incredibly bright red of the huckleberry, and the reddish brown of the bayberry, mingled with the bright and living green of small pitch pines, and also the duller green of the bayberry, boxberry, and plum, the yellowish green of the shrub oaks, and the various golden and yellow and fawn-colored tints of the birch and maple and aspen, each making its own figure, and, in the midst, the few yellow sand-slides on the sides of the hills looked like the white floor seen through rents in the rug. Coming from the country as I did, and many autumnal woods I had seen, this was perhaps the most novel and remarkable sight that I saw on the Cape. Probably the brightness of the tints was enhanced by contrast with the sand which surrounded this tract.

Cape Cod (1855–1865), in The Writings of Henry David Thoreau, vol. 4, pp. 193–194, Houghton Mifflin (1906).

See also AUTUMN

The houses were few and far between, besides being small and rusty, though they appeared to be kept in good repair, and their door-yards, which were the unfenced Cape, were tidy; or, rather, they looked as if the ground around them was blown clean by the wind. Perhaps the scarcity of wood here, and the consequent absence of the wood-pile and other wooden traps, had something to do with this appearance. They seemed, like mariners ashore, to have sat right down to enjoy the firmness of the land, without studying their postures or habiliments. To them it was merely *terra firma* and *cognita,* not yet *fertilis* and *jucunda.*

Cape Cod (1855–1865), in *The Writings of Henry David Thoreau,* vol. 4, p. 32, Houghton Mifflin (1906).

See also ARCHITECTURE

The single road which runs lengthwise the Cape, now winding over the plain, now through the shrubbery, which scrapes the wheels of the stage, was a mere cart-track in the sand, commonly without any fences to confine it, and continually changing from this side to that, to harder ground, or sometimes to avoid the tide. But the inhabitants travel in waste here and there pilgrim-wise and staff in hand, by narrow foot-paths, through which the sand flows out and reveals the nakedness of the land. We shuddered at the thought of living there and taking our afternoon walks over those barren swells, where we could overlook every step of our walk before taking it, and would have to pray for a fog or a snow-storm to conceal our destiny. The walker there must soon eat his heart.

Cape Cod (1855–1865), in *The Writings of Henry David Thoreau,* vol. 4, pp. 136–137, Houghton Mifflin (1906).

See also WALKING

CAREER, THOREAU'S

My life has been the poem I would have writ,
But I could not both live and utter it.

A Week on the Concord and Merrimack Rivers (1849), in *The Writings of Henry David Thoreau,* vol. 1, p. 365, Houghton Mifflin (1906).

See also POETRY AND POETS

CARLYLE, THOMAS

Every man will include in his list of worthies those whom he himself best represents. Carlyle, and our countryman Emerson, whose place and influence must ere long obtain a more distinct recognition, are, to a certain extent, the complement of each other. The age could not do with one of them, it cannot do with both. To make a broad and rude distinction ... the former, as critic, deals with the men of action ... the latter with the thinkers. . . . The one has more sympathy with the heroes, or practical reformers, the other with the observers, or philosophers. Put their worthies together, and you will have a pretty fair representation of mankind . . . with one or more memorable exceptions.

"Thomas Carlyle and His Works" (1847), in *The Writings of Henry David Thoreau*, vol. 4, p. 345, Houghton Mifflin (1906).

He utters substantial English thoughts in plainest English dialects. . . . Indeed, for fluency and skill in the use of the English tongue, he is a master unrivaled. His felicity and power of expression surpass even his special merits as historian and critic.

"Thomas Carlyle and His Works" (1847), in *The Writings of Henry David Thoreau*, vol. 4, p. 324, Houghton Mifflin (1906).

If Carlyle does not take two steps in philosophy, are there any who take three?

"Thomas Carlyle and His Works" (1847), in *The Writings of Henry David Thoreau*, vol. 4, p. 349, Houghton Mifflin (1906).

This man has something to communicate.

"Thomas Carlyle and His Works" (1847), in *The Writings of Henry David Thoreau*, vol. 4, p. 332, Houghton Mifflin (1906).

What else has been English news for so long a season? What else, of late years, has been England to us,—to us who read books, we mean? . . . Carlyle alone, since the death of Coleridge, has kept the promise of England. It is the best apology for all the bustle and the sin of commerce, that it has made us acquainted with the thoughts of this man.

"Thomas Carlyle and His Works" (1847), in *The Writings of Henry David Thoreau*, vol. 4, p. 320, Houghton Mifflin (1906).

See also ENGLAND AND THE ENGLISH

CATHOLICISM

In the morning, . . . I ran over to the Church of La Bonne Ste. Anne, whose matin bell we had heard, it being Sunday morning. Our book said that this church had "long been an object of interest, from the miraculous cures said to have been wrought on visitors to the shrine." There was a profusion of gilding, and I counted more than twenty-five crutches suspended on the walls, some for grown persons, some for children, which it was to be inferred so many sick had been able to dispense with; but they looked as if they had been made to order by the carpenter who made the church.

"A Yankee in Canada" (1853), in *The Writings of Henry David Thoreau*, vol. 5, p. 51, Houghton Mifflin (1906).

CHANCE

How many things are now at loose ends! Who knows which way the wind will blow tomorrow?

"Paradise (To Be) Regained" (1843), in *The Writings of Henry David Thoreau*, vol. 4, p. 283, Houghton Mifflin (1906).

CHANGE

Things do not change; we change.

Walden (1854), in *The Writings of Henry David Thoreau*, vol. 2, p. 361, Houghton Mifflin (1906).

See also INTEGRITY

CHARACTER

When will the world learn that a million men are of no importance compared with *one* man?

Letter, June 8, 1843, to Ralph Waldo Emerson, in *The Writings of Henry David Thoreau*, vol. 6, pp. 82–83, Houghton Mifflin (1906).

See also HUMAN NATURE

Your richest veins don't lie nearest the surface.

Letter, March 17, 1838, to John Thoreau, in *The Writings of Henry David Thoreau*, vol. 6, p. 20, Houghton Mifflin (1906).

Context suggests that Thoreau's comment is a general one, not one directed specifically at his brother.

We select granite for the underpinning of our houses and barns; we build fences of stone; but we do not ourselves rest on an underpinning of granitic truth, the lowest primitive rock. Our sills are rotten.

"Life Without Principle" (1863), in *The Writings of Henry David Thoreau*, vol. 4, p. 470, Houghton Mifflin (1906).

See also MORALITY

I confess, that practically speaking, when I have learned a man's real disposition, I have no hopes of changing it for the better or worse in this state of existence.

Walden (1854), in *The Writings of Henry David Thoreau*, vol. 2, p. 134, Houghton Mifflin (1906).

See also REFORM AND REFORMERS

We know but few men, a great many coats and breeches.

Walden (1854), in *The Writings of Henry David Thoreau*, vol. 2, p. 24, Houghton Mifflin (1906).

See also CLOTHING

CHASTITY

Chastity is the flowering of man; and what are called Genius, Heroism, Holiness, and the like, are but various fruits which succeed it.

Walden (1854), in *The Writings of Henry David Thoreau*, vol. 2, p. 243, Houghton Mifflin (1906).

CHAUCER, GEOFFREY

Chaucer had eminently the habits of a literary man and a scholar. There were never any times so stirring that there were not to be found some sedentary still. He was surrounded by the din of arms. The battles of Hallidon Hill and Neville's Cross, and the still more memorable battles of Cressy and Poictiers, were fought in his youth; but these did not concern our poet much, Wickliffe and his reform much more. He regarded himself always as one privileged to sit and converse with books. He helped to establish the literary class.

A *Week on the Concord and Merrimack Rivers* (1849), in *The Writings of Henry David Thoreau*, vol. 1, p. 394, Houghton Mifflin (1906).

See also STYLE

Chaucer is fresh and modern still, and no dust settles on his true passages. It lightens along the line, and we are reminded that flowers have bloomed, and birds sung, and hearts beaten in England. Before the earnest gaze of the reader, the rust and moss of time gradually drop off, and the original green life is revealed. He was a homely and domestic man, and did breathe quite as modern men do.

A *Week on the Concord and Merrimack Rivers* (1849), in *The Writings of Henry David Thoreau*, vol. 1, pp. 395–396, Houghton Mifflin (1906).

See also STYLE

Chaucer's remarkably trustful and affectionate character appears in his familiar, yet innocent and reverent, manner of speaking of his God. He comes into his thought without any false reverence, and with no more parade than the zephyr to his ear. . . . There is less love and simple, practical trust in Shakespeare and Milton. How rarely in our English tongue do we find expressed any affection for God! Herbert almost alone expresses it, "Ah, my dear God!"

A *Week on the Concord and Merrimack Rivers* (1849), in *The Writings of Henry David Thoreau*, vol. 1, pp. 398–399, Houghton Mifflin (1906).

Gentleness and delicacy of character are everywhere apparent in his verse. The simplest and humblest words come readily to his lips.

A *Week on the Concord and Merrimack Rivers* (1849), in *The Writings of Henry David Thoreau*, vol. 1, p. 398, Houghton Mifflin (1906).

See also STYLE

His genius does not soar like Milton's, but is genial and familiar. It shows great tenderness and delicacy, but not the heroic sentiment. It is only a greater portion of humanity with all its weakness.

A *Week on the Concord and Merrimack Rivers* (1849), in *The Writings of Henry David Thoreau*, vol. 1, pp. 397–398, Houghton Mifflin (1906).

Such pure and genuine and childlike love of Nature is hardly to be found in any poet.

A *Week on the Concord and Merrimack Rivers* (1849), in *The Writings of Henry David Thoreau*, vol. 1, p. 398, Houghton Mifflin (1906).

See also NATURE

We admire Chaucer for his sturdy English wit. . . . But though it is full of good sense and humanity, it is not transcendent poetry. For picturesque description of persons it is, perhaps, without a parallel in English poetry; yet it is essentially humorous, as the loftiest genius never is.

> *A Week on the Concord and Merrimack Rivers* (1849), in *The Writings of Henry David Thoreau*, vol. 1, p. 397, Houghton Mifflin (1906).

CHRISTIANITY AND CHRISTIANS

It is not every man who can be a Christian, even in a very moderate sense, whatever education you give him. It is a matter of constitution and temperament, after all. He may have to be born again many times. I have known many a man who pretended to be a Christian, in whom it was ridiculous, for he had no genius for it. It is not every man who can be a free man, even.

> "The Last Days of John Brown" (1860), in *The Writings of Henry David Thoreau*, vol. 4, p. 445, Houghton Mifflin (1906).

> See also FREEDOM

If it is not a tragical life we live, then I know not what to call it. Such a story as that of Jesus Christ,—the history of Jerusalem, say, being a part of the Universal History. The naked, the embalmed, unburied death of Jerusalem amid its desolate hills,—think of it. In Tasso's poem I trust some things are sweetly buried. Consider the snappish tenacity with which they preach Christianity still. What are time and space to Christianity, eighteen hundred years, and a new world?—that the humble life of a Jewish peasant should have force to make a New York bishop so bigoted. Forty-four lamps, the gift of kings, now burning in a place called the Holy Sepulchre; a church-bell ringing; some unaffected tears shed by a pilgrim on Mount Calvary within the week.

> *A Week on the Concord and Merrimack Rivers* (1849), in *The Writings of Henry David Thoreau*, vol. 1, pp. 67–68, Houghton Mifflin (1906).

> See also JESUS CHRIST

It is necessary not to be Christian to appreciate the beauty and significance of the life of Christ.

> *A Week on the Concord and Merrimack Rivers* (1849), in *The Writings of Henry David Thoreau*, vol. 1, p. 68, Houghton Mifflin (1906).

> See also JESUS CHRIST

One is sick at heart of this pagoda worship. It is like the beating of gongs in a Hindoo subterranean temple.

A Week on the Concord and Merrimack Rivers (1849), in The Writings of Henry David Thoreau, vol. 1, p. 78, Houghton Mifflin (1906).

One memorable addition to the old mythology is due to this era,—the Christian fable. With what pains, and tears, and blood these centuries have woven this and added it to the mythology of mankind! The new Prometheus. With what miraculous consent, and patience, and persistency has this mythus been stamped on the memory of the race! It would seem as if it were in the progress of our mythology to dethrone Jehovah, and crown Christ in his stead.

A Week on the Concord and Merrimack Rivers (1849), in The Writings of Henry David Thoreau, vol. 1, p. 67, Houghton Mifflin (1906).

See also JESUS CHRIST

The New Testament is an invaluable book, though I confess to having been slightly prejudiced against it in my very early days by the church and the Sabbath-school, so that it seemed, before I read it, to be the yellowest book in the catalogue. Yet I early escaped from their meshes. It is hard to get the commentaries out of one's head and taste its true flavor. . . . It would be a poor story to be prejudiced against the Life of Christ because the book has been edited by Christians. In fact, I love this book rarely, though it is a sort of castle in the air to me, which I am permitted to dream.

A Week on the Concord and Merrimack Rivers (1849), in The Writings of Henry David Thoreau, vol. 1, p. 72, Houghton Mifflin (1906).

See also JESUS CHRIST

CHURCHES

With a single companion, I soon found my way to the church of Notre Dame. . . . The Catholic are the only churches which I have seen worth remembering, which are not almost wholly profane. I do not speak only of the rich and splendid like this, but of the humblest of them as well. Coming from the hurrahing mob and the rattling carriages, we pushed aside the listed door of this church, and found ourselves instantly in an atmosphere which might be sacred to thought and religion, if one had any. There sat one or two women who had stolen a moment from the concerns of the day, as they were passing; but, if there had been fifty people there, it would still have been the most solitary place imaginable. They did not look up at us, nor did one regard another.... I was impressed by the quiet, religious atmosphere of the place. It was a great cave in the midst of a city; and what were the altars and the tinsel but the sparkling stalactites, into which you entered in a moment, and where the still atmosphere and the sombre light disposed to serious and profitable thought? Such a cave at hand, which you can enter any day, is worth a thousand of our churches which are open only Sundays, hardly long enough for an airing, and then filled with a bustling congregation,—a church where the priest is the least part, where you do your own preaching, where the universe preaches to you and can be heard. I am not sure but this Catholic religion would be an admirable one if the priest were quite omitted. I think that I might go to church myself some Monday, if I lived in a city where there was such a one to go to.... As for the Protestant churches, here or elsewhere, they did not interest me, for it is only as caves that churches interest me at all, and in that respect they were inferior.

"A Yankee in Canada" (1853), in *The Writings of Henry David Thoreau*, vol. 5, pp. 12–14, Houghton Mifflin (1906).

See also CATHOLICISM

CITIES AND CITY LIFE

Boston, New York, Philadelphia, Charleston, New Orleans, and the rest, are the names of wharves projecting into the sea (surrounded by the shops and dwellings of the merchants), good places to take in and to discharge a cargo (to land the products of other climes and load the exports of our own). I see a great many barrels and fig-drums,—piles of wood for umbrella-sticks,—blocks of granite and ice,—great heaps of goods, and the means of packing and conveying them,—much wrapping-paper and twine,—many crates and hogsheads and trucks,—and that is Boston. The more barrels, the more Boston. The museums and scientific societies and libraries are accidental. They gather around the sands to save carting.

Cape Cod (1855–1865), in *The Writings of Henry David Thoreau*, vol. 4, p. 268, Houghton Mifflin (1906).

CIVIL DISOBEDIENCE

All men recognize the right of revolution; that is, the right to refuse allegiance to, and to resist, the government, when its tyranny or its inefficiency are great and unendurable. But almost all say that such is not the case now. But such was the case, they think, in the Revolution of '75. If one were to tell me that this was a bad government because it taxed certain foreign commodities brought to its ports, it is most probable that I should not make an ado about it, for I can do without them. All machines have their friction; and possibly this does enough good to counterbalance the evil. At any rate, it is a great evil to make a stir about it. But when the friction comes to have its machine, and oppression and robbery are organized, I say, let us not have such a machine any longer. In other words, when a sixth of the population of a nation which has undertaken to be the refuge of liberty are slaves, and a whole country is unjustly overrun and conquered by a foreign army, and subjected to military law, I think that it is not too soon for honest men to rebel and revolutionize. What makes this duty the more urgent is the fact that the country so overrun is not our own, but ours is the invading army.

"Civil Disobedience," originally published as "Resistance to Civil Government" (1849), in *The Writings of Henry David Thoreau*, vol. 4, pp. 360–361, Houghton Mifflin (1906).

See also SLAVERY

As for adopting the ways which the State has provided for remedying the evil, I know not of such ways. They take too much time, and a man's life will be gone. I have other affairs to attend to. I came into this world, not chiefly to make this a good place to live in, but to live in it, be it good or bad. A man has not everything to do, but something; and because he cannot do *everything*, it is not necessary that he should do *something* wrong. It is not my business to be petitioning the Governor or the Legislature any more than it is theirs to petition me; and if they should not hear my petition, what should I do then? But in this case the State has provided no way: its very Constitution is evil.

"Civil Disobedience," originally published as "Resistance to Civil Government" (1849), in *The Writings of Henry David Thoreau*, vol. 4, p. 368, Houghton Mifflin (1906).

See also LIFE

Can there not be a government in which majorities do not virtually decide right and wrong, but conscience?—in which majorities decide only those questions to which the rule of expediency is applicable? Must the citizen even for a moment, or in the least degree, resign his conscience to the legislator? Why has every man a conscience then? I think that we should be men first, and subjects afterward. It is not desirable to cultivate a respect for the law, so much as for the right. The only obligation which I have a right to assume is to do at any time what I think right.

"Civil Disobedience," originally published as "Resistance to Civil Government" (1849), in *The Writings of Henry David Thoreau*, vol. 4, p. 358, Houghton Mifflin (1906).

See also CONSCIENCE

I do not hesitate to say, that those who call themselves Abolitionists should at once effectually withdraw their support, both in person and property, from the government of Massachusetts, and not wait until they constitute a majority of one, before they suffer the right to prevail through them. I think that it is enough if they have God on their side, without waiting for that other one. Moreover, any man more right than his neighbors constitutes a majority of one already.

"Civil Disobedience," originally published as "Resistance to Civil Government" (1849), in *The Writings of Henry David Thoreau*, vol. 4, p. 369, Houghton Mifflin (1906).

See also GOVERNMENT

I know this well, that if one thousand, if one hundred, if ten men whom I could name,—if ten *honest* men only,—ay, if *one* HONEST man, in this State of Massachusetts, *ceasing to hold slaves*, were actually to withdraw from this copartnership, and be locked up in the county jail therefor, it would be the abolition of slavery in America. For it matters not how small the beginning may seem to be: what is once well done is done forever.

"Civil Disobedience," originally published as "Resistance to Civil Government" (1849), in *The Writings of Henry David Thoreau*, vol. 4, p. 370, Houghton Mifflin (1906).

By "this copartnership" Thoreau means paying taxes.

See also SLAVERY

If the injustice is part of the necessary friction of the machine of government, let it go, let it go: perchance it will wear smooth,—certainly the machine will wear out. If the injustice has a spring, or a pulley, or a rope, or a crank, exclusively for itself, then perhaps you may consider whether the remedy will not be worse than the evil; but if it is of such a nature that it requires you to be the agent of injustice to another, then, I say, break the law. Let your life be a counter-friction to stop the machine. What I have to do is to see, at any rate, that I do not lend myself to the wrong which I condemn.

"Civil Disobedience," originally published as "Resistance to Civil Government" (1849), in *The Writings of Henry David Thoreau,* vol. 4, p. 368, Houghton Mifflin (1906).

See also JUSTICE

Some are petitioning the State to dissolve the Union, to disregard the requisitions of the President. Why do they not dissolve it themselves,—the union between themselves and the State,—and refuse to pay their quota into its treasury? Do not they stand in the same relation to the State that the State does to the Union? And have not the same reasons prevented the State from resisting the Union which have prevented them from resisting the State?

"Civil Disobedience," originally published as "Resistance to Civil Government" (1849), in *The Writings of Henry David Thoreau,* vol. 4, p. 366, Houghton Mifflin (1906).

See also GOVERNMENT

The mass of men serve the state thus, not as men mainly, but as machines, with their bodies. They are the standing army, and the militia, jailers, constables, *posse comitatus,* etc. In most cases there is no free exercise whatever of the judgment or of the moral sense; but they put themselves on a level with wood and earth and stones; and wooden men can perhaps be manufactured that will serve the purpose as well. Such command no more respect than men of straw or a lump of dirt. They have the same sort of worth only as horses and dogs. Yet such as these even are commonly esteemed good citizens. Others—as most legislators, politicians, lawyers, ministers, and office-holders—serve the state chiefly with their heads; and, as they rarely make any moral distinctions, they are as likely to serve the devil, without *intending* it, as God. A very few—as heroes, patriots, martyrs, reformers in the great sense, and *men*—serve the state with their consciences also, and so necessarily resist it for the most part; and are commonly treated as enemies by it.

"Civil Disobedience," originally published as "Resistance to Civil Government" (1849), in *The Writings of Henry David Thoreau,* vol. 4, pp. 359–360, Houghton Mifflin (1906).

See also CONSCIENCE

CIVILIZATION

We here overtook two Italian boys, who had waded thus far down the Cape through the sand, with their organs on their backs, and were going on to Provincetown. What a hard lot, we thought, if the Provincetown people should shut their doors against them! Whose yard would they go to next? Yet we concluded that they had chosen wisely to come here, where other music than that of the surf must be rare. Thus the great civilizer sends out his emissaries, sooner or later, to every sandy cape and lighthouse of the New World which the census-taker visits, and summons the savage there to surrender.

Cape Cod (1855–1865), in *The Writings of Henry David Thoreau,* vol. 4, p. 30, Houghton Mifflin (1906).

See also PROVINCIALISM

The civilized man is a more experienced and wiser savage.

Walden (1854), in *The Writings of Henry David Thoreau,* vol. 2, p. 44, Houghton Mifflin (1906).

While civilization has been improving our houses, it has not equally improved the men who are to inhabit them. It has created palaces, but it was not so easy to create noblemen and kings.

Walden (1854), in *The Writings of Henry David Thoreau,* vol. 2, p. 37, Houghton Mifflin (1906).

See also PROGRESS

CLASSICS, THE

Books must be read as deliberately and reservedly as they were written. It is not enough even to be able to speak the language of that nation by which they are written, for there is a memorable interval between the spoken and the written language, the language heard and the language read. The one is commonly transitory, a sound, a tongue, a dialect merely, almost brutish, and we learn it unconsciously, like the brutes, of our mothers. The other is the maturity and experience of that; if that is our mother tongue, this is our father tongue, a reserved and select expression, too significant to be heard by the ear, which we must be born again in order to speak. The crowds of men who merely *spoke* the Greek and Latin tongues in the Middle Ages were not entitled by the accident of birth to *read* the works of genius written in those languages; for these were not written in that Greek or Latin which they knew, but in the select language of literature. They had not learned the nobler dialects of Greece and Rome, but the very materials on which they were written were waste paper to them, and they prized instead a cheap contemporary literature. But when the several nations of Europe had acquired distinct though rude written languages of their own, sufficient for the purposes of their rising literatures, then first learning revived, and scholars were enabled to discern from that remoteness the treasures of antiquity. What the Roman and Grecian multitude could not *hear,* after the lapse of ages a few scholars *read,* and a few scholars only are still reading it.

Walden (1854), in *The Writings of Henry David Thoreau,* vol. 2, pp. 112–113, Houghton Mifflin (1906).

See also READING

It is worth the expense of youthful days and costly hours, if you learn only some words of an ancient language, which are raised out of the trivialness of the street, to be perpetual suggestions and provocations. It is not in vain that the farmer remembers and repeats the few Latin words which he has heard.

Walden (1854), in *The Writings of Henry David Thoreau,* vol. 2, pp. 111–112, Houghton Mifflin (1906).

Men sometimes speak as if the study of the classics would at length make way for more modern and practical studies; but the adventurous student will always study classics, in whatever language they may be written and however ancient they may be. For what are the classics but the noblest recorded thoughts of man? . . . We might as well omit to study Nature because she is old.

Walden (1854), in *The Writings of Henry David Thoreau,* vol. 2, p. 112, Houghton Mifflin (1906).

The heroic books, even if printed in the character of our mother tongue, will always be in a language dead to degenerate times; and we must laboriously seek the meaning of each word and line, conjecturing a larger sense than common use permits out of what wisdom and valor and generosity we have. The modern cheap and fertile press, with all its translations, has done little to bring us nearer to the heroic writers of antiquity. They seem as solitary, and the letter in which they are printed as rare and curious, as ever.

Walden (1854), in *The Writings of Henry David Thoreau,* vol. 2, p. 111, Houghton Mifflin (1906).

The student may read Homer or Æschylus in the Greek without danger of dissipation or luxuriousness, for it implies that he in some measure emulate their heroes, and consecrate morning hours to their pages.

Walden (1854), in *The Writings of Henry David Thoreau*, vol. 2, p. 111, Houghton Mifflin (1906).

See also HOMER

Those who have not learned to read the ancient classics in the language in which they were written must have a very imperfect knowledge of the history of the human race; for it is remarkable that no transcript of them has ever been made into any modern tongue, unless our civilization itself may be regarded as such a transcript. Homer has never yet been printed in English, nor Æschylus, nor Virgil even,—works as refined, as solidly done, and as beautiful almost as the morning itself; for later writers, say what we will of their genius, have rarely, if ever, equalled the elaborate beauty and finish and the lifelong and heroic literary labors of the ancients. They only talk of forgetting them who never knew them. It will be soon enough to forget them when we have the learning and the genius which will enable us to attend to and appreciate them.

Walden (1854), in *The Writings of Henry David Thoreau*, vol. 2, p. 115, Houghton Mifflin (1906).

See also TRANSLATION

I lately met with an old volume from a London bookshop, containing the Greek Minor Poets, and it was a pleasure to read once more only the words Orpheus, Linus, Musæus,—those faint poetic sounds and echoes of a name, dying away on the ears of us modern men; and those hardly more substantial sounds, Mimnermus, Ibycus, Alcæus, Stesichorus, Menander. They lived not in vain. We can converse with these bodiless fames without reserve or personality.

A Week on the Concord and Merrimack Rivers (1849), in *The Writings of Henry David Thoreau*, vol. 1, p. 238, Houghton Mifflin (1906).

CLERGY

The ecclesiastical history of this town interested us somewhat. It appears that . . . "in 1662, the town agreed that a part of every whale cast on shore be appropriated for the support of the ministry." No doubt there seemed to be some propriety in thus leaving the support of the ministers to Providence, whose servants they are, and who alone rules the storms; for, when few whales were cast up, they might suspect that their worship was not acceptable. The ministers must have sat upon the cliffs in every storm, and watched the shore with anxiety. And, for my part, if I were a minister, I would rather trust to the bowels of the billows, on the back side of Cape Cod, to cast up a whale for me, than to the generosity of many a country parish I know.

Cape Cod (1855–1865), in *The Writings of Henry David Thoreau,* vol. 4, p. 45, Houghton Mifflin (1906).

When you travel to the Celestial City, carry no letter of introduction. When you knock, ask to see God,—none of the servants.

Letter, March 27, 1848, to Harrison Blake, in *The Writings of Henry David Thoreau,* vol. 6, p. 164, Houghton Mifflin (1906).

See also SPIRITUALITY/PRAYER

The sort of morality which the priests inculcate is a very subtle policy, far finer than the politicians', and the world is very successfully ruled by them as the policemen.

A Week on the Concord and Merrimack Rivers (1849), in *The Writings of Henry David Thoreau,* vol. 1, p. 75, Houghton Mifflin (1906).

See also POLITICS AND POLITICIANS

CLOTHING

Every generation laughs at the old fashions, but follows religiously the new.

Walden (1854), in *The Writings of Henry David Thoreau,* vol. 2, p. 28, Houghton Mifflin (1906).

We worship not the Graces, nor the Parcæ, but Fashion. She spins and weaves and cuts with full authority. The head monkey at Paris puts on a traveller's cap, and all the monkeys in America do the same.

Walden (1854), in *The Writings of Henry David Thoreau,* vol. 2, p. 28, Houghton Mifflin (1906).

See also EUROPE VERSUS AMERICA

CLOUDS

As the light increased, I discovered around me an ocean of mist, which by chance reached up exactly to the base of the tower, and shut out every vestige of the earth, while I was left floating on this fragment of the wreck of a world, on my carved plank, in cloudland; a situation which required no aid from the imagination to render it impressive. As the light in the east steadily increased, it revealed to me more clearly the new world into which I had risen in the night, the new *terra firma* perchance of my future life. . . . All around beneath me was spread for a hundred miles on every side, as far as the eye could reach, an undulating country of clouds, answering in the varied swell of its surface to the terrestrial world it veiled. It was such a country as we might see in dreams, with all the delights of paradise.

A Week on the Concord and Merrimack Rivers (1849), in *The Writings of Henry David Thoreau*, vol. 1, pp. 197–198, Houghton Mifflin (1906).

When I consider the clouds stretched in stupendous masses across the sky, frowning with darkness or glowing with downy light, or gilded with the rays of the setting sun, like the battlements of a city in the heavens, their grandeur appears thrown away on the meanness of my employment; the drapery is altogether too rich for such poor acting. I am hardly worthy to be a suburban dweller outside those walls.

A Week on the Concord and Merrimack Rivers (1849), in *The Writings of Henry David Thoreau*, vol. 1, p. 407, Houghton Mifflin (1906).

COLONIALISM

That Cabot merely landed on the uninhabitable shore of Labrador gave the English no just title to New England, or to the United States generally, any more than to Patagonia.

Cape Cod (1855–1865), in *The Writings of Henry David Thoreau*, vol. 4, p. 233, Houghton Mifflin (1906).

COLUMBUS, CHRISTOPHER

Columbus felt the westward tendency more strongly than any before. He obeyed it, and found a New World for Castile and Leon.

"Walking" (1862), in *The Writings of Henry David Thoreau*, vol. 5, pp. 219–220, Houghton Mifflin (1906).

See also AMERICA AND AMERICANS

COMMON SENSE

There is absolutely no common sense; it is common nonsense.

"Paradise (To Be) Regained" (1843), in *The Writings of Henry David Thoreau*, vol. 4, p. 298, Houghton Mifflin (1906).

COMMUNICATION

We are in great haste to construct a magnetic telegraph from Maine to Texas; but Maine and Texas, it may be, have nothing important to communicate.

Walden (1854), in *The Writings of Henry David Thoreau*, vol. 2, p. 58, Houghton Mifflin (1906).

See also PROGRESS

COMPLAINTS

Some would find fault with the morning red, if they ever got up early enough.

Walden (1854), in *The Writings of Henry David Thoreau*, vol. 2, p. 358, Houghton Mifflin (1906).

The fault-finder will find faults even in paradise.

Walden (1854), in *The Writings of Henry David Thoreau*, vol. 2, p. 361, Houghton Mifflin (1906).

CONCORD, MASSACHUSETTS

I have travelled a good deal in Concord; and everywhere, in shops, and offices, and fields, the inhabitants have appeared to me to be doing penance in a thousand remarkable ways. . . . The twelve labors of Hercules were trifling in comparison with those which my neighbors have under-taken; for they were only twelve, and had an end; but I could never see that these men slew or captured any monster or finished any labor.

Walden (1854), *The Writings of Henry David Thoreau*, vol. 2, pp. 4–5, Houghton Mifflin (1906).

See also LABOR

CONCORD RIVER, MASSACHUSETTS

The Musketaquid, or Grass-ground River, though probably as old as the Nile or Euphrates, did not begin to have a place in civilized history until the fame of its grassy meadows and fish attracted settlers out of England in 1635, when it received the other but kindred name of CONCORD from the first plantation on its banks, which appears to have commenced in a spirit of peace and harmony. It will be Grass-ground River as long as grass grows and water runs here; it will be Concord River only while men lead peacable lives on its banks.

A Week on the Concord and Merrimack Rivers (1849), in The Writings of Henry David Thoreau, vol. 1, p. 3, Houghton Mifflin (1906).

See also NAMES

CONFORMITY

The greater number of men are merely corporals.

Cape Cod (1855–1865), in The Writings of Henry David Thoreau, vol. 4, p. 258, Houghton Mifflin (1906).

CONSCIENCE

Every gazette brings accounts of the untutored freaks of the wind,— shipwrecks and hurricanes which the mariner and planter accept as special or general providences; but they touch our consciences, they remind us of our sins. Another deluge would disgrace mankind.

"Paradise (To Be) Regained" (1843), in The Writings of Henry David Thoreau, vol. 4, pp. 282–283, Houghton Mifflin (1906).

I would remind my countrymen that they are to be men first, and Americans only at a late and convenient hour.

"Slavery in Massachusetts" (1854), in The Writings of Henry David Thoreau, vol. 4, p. 401, Houghton Mifflin (1906).

See also PATRIOTISM

It is not worth the while to let our imperfections disturb us always. The conscience really does not, and ought not to monopolize the whole of our lives, any more than the heart or the head. It is as liable to disease as any other part.

A Week on the Concord and Merrimack Rivers (1849), in *The Writings of Henry David Thoreau,* vol. 1, p. 75, Houghton Mifflin (1906).

CONSCIOUSNESS

Not till we are lost, in other words not till we have lost the world, do we begin to find ourselves, and realize where we are and the infinite extent of our relations.

Walden (1854), in *The Writings of Henry David Thoreau,* vol. 2, p. 190, Houghton Mifflin (1906).

See also KNOWLEDGE

The unconsciousness of man is the consciousness of God.

A Week on the Concord and Merrimack Rivers (1849), in *The Writings of Henry David Thoreau,* vol. 1, p. 351, Houghton Mifflin (1906).

See also GOD

CORPORATIONS

It is truly enough said that a corporation has no conscience; but a corporation of conscientious men is a corporation *with* a conscience.

"Civil Disobedience," originally published as "Resistance to Civil Government" (1849), in *The Writings of Henry David Thoreau,* vol. 4, p. 358, Houghton Mifflin (1906).

See also CONSCIENCE

COUNTRY LIFE

What should we think of the shepherd's life if his flocks always wandered to higher pastures than his thoughts?

Walden (1854), in *The Writings of Henry David Thoreau,* vol. 2, p. 98, Houghton Mifflin (1906).

CREEDS

I believe in the forest, and in the meadow, and in the night in which the corn grows.

"Walking" (1862), in *The Writings of Henry David Thoreau*, vol. 5, p. 225, Houghton Mifflin (1906).

See also NATURE

CRIME

We have heard that a few days after this, when the Provincetown Bank was robbed, speedy emissaries from Provincetown made particular inquiries concerning us at this lighthouse. Indeed, they traced us all the way down the Cape, and concluded that we came by this unusual route down the back side and on foot in order that we might discover a way to get off with our booty when we had committed the robbery. The Cape is so long and narrow, and so bare withal, that it is well-nigh impossible for a stranger to visit it without the knowledge of its inhabitants generally, unless he is wrecked on to it in the night. So, when this robbery occurred, all their suspicions seem to have at once centered on us two travelers who had just passed down it. If we had not chanced to leave the Cape so soon, we should probably have been arrested. The real robbers were two young men from Worcester County who traveled with a centre-bit, and are said to have done their work very neatly. But the only bank that we pried into was the great Cape Cod sand-bank, and we robbed it only of an old French crown piece, some shells and pebbles, and the materials of this story.

Cape Cod (1855–1865), in *The Writings of Henry David Thoreau*, vol. 4, pp. 176–177, Houghton Mifflin (1906).

CRITICISM, LITERARY

In this part of the world it is considered a ground for complaint if a man's writings admit of more than one interpretation.

Walden (1854), in *The Writings of Henry David Thoreau*, vol. 2, p. 358, Houghton Mifflin (1906).

See also CONFORMITY

CRUELTY

We slander the hyena; man is the fiercest and cruelest animal.

"Paradise (To Be) Regained" (1843), in *The Writings of Henry David Thoreau*, vol. 4, pp. 283–284, Houghton Mifflin (1906).

See also HUMANITY

CULTURE

It is not part of a true culture to tame tigers, any more than it is to make sheep ferocious.

"Walking" (1862), in *The Writings of Henry David Thoreau*, vol. 5, p. 236, Houghton Mifflin (1906).

DARK, THE

I believe that men are generally still a little afraid of the dark, though the witches are all hung, and Christianity and candles have been introduced.

Walden (1854), in *The Writings of Henry David Thoreau*, vol. 2, p. 145, Houghton Mifflin (1906).

DEATH

It is pleasant to walk over the beds of these fresh, crisp, and rustling leaves. How beautifully they go to their graves! how gently lay themselves down and turn to mould!—painted of a thousand hues, and fit to make the beds of us living. So they troop to their last resting-place, light and frisky. . . . They that soared so loftily, how contentedly they return to dust again, and are laid low, resigned to lie and decay at the foot of the tree, and afford nourishment to new generations of their kind, as well as to flutter on high! They teach us how to die. One wonders if the time will ever come when men, with their boasted faith in immortality, will lie down as gracefully and as ripe,—with such an Indian-summer serenity will shed their bodies, as they do their hair and nails.

"Autumnal Tints" (1862), in *The Writings of Henry David Thoreau*, vol. 5, pp. 269–270, Houghton Mifflin (1906).

See also AUTUMN

On the whole, it was not so impressive a scene as I might have expected. If I had found one body cast upon the beach in some lonely place, it would have affected me more. I sympathized rather with the winds and waves, as if to toss and mangle these poor human bodies was the order of the day. If this was the law of Nature, why waste any time in awe or pity? If the last day were come, we should not think so much about the separation of friends or the blighted prospects of individuals. I saw that corpses might be multiplied, as on the field of battle, till they no longer affected us in any degree as exceptions to the common lot of humanity. Take all the graveyards together, they are always the majority. It is the individual and private that demands our sympathy. A man can attend but one funeral in the course of this life, can behold but one corpse.

Cape Cod (1855–1865), in *The Writings of Henry David Thoreau*, vol. 4, pp. 11–12, Houghton Mifflin (1906).

See also SEA

Once also it was my business to go in search of the relics of a human body, mangled by sharks, which had just been cast up, a week after a wreck, having got the direction from a lighthouse: I should find it a mile or two distant over the sand, a dozen rods from the water, covered with a cloth, by a stick stuck up. I expected that I must look very narrowly to find so small an object, but the sandy beach, half a mile wide, and stretching farther than the eye could reach, was so perfectly smooth and bare, and the mirage toward the sea so magnifying, that when I was half a mile distant the insignificant sliver which marked the spot looked like a bleached spar, and the relics were conspicuous as if they lay in state on that sandy plain, or a generation had labored to pile up their cairn there. Close at hand they were simply some bones with a little flesh adhering to them, in fact only a slight inequality in the sweep of the shore. There was nothing at all remarkable about them, and they were singularly inoffensive both to the senses and the imagination. But as I stood there they grew more and more imposing. They were alone with the beach and the sea, whose hollow roar seemed addressed to them, and I was impressed as if there was an understanding between them and the ocean which necessarily left me out, with my snivelling sympathies. That dead body had taken possession of the shore, and reigned over it as no living one could, in the name of a certain majesty which belonged to it.

> *Cape Cod* (1855–1865), in *The Writings of Henry David Thoreau*, vol. 4, pp. 107–108, Houghton Mifflin (1906).

See also SEA

The mariner who makes the safest port in heaven, perchance, seems to his friends on earth to be shipwrecked, for they deem Boston Harbor the better place; though perhaps, invisible to them, a skillful pilot comes to meet him, and the fairest and balmiest gales blow off that coast, his good ship makes the land in halcyon days, and he kisses the shore in rapture there, while his old hulk tosses in the surf here. It is hard to part with one's body, but, no doubt, it is easy enough to do without it when once it is gone.

> *Cape Cod* (1855–1865), in *The Writings of Henry David Thoreau*, vol. 4, p. 13, Houghton Mifflin (1906).

We've wholly forgotten how to die. But be sure you do die nevertheless. Do your work, and finish it. If you know how to begin, you will know when to end.

> "A Plea for Captain John Brown" (1859), in *The Writings of Henry David Thoreau*, vol. 4, p. 435, Houghton Mifflin (1906).

See also LABOR

*D*ECADENCE

The civilized nations—Greece, Rome, England—have been sustained by the primitive forests which anciently rotted where they stand. They survive as long as the soil is not exhausted. Alas for human culture! little is to be expected of a nation, when the vegetable mould is exhausted, and it is compelled to make manure of the bones of its fathers. There the poet sustains himself merely by his own superfluous fat, and the philosopher comes down on his marrow-bones.

> "Walking" (1862), in *The Writings of Henry David Thoreau*, vol. 5, p. 229, Houghton Mifflin (1906).

See also NATURE

$\mathcal{D}$EEDS

If ever I *did* a man any good ... of course it was something exceptional and insignificant compared with the good or evil which I am constantly doing by being what I am.

Letter, February 27, 1853, to Harrison Blake, in *The Writings of Henry David Thoreau*, vol. 6, p. 212, Houghton Mifflin (1906).

See also MORALITY

$\mathcal{D}$EER

There were none of the small deer up there; they are more common about the settlements. One ran into the city of Bangor two years before, and jumped through a window of costly plate glass, and then into a mirror, where it thought it recognized one of its kind. . . . This the inhabitants speak of as the deer that went a-shopping.

"Chesuncook" (1858) in *The Maine Woods* (1864), in *The Writings of Henry David Thoreau*, vol. 3, p. 154, Houghton Mifflin (1906).

$\mathcal{D}$IET

I am more interested in the rosy cheek than I am to know what particular diet the maiden is fed on.

"Autumnal Tints" (1862), in *The Writings of Henry David Thoreau*, vol. 5, p. 250, Houghton Mifflin (1906).

Once I went so far as to slaughter a woodchuck which ravaged my bean-field,—effect his transmigration, as a Tartar would say,—and devour him, partly for experiment's sake; but though it afforded me a momentary enjoyment, notwithstanding a musky flavor, I saw that the longest use would not make that a good practice, however it might seem to have your woodchucks ready dressed by the village butcher.

Walden (1854), in *The Writings of Henry David Thoreau*, vol. 2, p. 66, Houghton Mifflin (1906).

See also PRIMITIVISM

There is a certain class of unbelievers who sometimes ask me such questions as, if I think that I can live on vegetable food alone; and to strike at the root of the matter at once,—for the root is faith,—I am accustomed to answer such, that I can live on board nails. If they cannot understand that, they cannot understand much that I have to say.

Walden (1854), in *The Writings of Henry David Thoreau,* vol. 2, p. 72, Houghton Mifflin (1906).

See also SIMPLICITY

DISASTER

There are more consequences to a shipwreck than the underwriters notice.

Cape Cod (1855–1865), in *The Writings of Henry David Thoreau,* vol. 4, p. 163, Houghton Mifflin (1906).

DISCOVERY

Do not engage to find things as you think they are.

Letter, August 9, 1850, to Harrison Blake, in *The Writings of Henry David Thoreau,* vol. 6, p. 186, Houghton Mifflin (1906).

See also OPTIMISM

DOGMA

Most people with whom I talk, men and women even of some originality and genius, have their scheme of the universe all cut and dried,—very *dry,* I assure you, to hear, dry enough to burn, dry-rotted and powder-post, methinks,—which they set up between you and them in the shortest intercourse; an ancient and tottering frame with all its boards blown off. They do not walk without their bed. Some, to me, seemingly very unimportant and unsubstantial things and relations are for them everlastingly settled,—as Father, Son, and Holy Ghost, and the like. These are like the everlasting hills to them. But in all my wanderings I never came across the least vestige of authority for these things. They have not left so distinct a trace as the delicate flower of a remote geological period on the coal in my grate.

A Week on the Concord and Merrimack Rivers (1849), in The Writings of Henry David Thoreau, vol. 1, p. 70, Houghton Mifflin (1906).

The wisest man preaches no doctrines; he has no scheme; he sees no rafter, not even a cobweb, against the heavens. It is clear sky.

A Week on the Concord and Merrimack Rivers (1849), in The Writings of Henry David Thoreau, vol. 1, pp. 70–71, Houghton Mifflin (1906).

DREAMS AND DREAMING

If you have built castles in the air, your work need not be lost; that is where they should be. Now put the foundations under them.

Walden (1854), in The Writings of Henry David Thoreau, vol. 2, p. 356, Houghton Mifflin (1906).

Dreams are the touchstones of our characters.

A Week on the Concord and Merrimack Rivers (1849), in The Writings of Henry David Thoreau, vol. 1, p. 315, Houghton Mifflin (1906).

See also CHARACTER

DUSTAN, HANNAH

According to the historian, they escaped as by a miracle all roving bands of Indians, and reached their homes in safety, with their trophies, for which the General Court paid them fifty pounds. The family of Hannah Dustan all assembled alive once more, except the infant whose brains were dashed out against the apple tree, and there have been many who in later time have lived to say that they have eaten of the fruit of that apple tree.

A Week on the Concord and Merrimack Rivers (1849), in The Writings of Henry David Thoreau, vol. 1, p. 345, Houghton Mifflin (1906).

"The Great and General Court" is the official name of the state legislature of the Commonwealth of Massachusetts.

On the thirty-first day of March, one hundred and forty-two years before this, probably about this time in the afternoon, there were hurriedly paddling down this part of the river, between the pine woods which then fringed these banks, two white women and a boy, who had left an island at the mouth of the Contoocook before daybreak. They were lightly clad for the season, in the English fashion, and handled their paddles unskillfully, but with nervous energy and determination, and at the bottom of their canoe lay the still bleeding scalps of ten of the aborigines. They were Hannah Dustan, and her nurse, Mary Neff, . . . and an English boy, named Samuel Lennardson, escaping from captivity among the Indians. On the 15th of March previous, Hannah Dustan had been compelled to rise from childbed, and half dressed, with one foot bare, accompanied by her nurse, commence an uncertain march, in still inclement weather, through the snow and the wilderness. She had seen her seven elder children flee with their father, but knew not of their fate. She had seen her infant's brains dashed out against an apple tree, and had left her own and her neighbors' dwellings in ashes. When she reached the wigwam of her captor, situated on an island in the Merrimack, more than twenty miles above where we now are, she had been told that she and her nurse were soon to be taken to a distant Indian settlement, and there made to run the gauntlet naked. . . . Having determined to attempt her escape, she instructed the boy to inquire of one of the men, how he should dispatch an enemy in the quickest manner, and take his scalp. "Strike 'em there," said he, placing his finger on his temple, and he also showed him how to take off the scalp. On the morning of the 31st she arose before daybreak, and awoke her nurse and the boy, and taking the Indians' tomahawks, they killed them all in their sleep, excepting one favorite boy, and one squaw who fled wounded with him to the woods. The English boy struck the Indian who had given him the information, on the temple, as he had been directed. They then collected all the provision they could find, and took their master's tomahawk and gun, and scuttling all the canoes but one, commenced their flight to Haverhill, distant about sixty miles by the river. But after having proceeded a short distance, fearing that her story would not be believed if she should escape to tell it, they returned to the silent wigwam, and taking off the scalps of the dead, put them into a bag as proofs of what they had done, and then, retracing their steps to the shore in the twilight, recommenced their voyage.

A Week on the Concord and Merrimack Rivers (1849), in The Writings of Henry David Thoreau, vol. 1, pp. 341–343, Houghton Mifflin (1906).

As Thoreau later makes clear, the "apple tree" in this passage signals that this story is a new world replication of the Fall of Adam and Eve.

This seems a long while ago, and yet it happened since Milton wrote his *Paradise Lost*. But its antiquity is not the less great for that, for we do not regulate our historical time by the English standard, nor did the English by the Roman, nor the Roman by the Greek. ... From this September afternoon, and from between these now cultivated shores, those times seemed more remote than the dark ages.

A Week on the Concord and Merrimack Rivers (1849), in The Writings of Henry David Thoreau, vol. 1, p. 345, Houghton Mifflin (1906).

EAST, THE

Ex oriente lux may still be the motto of scholars, for the Western world has not yet derived from the East all the light which it is destined to receive thence.

A Week on the Concord and Merrimack Rivers (1849), in The Writings of Henry David Thoreau, vol. 1, pp. 149–150, Houghton Mifflin (1906).

See also KNOWLEDGE

ECOLOGY

At this rate, we shall all be obliged to let our beards grow at least, if only to hide the nakedness of the land and make a sylvan appearance.

"Chesuncook" (1858) in The Maine Woods (1864), in The Writings of Henry David Thoreau, vol. 3, p. 171, Houghton Mifflin (1906).

Everything may serve a lower as well as a higher use.

"Chesuncook" (1858) in The Maine Woods (1864), in The Writings of Henry David Thoreau, vol. 3, p. 135, Houghton Mifflin (1906).

See also TRANSCENDENTALISM

Salmon, shad, and alewives were formerly abundant here, and taken in weirs by the Indians ... until the dam and afterward the canal at Billerica, and the factories at Lowell, put an end to their migrations hitherward; though it is thought that a few more enterprising shad may still occasionally be seen in this part of the river. ... Perchance, after a few thousands of years, if the fishes will be patient, and pass their summers elsewhere meanwhile, nature will have leveled the Billerica dam, and the Lowell factories, and the Grass-ground River run clear again, to be explored by new migratory shoals.

> *A Week on the Concord and Merrimack Rivers* (1849), in *The Writings of Henry David Thoreau*, vol. 1, p. 32, Houghton Mifflin (1906).

> Thoreau here translates the local Native American name, "Musketaquid" ("Grass-ground River"), for the Concord River.

EDUCATION

We seem to have forgotten that the expression "a *liberal* education" originally meant among the Romans one worthy of *free* men; while the learning of trades and professions by which to get your livelihood merely was considered worthy of *slaves* only. But taking a hint from the word, I would go a step further, and say that it is not the man of wealth and leisure simply, though devoted to art, or science, or literature, who, in a true sense, is *liberally* educated, but only the earnest and *free* man. In a slaveholding country like this, there can be no such thing as a *liberal* education tolerated by the State; and those scholars of Austria and France who, however learned they may be, are contented under their tyrannies have received only a *servile* education.

> "The Last Days of John Brown" (1860), in *The Writings of Henry David Thoreau*, vol. 4, p. 118, Houghton Mifflin (1906).

> See also FREEDOM

Those things for which the most money is demanded are never the things which the student most wants. Tuition, for instance, is an important item in the term bill, while for the far more valuable education which he gets by associating with the most cultivated of his contemporaries no charge is made.

> *Walden* (1854), in *The Writings of Henry David Thoreau*, vol. 2, pp. 55–56, Houghton Mifflin (1906).

> Thoreau here refers specifically to Harvard, his *alma mater.*

> See also HARVARD UNIVERSITY

We boast that we belong to the Nineteenth Century and are making the most rapid strides of any nation. But consider how little this village does for its own culture. I do not wish to flatter my townsmen, nor to be flattered by them, for that will not advance either of us. We need to be provoked,—goaded like oxen, as we are, into a trot. We have a comparatively decent system of common schools, schools for infants only; but excepting the half-starved Lyceum in the winter, and latterly the puny beginning of a library suggested by the State, no school for ourselves. We spend more on almost any article of bodily aliment or ailment than on our mental aliment. It is time that we had uncommon schools, that we did not leave off our education when we begin to be men and women. It is time that villages were universities, and their elder inhabitants the fellows of universities, with leisure—if they are, indeed, so well off—to pursue liberal studies the rest of their lives.

Walden (1854), in *The Writings of Henry David Thoreau*, vol. 2, pp. 120–121, Houghton Mifflin (1906).

See also CONCORD, MASSACHUSETTS

Can there be any greater reproach than an idle learning? Learn to split wood, at least.

A Week on the Concord and Merrimack Rivers (1849), in *The Writings of Henry David Thoreau*, vol. 1, p. 108, Houghton Mifflin (1906).

Emerson, Lidian Jackson

MY DEAR FRIEND,—I believe a good many conversations with you were left in an unfinished state, and now indeed I don't know where to take them up. But I will resume some of the unfinished silence. I shall not hesitate to know you. I think of you as some elder sister of mine, whom I could not have avoided,—a sort of lunar influence,—only of such age as the moon, whose time is measured by her light. You must know that you represent to me woman, for I have not traveled very far or wide,—and what if I had? . . . You have helped to keep my life "on loft," as Chaucer says of Griselda, and in a better sense. You always seemed to look down on me as from some elevation,—some of your high humilities,—and I was the better for having to look up. I felt taxed not to disappoint your expectation; for could there be any accident so sad as to be respected for something better than we are? It was a pleasure even to go away from you, as it is not to meet some, as it apprised me of my high relations; and such a departure is a sort of further introduction and meeting. Nothing makes the earth seem so spacious as to have friends at a distance; they make the latitudes and longitudes.

Letter, May 22, 1843, to Lidian Jackson Emerson, in *The Writings of Henry David Thoreau*, vol. 6, p. 76, Houghton Mifflin (1906).

See also FRIENDS AND FRIENDSHIP

ENGLAND AND THE ENGLISH

I look upon England today as an old gentleman who is travelling with a great deal of baggage, trumpery which has accumulated from long housekeeping, which he has not the courage to burn.

Walden (1854), in *The Writings of Henry David Thoreau*, vol. 2, p. 74, Houghton Mifflin (1906).

See also TRADITION

We now discovered that we were in a foreign country, in a station-house of another nation. . . . My attention was caught by the double advertisements in French and English, fastened to its posts, by the formality of the English, and the covert or open reference to their queen and the British lion. No gentlemanly conductor appeared, none whom you would know to be the conductor by his dress and demeanor; but ere long we began to see here and there a solid, red-faced, burly-looking Englishman, a little pursy perhaps, who made us ashamed of ourselves and our thin and nervous countrymen,—a grandfatherly personage, at home in his greatcoat, who looked as if he might be a stage proprietor, certainly a railroad director, and knew, or had a right to know, when the cars did start. . . . In the meanwhile some soldiers, redcoats, belonging to the barracks near by, were turned out to be drilled. At every important point in our route the soldiers showed themselves ready for us; though they were evidently rather raw recruits here, they manœuvred far better than our soldiers; yet as usual, I heard some Yankees talk as if they were no great shakes.

"A Yankee in Canada" (1853), in *The Writings of Henry David Thoreau*, vol. 5, p. 9, Houghton Mifflin (1906).

See also CANADA AND CANADIANS

ENTHUSIASM

Enthusiasm is a supernatural serenity.

A Week on the Concord and Merrimack Rivers (1849), in *The Writings of Henry David Thoreau*, vol. 1, p. 132, Houghton Mifflin (1906).

EPITAPHS

Friends and contemporaries should supply only the name and date, and leave it to posterity to write the epitaph.

A Week on the Concord and Merrimack Rivers (1849), in The Writings of Henry David Thoreau, vol. 1, p. 178, Houghton Mifflin (1906).

See also GRAVES

The rarest quality in an epitaph is truth.

A Week on the Concord and Merrimack Rivers (1849), in The Writings of Henry David Thoreau, vol. 1, p. 178, Houghton Mifflin (1906).

See also GRAVES

EUROPE VERSUS AMERICA

The old world stands serenely behind the new, as one mountain yonder towers behind another, more dim and distant. Rome imposes her story still upon this late generation.

"A Walk to Wachusett" (1843), in The Writings of Henry David Thoreau, vol. 5, pp. 138–139, Houghton Mifflin (1906).

See also HISTORY

EVANGELICALISM

The attention of those who frequent the camp-meetings at Eastham is said to be divided between the preaching of the Methodists and the preaching of the billows on the back side of the Cape, for they all stream over here in the course of their stay. I trust that in this case the loudest voice carries it. With what effect may we suppose the ocean to say, "My hearers!" to the multitude on the bank. On that side some John N. Maffit; on this, the Reverend Poluphloisboios Thalassa.

> *Cape Cod* (1855–1865), in *The Writings of Henry David Thoreau*, vol. 4, p. 67, Houghton Mifflin (1906).

> "Poluphloisboios Thalassa" is Thoreau's transliteration of a phrase (which translates as "the many ringing sea") in a line from Homer's *Odyssey* that he has just quoted.

> See also SEA

*E*VOLUTION

I love to see that Nature is so rife with life that myriads can be afforded to be sacrificed and suffered to prey on one another; that tender organizations can be so serenely squashed out of existence like pulp.

> *Walden* (1854), in *The Writings of Henry David Thoreau*, vol. 2, p. 350, Houghton Mifflin (1906).

> See also NATURE

*E*XAGGERATION

Exaggeration! was ever any virtue attributed to a man without exaggeration? was ever any vice, without infinite exaggeration? Do we not exaggerate ourselves to ourselves, or do we recognize ourselves for the actual men we are? Are we not all great men? Yet what are we actually, to speak of? We live by exaggeration.

> "Thomas Carlyle and His Works" (1847), in *The Writings of Henry David Thoreau*, vol. 4, pp. 352–353, Houghton Mifflin (1906).

> See also TRUTH

He who cannot exaggerate is not qualified to utter truth.

> "Thomas Carlyle and His Works" (1847), in *The Writings of Henry David Thoreau*, vol. 4, p. 353, Houghton Mifflin (1906).

> See also TRUTH

To a small man every greater is an exaggeration.

> "Thomas Carlyle and His Works" (1847), in *The Writings of Henry David Thoreau*, vol. 4, p. 353, Houghton Mifflin (1906).

> See also CARLYLE, THOMAS

EXERCISE

If you would get exercise, go in search of the springs of life.

"Walking" (1862), in *The Writings of Henry David Thoreau*, vol. 5, p. 209, Houghton Mifflin (1906).

EXISTENCE

I may add that I am enjoying existence as much as ever, and regret nothing.

Letter, March 21, 1862, to Myron B. Benton, in *The Writings of Henry David Thoreau*, vol. 6, p. 400, Houghton Mifflin (1906).

The last line in Thoreau's last letter, dictated to his sister, Sophia, six weeks before his death.

Here or nowhere is our heaven.

A Week on the Concord and Merrimack Rivers (1849), in *The Writings of Henry David Thoreau*, vol. 1, p. 405, Houghton Mifflin (1906).

EXISTENCE, HUMAN

Let us wander where we will, the universe is built round about us, and we are central still.

A Week on the Concord and Merrimack Rivers (1849), in *The Writings of Henry David Thoreau*, vol. 1, p. 353, Houghton Mifflin (1906).

See also UNIVERSE, THE

EXPERIENCE

It requires more than a day's devotion to know and to possess the wealth of a day.

"Life Without Principle" (1863), in *The Writings of Henry David Thoreau*, vol. 4, p. 471, Houghton Mifflin (1906).

For ourselves, we are too young for experience. Who is old enough?

"Paradise (To Be) Regained" (1843), in *The Writings of Henry David Thoreau*, vol. 4, p. 299, Houghton Mifflin (1906).

We can conceive of nothing more fair than something which we have experienced.

A Week on the Concord and Merrimack Rivers (1849), in *The Writings of Henry David Thoreau*, vol. 1, p. 406, Houghton Mifflin (1906).

See also IMAGINATION

*E*XPLORATION

So far as inland discovery was concerned, the adventurous spirit of the English was that of sailors who land but for a day, and their enterprise the enterprise of traders.

Cape Cod (1855–1865), in *The Writings of Henry David Thoreau*, vol. 4, p. 235, Houghton Mifflin (1906).

The heroes and discoverers have found true more than was previously believed, only when they were expecting and dreaming of something more than their contemporaries dreamed of, or even themselves discovered, that is, when they were in a frame of mind fitted to behold the truth. Referred to the world's standard, they are always insane. Even savages have indirectly surmised as much.

Cape Cod (1855–1865), in *The Writings of Henry David Thoreau*, vol. 4, p. 121, Houghton Mifflin (1906).

See also DISCOVERY

The nearest beach to us on the other side, whither we looked, due east, was on the coast of Galicia, in Spain, whose capital is Santiago, though by old poets' reckoning it should have been Atlantis or the Hesperides; but heaven is found to be farther west now. . . . A little south of east was Palos, where Columbus weighed anchor, and farther yet the pillars which Hercules set up; concerning which when we inquired at the top of our voices what was written on them,—for we had the morning sun in our faces, and could not see distinctly,—the inhabitants shouted *Ne plus ultra* (no more beyond), but the wind bore to us the truth only, *plus ultra* (more beyond), and over the Bay westward was echoed *ultra* (beyond).

We spoke to them through the surf about the Far West, the true Hesperia, *heos peras* or end of the day, the This Side Sundown, where the sun was extinguished in the *Pacific,* and we advised them to pull up stakes and plant those pillars of theirs on the shore of California, whither all our folks were gone,—the only *ne* plus ultra now. Whereat they looked crestfallen on their cliffs, for we had taken the wind out of all their sails.

Cape Cod (1855–1865), in *The Writings of Henry David Thoreau,* vol. 4, pp. 177–179, Houghton Mifflin (1906).

See also COLUMBUS, CHRISTOPHER

Where is the "unexplored land" but in our own untried enterprises? To an adventurous spirit any place—London, New York, Worcester, or his own yard—is "unexplored land," to seek which Frémont and Kane travel so far. To a sluggish and defeated spirit even the Great Basin and the Polaris are trivial places.

Letter, May 20, 1860, to Harrison Blake, in *The Writings of Henry David Thoreau,* vol. 6, p. 362, Houghton Mifflin (1906).

*F*ACTS

Let us not underrate the value of a fact; it will one day flower in a truth. It is astonishing how few facts of importance are added in a century to the natural history of any animal. The natural history of man himself is still being gradually written.

"Natural History of Massachusetts" (1842), in *The Writings of Henry David Thoreau,* vol. 5, p. 130, Houghton Mifflin (1906).

See also NATURAL HISTORY

We read that the traveller asked the boy if the swamp before him had a hard bottom. The boy replied that it had. But presently the traveller's horse sank in up to the girths, and he observed to the boy, "I thought you said that this bog had a hard bottom." "So it has," answered the latter, "but you have not got half way to it yet." So it is with the bogs and quicksands of society; but he is an old boy that knows it.

Walden (1854), in *The Writings of Henry David Thoreau,* vol. 2, p. 363, Houghton Mifflin (1906).

See also SOCIETY

FAITH

Faith never makes a confession.

> Letter, October 16, 1843, to Lidian Jackson Emerson, in *The Writings of Henry David Thoreau*, vol. 6, p. 112, Houghton Mifflin (1906).

Faith, indeed, is all the reform that is needed; it is itself a reform.

> "Paradise (To Be) Regained" (1843), in *The Writings of Henry David Thoreau*, vol. 4, p. 300, Houghton Mifflin (1906).
>
> See also REFORM AND REFORMERS

We are older by faith than by experience.

> "Paradise (To Be) Regained" (1843), in *The Writings of Henry David Thoreau*, vol. 4, p. 299, Houghton Mifflin (1906).
>
> See also EXPERIENCE

A healthy man, with steady employment, as wood-chopping at fifty cents a cord, and a camp in the woods, will not be a good subject for Christianity. The New Testament may be a choice book to him on some, but not on all or most of his days. He will rather go a-fishing in his leisure hours. The Apostles, though they were fishers too, were of the solemn race of sea-fishers, and never trolled for pickerel on inland streams.

> *A Week on the Concord and Merrimack Rivers* (1849), in *The Writings of Henry David Thoreau*, vol. 1, pp. 74–75, Houghton Mifflin (1906).
>
> See also FISHING

FAME

Fame itself is but an epitaph; as late, as false, as true.

> *A Week on the Concord and Merrimack Rivers* (1849), in *The Writings of Henry David Thoreau*, vol. 1, p. 178, Houghton Mifflin (1906).
>
> See also EPITAPHS

FARMERS AND FARMING

I see young men, my townsmen, whose misfortune it is to have inherited farms, houses, barns, cattle, and farming tools; for these are more easily acquired than got rid of. Better if they had been born in the open pasture and suckled by a wolf, that they might have seen with clearer eyes what field they were called to labor in. Who made them serfs of the soil? Why should they eat their sixty acres, when man is condemned to eat only his peck of dirt? Why should they begin digging their graves as soon as they are born?

Walden (1854), in *The Writings of Henry David Thoreau*, vol. 2, p. 5, Houghton Mifflin (1906).

See also CONCORD, MASSACHUSETTS

Every one finds by his own experience, as well as in history, that the era in which men cultivate the apple, and the amenities of the garden, is essentially different from that of the hunter and forest life, and neither can displace the other without loss.

A Week on the Concord and Merrimack Rivers (1849), in *The Writings of Henry David Thoreau*, vol. 1, p. 54, Houghton Mifflin (1906).

See also GARDENS AND GARDENING

*F*AT*E*

Every path but your own is the path of fate. Keep on your own track, then.

Walden (1854), in *The Writings of Henry David Thoreau*, vol. 2, p. 131, Houghton Mifflin (1906).

*F*AT*HERS*

No people ever lived by cursing their fathers, however great a curse their fathers might have been to them.

Cape Cod (1855–1865), in *The Writings of Henry David Thoreau*, vol. 4, p. 22, Houghton Mifflin (1906).

*F*IELD, *JOHN*

An honest, hard-working, but shiftless man plainly was John Field.

Walden (1854), in *The Writings of Henry David Thoreau*, vol. 2, p. 226, Houghton Mifflin (1906).

Poor John Field!—I trust he does not read this, unless he will improve by it,—thinking to live by some derivative old-country mode in this primitive new country. . . . With his horizon all his own, yet he a poor man, born to be poor, with his inherited Irish poverty or poor life, his Adam's grandmother and boggy ways, not to rise in this world, he nor his posterity, till their wading webbed bog-trotting feet get *talaria* to their heels.

Walden (1854), in *The Writings of Henry David Thoreau*, vol. 2, p. 231, Houghton Mifflin (1906).

*F*IRE

It was, perhaps, even a more grand and desolate place for a night's lodging than the summit would have been, being in the neighborhood of those wild trees, and of the torrent. Some more ærial and finer-spirited winds rushed and roared through the ravine all night, from time to time arousing our fire, and dispersing the embers about. It was as if we lay in the very nest of a young whirlwind. At midnight, one of my bed-fellows, being startled in his dreams by the sudden blazing up to its top of a fir tree, whose green boughs were dried by the heat, sprang up, with a cry, from his bed, thinking the world on fire, and drew the whole camp after him.

"Ktaadn" (1848) in *The Maine Woods* (1864), in *The Writings of Henry David Thoreau*, vol. 3, pp. 68–69, Houghton Mifflin (1906).

See also KTAADN, MOUNT

We could not well camp higher, for want of fuel; and the trees here seemed so evergreen and sappy, that we almost doubted if they would acknowledge the influence of fire; but fire prevailed at last, and blazed here, too, like a good citizen of the world.

"Ktaadn" (1848) in *The Maine Woods* (1864), in *The Writings of Henry David Thoreau*, vol. 3, p. 68, Houghton Mifflin (1906).

See also KTAADN, MOUNT

I sometimes left a good fire when I went to take a walk in a winter afternoon; and when I returned, three or four hours afterward, it would be still alive and glowing. My house was not empty though I was gone. It was as if I had left a cheerful housekeeper behind. It was I and Fire that lived there; and commonly my housekeeper proved trustworthy.

Walden (1854), in *The Writings of Henry David Thoreau*, vol. 2, p. 279, Houghton Mifflin (1906).

*F*ISH

Who hears the fishes when they cry?

A Week on the Concord and Merrimack Rivers (1849), in *The Writings of Henry David Thoreau*, vol. 1, p. 36, Houghton Mifflin (1906).

*F*ISHING

I confess I was surprised to find that so many men spent their whole day, ay, their whole lives almost, a-fishing. It is remarkable what a serious business men make of getting their dinners, and how universally shiftlessness and a groveling taste take refuge in a merely ant-like industry. Better go without your dinner, I thought, than be thus everlastingly fishing for it like a cormorant. Of course, *viewed from the shore*, our pursuits in the country appear not a whit less frivolous.

Cape Cod (1855–1865), in *The Writings of Henry David Thoreau*, vol. 4, p. 182, Houghton Mifflin (1906).

See also LABOR

In the night I dreamed of trout-fishing; and, when at length I awoke, it seemed a fable that this painted fish swam there so near my couch, and rose to our hooks the last evening, and I doubted if I had not dreamed it all. So I arose before dawn to test its truth, while my companions were still sleeping. There stood Ktaadn with distinct and cloudless outline in the moonlight; and the rippling of the rapids was the only sound to break the stillness. Standing on the shore, I once more cast my line into the stream, and found the dream to be real and the fable true. The speckled trout and silvery roach, like flying-fish, sped swiftly through the moonlight air, describing bright arcs on the dark side of Ktaadn, until moonlight, now fading into daylight, brought satiety to my mind, and the minds of my companions, who had joined me.

"Ktaadn" (1848) in *The Maine Woods* (1864), in *The Writings of Henry David Thoreau*, vol. 3, p. 61, Houghton Mifflin (1906).

See also DREAMS AND DREAMING

The dullest soul cannot go upon such an expedition without some of the spirit of adventure; as if he had stolen the boat of Charon and gone down the Styx on a midnight expedition in the realms of Pluto. . . . The silent navigator shoves his craft gently over the water, with a smothered pride and sense of benefaction, as if he were phosphor, or light-bringer, to these dusky realms, or some sister moon, blessing the spaces with her light. The waters, for a rod or two on either hand and several feet in depth, are lit up with more than noonday distinctness, and he enjoys the opportunity which so many have desired, for the roofs of a city are indeed raised, and he surveys the midnight economy of the fishes.

"Natural History of Massachusetts" (1842), in *The Writings of Henry David Thoreau*, vol. 5, p. 122, Houghton Mifflin (1906).

When the ice is covered with snow, I do not suspect the wealth under my feet; that there is as good as a mine under me wherever I go. How many pickerel are poised on easy fin fathoms below the loaded wain! The revolution of the seasons must be a curious phenomenon to them. At length the sun and wind brush aside their curtain, and they see the heavens again.

"Natural History of Massachusetts" (1842), in *The Writings of Henry David Thoreau*, vol. 5, p. 119, Houghton Mifflin (1906).

Shall I go to heaven or a-fishing?

Walden (1854), in *The Writings of Henry David Thoreau*, vol. 2, p. 249, Houghton Mifflin (1906).

*F*OOD AND EATING

To meet the objections of some inveterate cavillers, I may as well state, that if I dined out occasionally, as I always had done, and I trust shall have opportunities to do again, it was frequently to the detriment of my domestic arrangements.

Walden (1854), in *The Writings of Henry David Thoreau*, vol. 2, p. 67, Houghton Mifflin (1906).

See also SOLITUDE

*F*ORESTS

If it were not for the rivers (and he might go round their heads), a squirrel could here travel thus the whole breadth of the country.

"Chesuncook" (1858) in *The Maine Woods* (1864), in *The Writings of Henry David Thoreau*, vol. 3, p. 169, Houghton Mifflin (1906).

See also WILDERNESS

What were the "forests" of England to these?

"Chesuncook" (1858) in *The Maine Woods* (1864), in *The Writings of Henry David Thoreau*, vol. 3, p. 169, Houghton Mifflin (1906).

See also WILDERNESS

The very timber and boards and shingles of which our houses are made grew but yesterday in a wilderness where the Indian still hunts and the moose runs wild.

"Ktaadn" (1848) in *The Maine Woods* (1864), in *The Writings of Henry David Thoreau*, vol. 3, p. 90, Houghton Mifflin (1906).

See also NATIVE AMERICANS

There stands the city of Bangor, fifty miles up the Penobscot, at the head of navigation for vessels of the largest class, the principal lumber depot on this continent, with a population of twelve thousand, like a star on the edge of night, still hewing at the forests of which it is built, already overflowing with the luxuries and refinement of Europe, and sending its vessels to Spain, to England, and to the West Indies for its groceries,—and yet only a few axemen have gone "up river," into the howling wilderness which feeds it. The bear and deer are still found within its limits; and the moose, as he swims the Penobscot, is entangled amid its shipping, and taken by foreign sailors in its harbor. . . . Sixty miles above, the country is virtually unmapped and unexplored, and there still waves the virgin forest of the New World.

"Ktaadn" (1848) in *The Maine Woods* (1864), in *The Writings of Henry David Thoreau*, vol. 3, pp. 91–92, Houghton Mifflin (1906).

See also NATURE VERSUS CIVILIZATION

*F*OXES

Perhaps of all our untamed quadrupeds, the fox has obtained the widest and most familiar reputation. . . . His recent tracks still give variety to a winter's walk. I tread in the steps of the fox that has gone before me by some hours, or which perhaps I have started, with such a tip-toe of expectation as if I were on the trail of the Spirit itself which resides in the wood, and expected soon to catch it in its lair.

"Natural History of Massachusetts" (1842), in *The Writings of Henry David Thoreau*, vol. 5, p. 117, Houghton Mifflin (1906).

FREEDOM

The man who takes the liberty to live is superior to all the laws, by virtue of his relation to the lawmaker.

"Walking" (1862), in *The Writings of Henry David Thoreau*, vol. 5, pp. 240–241, Houghton Mifflin (1906).

See also GOD

Every sacred book, successively, has been accepted in the faith that it was to be the final resting-place of the sojourning soul; but after all, it was but a caravansary which supplied refreshment to the traveler, and directed him farther on his way to Isphahan or Bagdat. Thank God, no Hindoo tyranny prevailed at the framing of the world, but we are freemen of the universe, and not sentenced to any caste.

A Week on the Concord and Merrimack Rivers (1849), in *The Writings of Henry David Thoreau*, vol. 1, p. 155, Houghton Mifflin (1906).

See also RELIGION

FRIENDS AND FRIENDSHIP

After years of vain familiarity, some distant gesture or unconscious behavior, which we remember, speaks to us with more emphasis than the wisest or kindest words. We are sometimes made aware of a kindness long passed, and realize that there have been times when our Friends' thoughts of us were of so pure and lofty a character that they passed over us like the winds of heaven unnoticed; when they treated us not as what we were, but as what we aspired to be.

A Week on the Concord and Merrimack Rivers (1849), in *The Writings of Henry David Thoreau*, vol. 1, p. 275, Houghton Mifflin (1906).

See also LOVE

Even the utmost goodwill and harmony and practical kindness are not sufficient for Friendship, for Friends do not live in harmony merely, as some say, but in melody. We do not wish for Friends to feed and clothe our bodies,—neighbors are kind enough for that,—but to do the like office to our spirits. For this few are rich enough, however well disposed they may be.

A Week on the Concord and Merrimack Rivers (1849), in *The Writings of Henry David Thoreau*, vol. 1, p. 283, Houghton Mifflin (1906).

Friendship is never established as an understood relation. . . . It is a miracle which requires constant proofs. It is an exercise of the purest imagination and the rarest faith.

> *A Week on the Concord and Merrimack Rivers* (1849), in *The Writings of Henry David Thoreau*, vol. 1, p. 289, Houghton Mifflin (1906).
>
> See also FAITH

I would that I were worthy to be any man's Friend.

> *A Week on the Concord and Merrimack Rivers* (1849), in *The Writings of Henry David Thoreau*, vol. 1, p. 282, Houghton Mifflin (1906).

It is a truer truth, it is better and fairer news, and no time will ever shame it, or prove it false.

> *A Week on the Concord and Merrimack Rivers* (1849), in *The Writings of Henry David Thoreau*, vol. 1, p. 291, Houghton Mifflin (1906).
>
> See also TIME

It is impossible to say all that we think, even to our truest Friend. We may bid him farewell forever sooner than complain, for our complaint is too well grounded to be uttered.

> *A Week on the Concord and Merrimack Rivers* (1849), in *The Writings of Henry David Thoreau*, vol. 1, p. 300, Houghton Mifflin (1906).
>
> See also COMMUNICATION

My Friend is that one whom I can associate with my choicest thought.

> *A Week on the Concord and Merrimack Rivers* (1849), in *The Writings of Henry David Thoreau*, vol. 1, p. 288, Houghton Mifflin (1906).
>
> See also THINKING AND THOUGHTS

The only danger in Friendship is that it will end.

> *A Week on the Concord and Merrimack Rivers* (1849), in *The Writings of Henry David Thoreau*, vol. 1, p. 294, Houghton Mifflin (1906).

There are times when we have had enough even of our Friends.

> *A Week on the Concord and Merrimack Rivers* (1849), in *The Writings of Henry David Thoreau*, vol. 1, p. 288, Houghton Mifflin (1906).

They cherish each other's hopes. They are kind to each other's dreams.

> *A Week on the Concord and Merrimack Rivers* (1849), in *The Writings of Henry David Thoreau*, vol. 1, p. 286, Houghton Mifflin (1906).

To say that a man is your Friend means commonly no more than this, that he is not your enemy.

A Week on the Concord and Merrimack Rivers (1849), in The Writings of Henry David Thoreau, vol. 1, p. 282, Houghton Mifflin (1906).

We must accept or refuse one another as we are. I could tame a hyena more easily than my Friend. He is a material which no tool of mine will work.

A Week on the Concord and Merrimack Rivers (1849), in The Writings of Henry David Thoreau, vol. 1, p. 301, Houghton Mifflin (1906).

*F*RONTIERS

The frontiers are not east or west, north or south; but wherever a man *fronts* a fact, though that fact be a neighbor, there is an unsettled wilderness between him and Canada, between him and the setting sun, or, farther still, between him and *it*. Let him build himself a log house with the bark on where he is, *fronting* IT, and wage there an Old French war for seven or seventy years, with Indians and Rangers, or whatever else may come between him and the reality, and save his scalp if he can.

A Week on the Concord and Merrimack Rivers (1849), in The Writings of Henry David Thoreau, vol. 1, pp. 323–324, Houghton Mifflin (1906).

See also FACTS

*F*ULLER, MARGARET

The ship struck at ten minutes after four A.M., and all hands, being mostly in their nightclothes, made haste to the forecastle, the water coming in at once. There they remained; the passengers *in* the forecastle, the crew above it, doing what they could. Every wave lifted the forecastle roof and washed over those within. The first man got ashore at nine; many from nine to noon. At flood-tide, about half past three o'clock, when the ship broke up entirely, they came out of the forecastle, and Margaret sat with her back to the foremast, with her hands on her knees, her husband and child already drowned. A great wave came and washed her aft. The steward (?) had just before taken her child and started for shore. Both were drowned.

> Letter, July 25, 1850, to Ralph Waldo Emerson, in *The Writings of Henry David Thoreau*, vol. 6, pp. 183–184, Houghton Mifflin (1906).

> Recounting the deaths of Margaret Fuller, her husband, The Marquis of Ossoli, and their child.

*F*UTURE, THE

We shall be reduced to gnaw the very crust of the earth for nutriment.

> "Chesuncook" (1858) in *The Maine Woods* (1864), in *The Writings of Henry David Thoreau*, vol. 3, p. 170, Houghton Mifflin (1906).

> See also CIVILIZATION

It would be no reproach to a philosopher, that he knew the future better than the past, or even than the present. It is better worth knowing.

> "Thomas Carlyle and His Works" (1847), in *The Writings of Henry David Thoreau*, vol. 4, p. 348, Houghton Mifflin (1906).

> See also PAST, THE

*G*ARDENS AND GARDENING

Gardening is civil and social, but it wants the vigor and freedom of the forest and the outlaw.

> *A Week on the Concord and Merrimack Rivers* (1849), in *The Writings of Henry David Thoreau*, vol. 1, p. 55, Houghton Mifflin (1906).

> See also WILDERNESS

*G*ENERATIONS

One generation abandons the enterprises of another like stranded vessels.

> *Walden* (1854), in *The Writings of Henry David Thoreau*, vol. 2, p. 12, Houghton Mifflin (1906).

> See also OLD AGE

GENIUS

Follow your genius closely enough, and it will not fail to show you a fresh prospect every hour.

> *Walden* (1854), in *The Writings of Henry David Thoreau*, vol. 2, p. 125, Houghton Mifflin (1906).

Genius is not a retainer to any emperor.

> *Walden* (1854), in *The Writings of Henry David Thoreau*, vol. 2, p. 63, Houghton Mifflin (1906).
>
> See also INDEPENDENCE

No man ever followed his genius till it misled him.

> *Walden* (1854), in *The Writings of Henry David Thoreau*, vol. 2, p. 239, Houghton Mifflin (1906).

GOD

Have you learned the alphabet of heaven and can count three? Do you know the number of God's family? Can you put mysteries into words? Do you presume to fable of the ineffable? Pray, what geographer are you, that speak of heaven's topography? Whose friend are you, that speak of God's personality? . . . Yet we have a sort of family history of our God,—so have the Tahitians of theirs,—and some old poet's grand imagination is imposed on us as adamantine everlasting truth, and God's own word. Pythagoras says, truly enough, "A true assertion respecting God is an assertion of God"; but we may well doubt if there is any example of this in literature.

> *A Week on the Concord and Merrimack Rivers* (1849), in *The Writings of Henry David Thoreau*, vol. 1, pp. 71–72, Houghton Mifflin (1906).
>
> See also RELIGION

It seems to me that the god that is commonly worshiped in civilized countries is not at all divine, though he bears a divine name, but is the overwhelming authority and respectability of mankind combined. Men reverence one another, not yet God.

> *A Week on the Concord and Merrimack Rivers* (1849), in *The Writings of Henry David Thoreau*, vol. 1, pp. 65–66, Houghton Mifflin (1906).
>
> See also RELIGION

GOETHE, JOHANN WOLFGANG VON

Above all, he possessed a hearty good-will to all men, and never wrote a cross or even careless word.

> *A Week on the Concord and Merrimack Rivers* (1849), in *The Writings of Henry David Thoreau*, vol. 1, p. 348, Houghton Mifflin (1906).

GOLD

I did not know that mankind was suffering for want of gold.

> "Life Without Principle" (1863), in *The Writings of Henry David Thoreau*, vol. 4, p. 464, Houghton Mifflin (1906).

GOLD RUSH (CALIFORNIA)

The gold-digger in the ravines of the mountains is as much a gambler as his fellow in the saloons of San Francisco. What difference does it make whether you shake dirt or shake dice? If you win, society is the loser.

> "Life Without Principle" (1863), in *The Writings of Henry David Thoreau*, vol. 4, p. 464, Houghton Mifflin (1906).

GOSSIP

Every day or two I strolled to the village to hear some of the gossip which is incessantly going on there, circulating either from mouth to mouth, or from newspaper to newspaper, and which, taken in homœopathic doses, was really as refreshing in its way as the rustle of leaves and the peeping of frogs.

> *Walden* (1854), in *The Writings of Henry David Thoreau*, vol. 2, p. 185, Houghton Mifflin (1906).

GOVERNMENT

But, to speak practically and as a citizen, unlike those who call themselves no-government men, I ask for, not at once no government, but *at once* a better government. Let every man make known what kind of government would command his respect, and that will be one step toward obtaining it.

"Civil Disobedience," originally published as "Resistance to Civil Government" (1849), in *The Writings of Henry David Thoreau*, vol. 4, p. 357, Houghton Mifflin (1906).

Government is at best but an expedient; but most governments are usually, and all governments are sometimes, inexpedient.

"Civil Disobedience," originally published as "Resistance to Civil Government" (1849), in *The Writings of Henry David Thoreau*, vol. 4, p. 356, Houghton Mifflin (1906).

I heartily accept the motto, "That government is best which governs least"; and I should like to see it acted up to more rapidly and systematically. Carried out, it finally amounts to this, which also I believe,—"That government is best which governs not at all"; and when men are prepared for it, that will be the kind of government which they will have.

"Civil Disobedience," originally published as "Resistance to Civil Government" (1849), in *The Writings of Henry David Thoreau*, vol. 4, p. 356, Houghton Mifflin (1906).

The State never intentionally confronts a man's sense, intellectual or moral, but only his body, his senses. It is not armed with superior wit or honesty, but with superior physical strength.

"Civil Disobedience," originally published as "Resistance to Civil Government" (1849), in *The Writings of Henry David Thoreau*, vol. 4, p. 376, Houghton Mifflin (1906).

When I meet a government which says to me, "Your money or your life," why should I be in haste to give it my money?

"Civil Disobedience," originally published as "Resistance to Civil Government" (1849), in *The Writings of Henry David Thoreau*, vol. 4, p. 376, Houghton Mifflin (1906).

See also MONEY

Is it not possible that an individual may be right and a government wrong? Are laws to be enforced simply because they were made? or declared by any number of men to be good, if they are *not* good? Is there any necessity for a man's being a tool to perform a deed of which his better nature disapproves?

"A Plea for Captain John Brown" (1859), in *The Writings of Henry David Thoreau*, vol. 4, pp. 437–438, Houghton Mifflin (1906).

See also CONSCIENCE

The only government that I recognize—and it matters not how few are at the head of it, or how small its army—is that power that establishes justice in the land, never that which establishes injustice.

"A Plea for Captain John Brown" (1859), in *The Writings of Henry David Thoreau*, vol. 4, p. 430, Houghton Mifflin (1906).

See also JUSTICE

The effect of a good government is to make life more valuable; of a bad one, to make it less valuable.

"Slavery in Massachusetts" (1854), in *The Writings of Henry David Thoreau*, vol. 4, p. 405, Houghton Mifflin (1906).

See also JUSTICE

The government of the world I live in was not framed, like that of Britain, in after-dinner conversations over the wine.

Walden (1854), in *The Writings of Henry David Thoreau*, vol. 2, p. 366, Houghton Mifflin (1906).

GRACE

The gifts of Heaven are never quite gratuitous.

A Week on the Concord and Merrimack Rivers (1849), in *The Writings of Henry David Thoreau*, vol. 1, p. 375, Houghton Mifflin (1906).

GRAVES

Nothing but great antiquity can make graveyards interesting to me. I have no friends there.

A Week on the Concord and Merrimack Rivers (1849), in *The Writings of Henry David Thoreau*, vol. 1, p. 178, Houghton Mifflin (1906).

See also FRIENDS AND FRIENDSHIP

HABIT

It is remarkable how easily and insensibly we fall into a particular route, and make a beaten track for ourselves. I had not lived there a week before my feet wore a path from my door to the pond-side; and though it is five or six years since I trod it, it is still quite distinct. It is true, I fear, that others may have fallen into it, and so helped to keep it open.

Walden (1854), in *The Writings of Henry David Thoreau*, vol. 2, pp. 355–356, Houghton Mifflin (1906).

See also CONFORMITY

HAPPINESS

I am too easily contented with a slight and almost animal happiness. My happiness is a good deal like that of the woodchucks.

Letter, May 2, 1848, to Harrison Blake, in *The Writings of Henry David Thoreau*, vol. 6, p. 168, Houghton Mifflin (1906).

HARPER'S FERRY, WEST VIRGINIA, JOHN BROWN'S RAID

I foresee the time when the painter will paint that scene, no longer going to Rome for a subject; the poet will sing it; the historian record it; and, with the Landing of the Pilgrims and the Declaration of Independence, it will be the ornament of some future national gallery, when at least the present form of slavery shall be no more here. We shall then be at liberty to weep for Captain Brown. Then, and not till then, we will take our revenge.

"A Plea for Captain John Brown" (1859), in *The Writings of Henry David Thoreau*, vol. 4, p. 440, Houghton Mifflin (1906).

See also BROWN, JOHN

$\mathcal{H}$ARVARD UNIVERSITY

They have been foolish enough to put at the end of all this earnest the old joke of a diploma. Let every sheep keep but his own skin, I say.

> Letter, November 14, 1847, to Ralph Waldo Emerson, in *The Writings of Henry David Thoreau*, vol. 6, p. 138, Houghton Mifflin (1906).

> In the context of a description of the intellectual (especially scientific) progress of his *alma mater*, Thoreau here laments the fact that Harvard University still followed the Oxford and Cambridge custom of awarding an unearned Master's degree to all *alumni* five years after graduation. His remark about sheep and their skins echoes his own refusal to accept such a degree when offered it.

$\mathcal{H}$AWKS

It appeared to have no companion in the universe,—sporting there alone,—and to need none but the morning and the ether with which it played. It was not lonely, but made all the earth lonely beneath it. Where was the parent which hatched it, its kindred, and its father in the heavens? The tenant of the air, it seemed related to the earth but by an egg hatched some time in the crevice of a crag;—or was its native nest made in the angle of a cloud, woven of the rainbow's trimmings and the sunset sky, and lined with some soft midsummer haze caught up from earth? Its eyry now some cliffy cloud.

> *Walden* (1854), in *The Writings of Henry David Thoreau*, vol. 2, p. 349, Houghton Mifflin (1906).

> See also INDEPENDENCE

On the 29th of April, as I was fishing . . . I heard a singular rattling sound, somewhat like that of the sticks which boys play with their fingers, when, looking up, I observed a very slight and graceful hawk, like a nighthawk, alternately soaring like a ripple and tumbling a rod or two over and over, showing the underside of its wings, which gleamed like a satin ribbon in the sun, or like the pearly inside of a shell. This sight reminded me of falconry and what nobleness and poetry are associated with that sport. The merlin it seemed to me it might be called: but I care not for its name. It was the most ethereal flight I had ever witnessed.

> *Walden* (1854), in *The Writings of Henry David Thoreau*, vol. 2, pp. 348–349, Houghton Mifflin (1906).

$\mathcal{H}$EALTH

All health and success does me good, however far off and withdrawn it may appear; all disease and failure helps to make me sad and does me evil, however much sympathy it may have with me or I with it.

Walden (1854), in *The Writings of Henry David Thoreau*, vol. 2, p. 87, Houghton Mifflin (1906).

See also SUCCESS

$\mathcal{H}$EROES AND HEROISM

I am less affected by their heroism who stood up for half an hour in the front line at Buena Vista, than by the steady and cheerful valor of the men who inhabit the snow-plow for their winter quarters; who have not merely the three-o'-clock-in-the-morning courage, which Bonaparte thought was the rarest, but whose courage does not go to rest so early, who go to sleep only when the storm sleeps or the sinews of their iron steed are frozen.

Walden (1854), in *The Writings of Henry David Thoreau*, vol. 2, pp. 131–132, Houghton Mifflin (1906).

See also WORKERS

The hero is commonly the simplest and obscurest of men.

"Walking" (1862), in *The Writings of Henry David Thoreau*, vol. 5, p. 224, Houghton Mifflin (1906).

This observation ends a long meditation on the Rhine versus the Mississippi, as they symbolize, respectively, the chivalric age of mediaeval Europe and the heroic age of modern, democratic America.

See also SIMPLICITY

$\mathcal{H}$INDUISM

As our domestic fowls are said to have their original in the wild pheasant of India, so our domestic thoughts have their prototypes in the thoughts of her philosophers.

A Week on the Concord and Merrimack Rivers (1849), in *The Writings of Henry David Thoreau*, vol. 1, p. 156, Houghton Mifflin (1906).

See also PHILOSOPHY AND PHILOSOPHERS

These philosophers dwell on the inevitability and unchangeableness of laws, on the power of temperament and constitution, the three *goon,* or qualities, and the circumstances, or birth and affinity. The end is an immense consolation; eternal absorption in Brahma.

A Week on the Concord and Merrimack Rivers (1849), in *The Writings of Henry David Thoreau,* vol. 1, pp. 140–141, Houghton Mifflin (1906).

$\mathcal{H}$ISTORY

Consider what stuff history is made of,—that for the most part it is merely a story agreed on by posterity. Who will tell us even how many Russians were engaged in the battle of Chernaya, the other day? Yet, no doubt, Mr. Scriblerus, the historian, will fix on a definite number for the schoolboys to commit to their excellent memories. What, then, of the number of Persians at Salamis? The historian whom I read knew as much about the position of the parties and their tactics in the last-mentioned affair as they who describe a recent battle in an article for the press nowadays before the particulars have arrived. I believe that, if I were to live the life of mankind over again myself (which I would not be hired to do), with the Universal History in my hands, I should not be able to tell what was what.

Cape Cod (1855–1865), in *The Writings of Henry David Thoreau,* vol. 4, p. 250, Houghton Mifflin (1906).

See also JOURNALISM AND JOURNALISTS

Exaggerated history is poetry, and truth referred to a new standard.

"Thomas Carlyle and His Works" (1847), in *The Writings of Henry David Thoreau,* vol. 4, p. 353, Houghton Mifflin (1906).

See also POETRY AND POETS

All the events which make the annals of the nations are but the shadows of our private experiences.

A Week on the Concord and Merrimack Rivers (1849), in *The Writings of Henry David Thoreau,* vol. 1, p. 310, Houghton Mifflin (1906).

Critical acumen is exerted in vain to uncover the past; the *past* cannot be *presented;* we cannot know what we are not. But one veil hangs over past, present, and future, and it is the province of the historian to find out, not what was, but what is. Where a battle has been fought, you will find nothing but the bones of men and beasts; where a battle is being fought, there are hearts beating.

A Week on the Concord and Merrimack Rivers (1849), in *The Writings of Henry David Thoreau*, vol. 1, p. 162, Houghton Mifflin (1906).

See also SCHOLARS AND SCHOLARSHIP

Such were garrulous and noisy eras, which no longer yield any sound, but the Grecian or silent and melodious era is ever sounding and resounding in the ears of men.

A Week on the Concord and Merrimack Rivers (1849), in *The Writings of Henry David Thoreau*, vol. 1, p. 419, Houghton Mifflin (1906).

See also SILENCE

*H*OMER

He conveys the least information, even the hour of the day, with such magnificence and vast expense of natural imagery, as if it were a message from the gods.

A Week on the Concord and Merrimack Rivers (1849), in *The Writings of Henry David Thoreau*, vol. 1, p. 95, Houghton Mifflin (1906).

*H*OUSES AND HOMES

I dug my cellar in the side of a hill sloping to the south, where a woodchuck had formerly dug his burrow, down through sumach and blackberry roots, and the lowest stain of vegetation, six feet square by seven deep, to a fine sand where potatoes would not freeze in any winter. . . . I took particular pleasure in this breaking of ground, for in almost all latitudes men dig into the earth for an equable temperature. Under the most splendid house in the city is still to be found the cellar where they store their roots as of old, and long after the superstructure has disappeared posterity remark its dent in the earth. The house is still but a sort of porch at the entrance of a burrow.

Walden (1854), in *The Writings of Henry David Thoreau*, vol. 2, p. 49, Houghton Mifflin (1906).

See also ARCHITECTURE

$\mathcal{H}$UMAN NATURE

Men are in the main alike, but they were made several in order that they might be various. If a low use is to be served, one man will do nearly quite as well as another; if a high one, individual excellence is to be regarded.

"Walking" (1862), in *The Writings of Henry David Thoreau*, vol. 5, p. 235, Houghton Mifflin (1906).

How cheap must be the material of which so many men are made!

A Week on the Concord and Merrimack Rivers (1849), in *The Writings of Henry David Thoreau*, vol. 1, p. 361, Houghton Mifflin (1906).

See also CHARACTER

$\mathcal{H}$UMANE HOUSES

At length, by mid-afternoon, after we had had two or three rainbows over the sea, the showers ceased, and the heavens gradually cleared up, though the wind still blowed as hard and the breakers ran as high as before. Keeping on, we soon after came to a charity-house, which we looked into to see how the shipwrecked mariners might fare. Far away in some desolate hollow by the seaside, just within the bank, stands a lonely building on piles driven into the sand, with a slight nail put through the staple, which a freezing man can bend, with some straw, perchance, on the floor on which he may lie, or which he may burn in the fireplace to keep him alive. Perhaps this hut has never been required to shelter a shipwrecked man, and the benevolent person who promised to inspect it annually, to see that the straw and matches are here, and that the boards will keep off the wind, has grown remiss and thinks that storms and shipwrecks are over; and this very night a perishing crew may pry open its door with their numbed fingers and leave half their number dead here by morning. When I thought what must be the condition of the families which alone would ever occupy or had occupied them, what must have been the tragedy of the winter evenings spent by human beings around their hearths, these houses, though they were meant for human dwellings, did not look cheerful to me. They appeared but a stage to the grave. The gulls flew around and screamed over them; the roar of the ocean in storms, and the lapse of its waves in calms, alone resounds through them, all dark and empty within, year in, year out, except, perchance, on one memorable

night. Houses of entertainment for shipwrecked men! What kind of sail-
or's homes were they?

Cape Cod (1855–1865), in *The Writings of Henry David Thoreau*, vol. 4, pp. 74–75, Houghton Mifflin (1906).

This "charity-house," as the wrecker called it, this "Humane house," as
some call it, that is, the one to which we first came, had neither window
nor sliding shutter, nor clapboards, nor paint. As we have said, there was
a rusty nail put through the staple. However, as we wished to get an idea
of a Humane house, and we hoped that we should never have a better
opportunity, we put our eyes, by turns, to a knot-hole in the door, and,
after long looking, without seeing, into the dark,—not knowing how many
shipwrecked men's bones we might see at last, looking with the eye of
faith, knowing that, though to him that knocketh it may not always be
opened, yet to him that looketh long enough through a knot-hole the
inside shall be visible,—for we had had some practice at looking inward,—
by steadily keeping our other ball covered from the light meanwhile,
putting the outward world behind us, ocean and land, and the beach,—
till the pupil became enlarged and collected the rays of light that were
wandering in that dark (for the pupil shall be enlarged by looking; there
was never so dark a night but a faithful and patient eye, however small,
might at last prevail over it),—after all this, I say, things began to take
shape to our vision,—if we may use this expression where there was
nothing but emptiness,—and we obtained the long-wished-for insight.
Though we thought at first that it was a hopeless case, after several
minutes' steady exercise of the divine faculty, our prospects began steadily
to brighten, and we were ready to exclaim with the blind bard of "Paradise
Lost and Regained,"—

> "Hail, holy Light! offspring of Heaven first-born,
> Or of the Eternal coeternal beam
> May I express thee unblamed?"

A little longer, and a chimney rushed red on our sight. In short, when
our vision had grown familiar with the darkness, we discovered that there
were some stones and some loose wads of wool on the floor, and an empty
fireplace at the further end; but it *was not* supplied with matches, or straw,
or hay, that we could see, nor "accommodated with a bench." Indeed, it
was the wreck of all cosmical beauty there within.

Turning our backs on the outward world, we thus looked through the
knot-hole into the Humane house, into the very bowels of mercy; and for
bread we found a stone. It was literally a great cry (of sea-mews outside),

and a little wool. However, we were glad to sit outside, under the lee of the Humane house, to escape the piercing wind; and there we thought how cold is charity! how inhumane humanity! This, then, is what charity hides! Virtues antique and far away, with ever a rusty nail over the latch; and very difficult to keep in repair, withal, it is so uncertain whether any will ever gain the beach near you. So we shivered round about, not being able to get into it, ever and anon looking through the knot-hole into that night without a star, until we concluded that it was not a *humane* house at all, but a seaside box, now shut up, belonging to some of the family of Night or Chaos, where they spent their summers by the sea, for the sake of the sea-breeze, and that it was not proper for us to be prying into their concerns.

Cape Cod (1855–1865), in *The Writings of Henry David Thoreau*, vol. 4, pp. 76–78, Houghton Mifflin (1906).

$\mathcal{H}$UMANITY

I picked up a bottle half buried in the wet sand, covered with barnacles, but stoppled tight, and half full of red ale, which still smacked of juniper,—all that remained I fancied from the wreck of a rowdy world,—that great salt sea on the one hand, and this little sea of ale on the other, preserving their separate characters. What if it could tell us its adventures over countless ocean waves! Man could not be man through such ordeals as it had passed. But as I poured it slowly out on to the sand, it seemed to me that man himself was like a half-emptied bottle of pale ale, which Time had drunk so far, yet stoppled tight for a while, and drifting about in the ocean of circumstances, but destined ere-long to mingle with the surrounding waves, or be spilled amid the sands of a distant shore.

Cape Cod (1855–1865), in *The Writings of Henry David Thoreau*, vol. 4, p. 117, Houghton Mifflin (1906).

The age of the world is great enough for our imaginations, even according to the Mosaic account, without borrowing any years from the geologist. From Adam and Eve at one leap sheer down to the deluge, and then through the ancient monarchies, through Babylon and Thebes, Brahma and Abraham, to Greece and the Argonauts; whence we might start again with Orpheus, and the Trojan war, the Pyramids and the Olympic games, and Homer and Athens, for our stages; and after a breathing space at the building of Rome, continue our journey down through Odin and Christ to——America. It is a wearisome while. And yet the lives of but sixty old women, such as live under the hill, say of a century each, strung together, are sufficient to reach over the whole ground. Taking hold of hands they would span the interval from Eve to my own mother. A respectable tea-party merely,—whose gossip would be Universal History. The fourth old woman from myself suckled Columbus,—the ninth was nurse to the Norman Conqueror,—the nineteenth was the Virgin Mary—the twenty-fourth was the Cumæan Sibyl,—the thirtieth was at the Trojan war and Helen her name,—the thirty-eighth was Queen Semiramis,—the sixtieth was Eve, the mother of mankind. So much for the

> "Old woman that lives under the hill,
> And if she's not gone she lives there still."

It will not take a very great-granddaughter of hers to be in at the death of Time.

A Week on the Concord and Merrimack Rivers (1849), in *The Writings of Henry David Thoreau*, vol. 1, pp. 346–347, Houghton Mifflin (1906).

See also HISTORY

$\mathcal{H}$UNTING

The afternoon's tragedy, and my share in it, as it affected the innocence, destroyed the pleasure of my adventure. It is true, I came as near as is possible to come to being a hunter and miss it, myself; and as it is, I think that I could spend a year in the woods, fishing and hunting just enough to sustain myself, with satisfaction. This would be next to living like a philosopher on the fruits of the earth which you had raised, which also attracts me. But this hunting of the moose merely for the satisfaction of killing him,—not even for the sake of his hide,—without making any extraordinary exertion or running any risk yourself, is too much like going out by night to some wood-side pasture and shooting your neighbor's horses.

"Chesuncook" (1858) in *The Maine Woods* (1864), in *The Writings of Henry David Thoreau*, vol. 3, p. 132, Houghton Mifflin (1906).

See also MOOSE

*H*YPOCRISY

The Indian thought that we should lie by on Sunday. Said he, "We come here lookum things, look all around; but come Sunday, lock up all that, and then Monday look again." . . . However, the Indian added, plying the paddle all the while, that if we would go along, he must go with us, he our man, and he suppose that if he no takum pay for what he do Sunday, then ther's no harm, but if he takum pay, then wrong. I told him that he was stricter than white men. Nevertheless, I noticed that he did not forget to reckon in the Sundays at last.

"The Allegash and East Branch" (1864) in *The Maine Woods* (1864), in *The Writings of Henry David Thoreau*, vol. 3, pp. 214–215, Houghton Mifflin (1906).

See also POLIS, JOE

There are thousands who are *in opinion* opposed to slavery and to the war, who yet in effect do nothing to put an end to them; who, esteeming themselves children of Washington and Franklin, sit down with their hands in their pockets, and say that they know not what to do, and do nothing; who even postpone the question of freedom to the question of free trade, and quietly read the prices-current along with the latest advices from Mexico, after dinner, and it may be, fall asleep over them both. What is the price-current of an honest man and patriot to-day? They hesitate, and they regret, and sometimes they petition; but they do nothing in earnest and with effect. They will wait, well disposed, for others to remedy the evil, that they may no longer have to regret. At most, they give only a cheap vote, and a feeble countenance and God-speed, to the right, as it goes by them. There are nine hundred and ninety-nine patrons of virtue to one virtuous man. But it is easier to deal with the real possessor of a thing than with the temporary guardian of it.

"Civil Disobedience," originally published as "Resistance to Civil Government" (1849), in *The Writings of Henry David Thoreau*, vol. 4, pp. 362–363, Houghton Mifflin (1906).

See also MORALITY

*I*CE

In the winter of '46–7 there came a hundred men of Hyperborean extraction swoop down on to our pond one morning, with many carloads of ungainly-looking farming tools. . . . I did not know whether they had come to sow a crop of winter rye, or some other kind of grain recently introduced from Iceland. As I saw no manure, I judged that they meant to skim the land, as I had done, thinking the soil was deep and had lain fallow long enough. They said that a gentleman farmer, who was behind the scenes, wanted to double his money, which, as I understood, amounted to half a million already; but in order to cover each one of his dollars with another, he took off the only coat, ay, the skin itself, of Walden Pond in the midst of a hard winter.

Walden (1854), in *The Writings of Henry David Thoreau*, vol. 2, pp. 324–325, Houghton Mifflin (1906).

See also ECOLOGY

One pleasant morning after a cold night, February 24th, 1850, having gone to Flint's Pond to spend the day, I noticed with surprise, that when I struck the ice with the head of my axe, it resounded like a gong for many rods around, or as if I had struck on a tight drum-head. The pond began to boom about an hour after sunrise, when it felt the influence of the sun's rays slanted upon it from over the hills; it stretched itself and yawned like a waking man with a gradually increasing tumult, which was kept up three or four hours. It took a short siesta at noon, and boomed once more toward night, as the sun was withdrawing his influence.

Walden (1854), in *The Writings of Henry David Thoreau*, vol. 2, pp. 332–333, Houghton Mifflin (1906).

See also SPRING

The phenomena of the year take place every day in a pond on a small scale. Every morning, generally speaking, the shallow water is being warmed more rapidly than the deep, though it may not be made so warm after all, and every evening it is being cooled more rapidly until the morning. The day is an epitome of the year. The night is the winter, the morning and evening are the spring and fall, and the noon is the summer. The cracking and booming of the ice indicate a change of temperature.

Walden (1854), in *The Writings of Henry David Thoreau*, vol. 2, p. 332, Houghton Mifflin (1906).

See also SPRING

Thus it appears that the sweltering inhabitants of Charleston and New Orleans, of Madras and Bombay and Calcutta, drink at my well. In the morning I bathe my intellect in the stupendous and cosmogonal philosophy of the Bhagvat-Geeta, since whose composition years of the gods have elapsed, and in comparison with which our modern world and its literature seem puny and trivial; and I doubt if that philosophy is not to be referred to a previous state of existence, so remote is its sublimity from our conceptions. I lay down the book and go to my well for water, and lo!

there I meet the servant of the Bramin, priest of Brahma and Vishnu and Indra, who still sits in his temple on the Ganges reading the Vedas, or dwells at the root of a tree with his crust and water jug. I meet his servant come to draw water for his master, and our buckets as it were grate together in the same well. The pure Walden water is mingled with the sacred water of the Ganges. With favoring winds it is wafted past the site of the fabulous islands of Atlantis and the Hesperides, makes the periplus of Hanno, and, floating by Ternate and Tidore and the mouth of the Persian Gulf, melts in the tropic gales of the Indian seas, and is landed in ports of which Alexander only heard the names.

Walden (1854), in *The Writings of Henry David Thoreau,* vol. 2, pp. 328–329, Houghton Mifflin (1906).

See also WALDEN POND

*I*MAGINATION

The imagination, give it the least license, dives deeper and soars higher than Nature goes.

Walden (1854), in *The Writings of Henry David Thoreau,* vol. 2, p. 318, Houghton Mifflin (1906).

See also NATURE

*I*NDEPENDENCE

Do what nobody else can do for you. Omit to do anything else.

Letter, August 9, 1850, to Harrison Blake, in *The Writings of Henry David Thoreau,* vol. 6, p. 186, Houghton Mifflin (1906).

See also ACTION

All great enterprises are self-supporting.

"Life Without Principle" (1863), in *The Writings of Henry David Thoreau,* vol. 4, p. 461, Houghton Mifflin (1906).

See also LABOR

I would rather sit on a pumpkin and have it all to myself than be crowded on a velvet cushion. I would rather ride on earth in an ox cart, with a free circulation, than go to heaven in the fancy car of an excursion train and breathe a *malaria* all the way.

Walden (1854), in *The Writings of Henry David Thoreau,* vol. 2, p. 41, Houghton Mifflin (1906).

One young man of my acquaintance, who has inherited some acres, told me that he thought he should live as I did, *if he had the means.* I would not have any one adopt *my* mode of living on any account; for, beside that before he has fairly learned it I may have found out another for myself, I desire that there may be as many different persons in the world as possible; but I would have each one be very careful to find out and pursue *his own* way, and not his father's or his mother's or his neighbor's instead. The youth may build or plant or sail, only let him not be hindered from doing that which he tells me he would like to do.

Walden (1854), in *The Writings of Henry David Thoreau*, vol. 2, pp. 78–79, Houghton Mifflin (1906).

Why should we be in such desperate haste to succeed and in such desperate enterprises? If a man does not keep pace with his companions, perhaps it is because he hears a different drummer. Let him step to the music which hears, however measured or far away.

Walden (1854), in *The Writings of Henry David Thoreau*, vol. 2, pp. 358–359, Houghton Mifflin (1906).

See also CONFORMITY

*I*NNOCENCE

The Eastern steamboat passed us with music and a cheer, as if they were going to a ball, when they might be going to—Davy's locker.

Cape Cod (1855–1865), in *The Writings of Henry David Thoreau*, vol. 4, p. 266, Houghton Mifflin (1906).

See also DEATH

Through our own recovered innocence we discern the innocence of our neighbors.

Walden (1854), in *The Writings of Henry David Thoreau*, vol. 2, pp. 346–347, Houghton Mifflin (1906).

Men are as innocent as the morning to the unsuspicious.

A Week on the Concord and Merrimack Rivers (1849), in *The Writings of Henry David Thoreau*, vol. 1, p. 134, Houghton Mifflin (1906).

See also MORNING

To the innocent there are neither cherubim nor angels.

A Week on the Concord and Merrimack Rivers (1849), in *The Writings of Henry David Thoreau*, vol. 1, p. 394, Houghton Mifflin (1906).

See also MORALITY

*I*NSTINCT

It appeared as if ... he found his way very much as an animal does. Perhaps what is commonly called instinct in an animal, in this case is merely a sharpened and educated sense. Often, when an Indian says, "I don't know," in regard to the route he is to take, he does not mean what a white man would by those words, for his Indian instinct may tell him still as much as the most confident white man knows. He does not carry things in his head, nor remember the route exactly, like a white man, but relies on himself at the moment. Not having experienced the need of the other sort of knowledge, all labeled and arranged, he has not acquired it.

"The Allegash and East Branch" (1864) in *The Maine Woods* (1864), in *The Writings of Henry David Thoreau,* vol. 3, p. 205, Houghton Mifflin (1906).

See also POLIS, JOE

*I*NSTITUTIONS

In my short experience of human life, the *outward* obstacles, if there were any such, have not been living men, but the institutions of the dead.

A Week on the Concord and Merrimack Rivers (1849), in *The Writings of Henry David Thoreau,* vol. 1, p. 134, Houghton Mifflin (1906).

See also TRADITION

*I*NTEGRITY

It makes no odds where a man goes or stays, if he is only about his business.

Letter, February 7, 1855, to Thomas Cholmondeley, in *The Writings of Henry David Thoreau,* vol. 6, p. 251, Houghton Mifflin (1906).

See also TRAVELING AND TRAVELERS

I learned this, at least, by my experiment: that if one advances confidently in the direction of his dreams, and endeavors to live the life which he has imagined, he will meet with a success unexpected in common hours. He will put some things behind, will pass an invisible boundary; new, universal, and more liberal laws will begin to establish themselves around and within him; or the old laws be expanded, and interpreted in his favor in a more liberal sense, and he will live with the license of a higher order of beings. In proportion as he simplifies his life, the laws of the universe will appear less complex, and solitude will not be solitude, nor poverty poverty, nor weakness weakness.

Walden (1854), in *The Writings of Henry David Thoreau,* vol. 2, p. 356, Houghton Mifflin (1906).

See also SIMPLICITY

Sell your clothes and keep your thoughts. God will see that you do not want society.

Walden (1854), in *The Writings of Henry David Thoreau,* vol. 2, p. 361, Houghton Mifflin (1906).

See also PROPERTY

ℐRELAND AND THE IRISH

Alas! the culture of an Irishman is an enterprise to be undertaken with a sort of moral bog hoe.

Walden (1854), in *The Writings of Henry David Thoreau,* vol. 2, p. 228, Houghton Mifflin (1906).

ℐAMES, HENRY, SR.

I have been to see Henry James, and like him very much. It was a great pleasure to meet him. It makes humanity seem more erect and respectable. I never was more kindly and faithfully catechised. It made me respect myself more to be thought worthy of such wise questions.

Letter, June 8, 1843, to Ralph Waldo Emerson, in *The Writings of Henry David Thoreau,* vol. 6, p. 80, Houghton Mifflin (1906).

ℐESUS CHRIST

Christ is the prince of Reformers and Radicals.

A Week on the Concord and Merrimack Rivers (1849), in *The Writings of Henry David Thoreau,* vol. 1, p. 142, Houghton Mifflin (1906).

See also REFORM AND REFORMERS

Christ was a sublime actor on the stage of the world. He knew what he was thinking of when he said, "Heaven and earth shall pass away, but my words shall not pass away." I draw near to him at such a time. Yet he taught mankind but imperfectly how to live; his thoughts were all directed toward another world. There is another kind of success than his. Even here we have a sort of living to get, and must buffet it somewhat longer. There are various tough problems yet to solve, and we must shift to live, betwixt spirit and matter, such a human life as we can.

A Week on the Concord and Merrimack Rivers (1849), in The Writings of Henry David Thoreau, vol. 1, p. 74, Houghton Mifflin (1906).

See also MORALITY

*J*OURNALISM AND JOURNALISTS

Could slavery suggest a more complete servility than some of these journals exhibit? Is there any dust which their conduct does not lick, and make fouler still with its slime?

"Slavery in Massachusetts" (1854), in The Writings of Henry David Thoreau, vol. 4, p. 399, Houghton Mifflin (1906).

Thoreau refers to the response of the Boston newspapers to the return of fugitive slaves to the South.

The press is, almost without exception, corrupt.

"Slavery in Massachusetts" (1854), in The Writings of Henry David Thoreau, vol. 4, p. 397, Houghton Mifflin (1906).

*J*OY

Surely joy is the condition of life.

"Natural History of Massachusetts" (1842), in The Writings of Henry David Thoreau, vol. 5, p. 106, Houghton Mifflin (1906).

A declaration inspired by Thoreau's contemplation of the sheer variety and liveliness of creatures in nature.

See also LIFE

JUSTICE

If I have unjustly wrested a plank from a drowning man, I must restore it to him though I drown myself.

"Civil Disobedience," originally published as "Resistance to Civil Government" (1849), in *The Writings of Henry David Thoreau*, vol. 4, p. 361, Houghton Mifflin (1906).

I wish my countrymen to consider that whatever the human law may be, neither an individual nor a nation can ever commit the least act of injustice against the obscurest individual without having to pay the penalty for it. A government which deliberately enacts injustice, and persists in it, will at length even become the laughing-stock of the world.

"Slavery in Massachusetts" (1854), in *The Writings of Henry David Thoreau*, vol. 4, p. 394, Houghton Mifflin (1906).

See also GOVERNMENT

KNOWLEDGE

It is better to have your head in the clouds, and know where you are . . . than to breathe the clearer atmosphere below them, and think that you are in paradise.

Letter, April 10, 1853, to Harrison Blake, in *The Writings of Henry David Thoreau*, vol. 6, p. 219, Houghton Mifflin (1906).

See also CLOUDS

Knowledge does not come to us by details, but in flashes of light from heaven.

"Life Without Principle" (1863), in *The Writings of Henry David Thoreau*, vol. 4, p. 476, Houghton Mifflin (1906).

We bless and curse ourselves.

A Week on the Concord and Merrimack Rivers (1849), in *The Writings of Henry David Thoreau*, vol. 1, p. 315, Houghton Mifflin (1906).

Thoreau here refers to the self-understanding that may come in dreams.

See also CONSCIOUSNESS

Such is always the pursuit of knowledge. The celestial fruits, the golden apples of the Hesperides, are ever guarded by a hundred-headed dragon which never sleeps, so that it is an Herculean labor to pluck them.

"Wild Apples" (1862), in *The Writings of Henry David Thoreau*, vol. 5, p. 307, Houghton Mifflin (1906).

Thoreau refers here to one of the labors of Hercules in Greek mythology.

See also APPLES AND APPLE TREES

$\mathcal{K}$TAADN, MOUNT

At length I entered within the skirts of the cloud which seemed forever drifting over the summit, and yet would never be gone. . . . It reminded me of the creations of the old epic and dramatic poets, of Atlas, Vulcan, the Cyclops, and Prometheus. Such was Caucasus and the rock where Prometheus was bound. Æschylus had no doubt visited such scenery as this. It was vast, Titanic, and such as man never inhabits. Some part of the beholder, even some vital part, seems to escape through the loose grating of his ribs as he ascends. He is more lone than you can imagine. There is less of substantial thought and fair understanding in him than in the plains where men inhabit. His reason is dispersed and shadowy, more thin and subtle, like the air. Vast, Titanic, inhuman Nature has got him at disadvantage, caught him alone, and pilfers him of some of his divine faculty. She does not smile on him as in the plains. She seems to say sternly, Why came ye here before your time? This ground is not prepared for you. Is it not enough that I smile in the valleys?

"Ktaadn" (1848) in *The Maine Woods* (1864), in *The Writings of Henry David Thoreau*, vol. 3, pp. 70–71, Houghton Mifflin (1906).

See also NATURE

Perhaps I most fully realized that this was primeval, untamed, and forever untamable, *Nature*. . . . It is difficult to conceive of a region uninhabited by man. We habitually presume his presence and influence everywhere. And yet we have not seen pure Nature, unless we have seen her thus vast and drear and inhuman, though in the midst of cities. Nature was here something savage and awful, though beautiful. I looked with awe at the ground I trod on, to see what the Powers had made there, the form and fashion and material of their work. This was that Earth of which we have heard, made out of Chaos and Old Night. Here was no man's garden, but the unhandseled globe. It was not lawn, nor pasture, nor mead, nor woodland, nor lea, nor arable, nor waste land. It was the fresh and natural surface of the planet Earth, as it was made forever and ever,—to be the dwelling of man, we say,—so Nature made it, and man may use it if he can. Man was not to be associated with it. It was Matter, vast, terrific,— not his Mother Earth that we have heard of, not for him to tread on, or be buried in,—no, it were being too familiar even to let his bones lie there,—the home this, of Necessity and Fate. There was clearly felt the presence of a force not bound to be kind to man. It was a place for heathenism and superstitious rites,—to be inhabited by men nearer of kin to the rocks and to wild animals than we.

"Ktaadn" (1848) in *The Maine Woods* (1864), in *The Writings of Henry David Thoreau*, vol. 3, pp. 77–78, Houghton Mifflin (1906).

See also NATURE

Seen from this point, a bare ridge at the extremity of the open land, Ktaadn presented a different aspect from any mountain I have seen, there being a greater proportion of naked rock rising abruptly from the forest; and we looked up at this blue barrier as if it were some fragment of a wall which anciently bounded the earth in that direction.

"Ktaadn" (1848) in *The Maine Woods* (1864), in *The Writings of Henry David Thoreau*, vol. 3, p. 62, Houghton Mifflin (1906).

We were soon in the smooth water of the Quakish Lake, ... and we had our first, but a partial view of Ktaadn, its summit veiled in clouds, like a dark isthmus in that quarter, connecting the heavens with the earth.

"Ktaadn" (1848) in *The Maine Woods* (1864), in *The Writings of Henry David Thoreau*, vol. 3, p. 36, Houghton Mifflin (1906).

While my companions were seeking a suitable spot ... I improved the little daylight that was left in climbing the mountain alone. ... I began to work my way, scarcely less arduous than Satan's anciently through Chaos, up the nearest though not the highest peak, at first scrambling on all fours over the tops of ancient black spruce trees (*Abies nigra*), old as the flood, from two to ten or twelve feet in height, their tops flat and spreading, and their foliage blue, and nipped with cold, as if for centuries they had ceased growing upward against the bleak sky, the solid cold. ... This was the sort of garden I made my way *over*, for an eighth of a mile, at the risk, it is true, of treading on some of the plants, not seeing any path *through* it,— certainly the most treacherous and porous country I ever traveled.

"Nigh foundered on he fares,
Treading the crude consistence, half on foot,
Half flying."

"Ktaadn" (1848) in *The Maine Woods* (1864), in *The Writings of Henry David Thoreau*, vol. 3, pp. 66–68, Houghton Mifflin (1906).

LABOR

A man had better starve at once than lose his innocence in the process of getting his bread.

"Life Without Principle" (1863), in *The Writings of Henry David Thoreau*, vol. 4, p. 468, Houghton Mifflin (1906).

See also MORALITY

I wish to suggest that a man may be very industrious, and yet not spend his time well. There is no more fatal blunderer than he who consumes the greater part of his life getting his living.

"Life Without Principle" (1863), in *The Writings of Henry David Thoreau*, vol. 4, p. 461, Houghton Mifflin (1906).

See also LIFE

If the laborer gets no more than the wages which his employer pays him, he is cheated, he cheats himself.

"Life Without Principle" (1863), in *The Writings of Henry David Thoreau*, vol. 4, p. 458, Houghton Mifflin (1906).

See also MONEY

Most men would feel insulted if it were proposed to employ them in throwing stones over a wall, and then in throwing them back, merely that they might earn their wages. But many are no more worthily employed now.

"Life Without Principle" (1863), in *The Writings of Henry David Thoreau*, vol. 4, p. 457, Houghton Mifflin (1906).

This world is a place of business. What an infinite bustle! I am awaked almost every night by the panting of the locomotive. It interrupts my dreams. There is no sabbath. It would be glorious to see mankind at leisure for once. It is nothing but work, work, work.

"Life Without Principle" (1863), in *The Writings of Henry David Thoreau*, vol. 4, p. 456, Houghton Mifflin (1906).

But men labor under a mistake. The better part of the man is soon ploughed into the soil for compost. By a seeming fate, commonly called necessity, they are employed, as it says in an old book, laying up treasures which moth and rust will corrupt and thieves break through and steal. It is a fool's life, as they will find when they get to the end of it, if not before.

Walden (1854), in The Writings of Henry David Thoreau, vol. 2, p. 6, Houghton Mifflin (1906).

See also PROPERTY

Drive a nail home and clinch it so faithfully that you can wake up in the night and think of your work with satisfaction,—a work at which you would not be ashamed to invoke the Muse.

Walden (1854), in The Writings of Henry David Thoreau, vol. 2, p. 364, Houghton Mifflin (1906).

See also INTEGRITY

For more than five years I maintained myself thus solely by the labor of my hands, and I found that, by working about six weeks in a year, I could meet all the expenses of living. The whole of my winters, as well as most of my summers, I had free and clear for study.

Walden (1854), in The Writings of Henry David Thoreau, vol. 2, p. 76, Houghton Mifflin (1906).

LAKES

It is an agreeable change to cross a lake, after you have been shut up in the woods, not only on account of the greater expanse of water, but also of sky. It is one of the surprises which Nature has in store for the traveler in the forest. To look down, in this case, over eighteen miles of water, was liberating and civilizing even.

"The Allegash and East Branch" (1864) in The Maine Woods (1864), in The Writings of Henry David Thoreau, vol. 3, pp. 218–219, Houghton Mifflin (1906).

See also FORESTS

That which we kept off, and toward which the waves were driving, was as dreary and harborless a shore as you can conceive. For half a dozen rods in width it was a perfect maze of submerged trees, all dead and bare and bleaching, some standing half their original height, others prostrate, and criss-across, above or beneath the surface, and mingled with them were loose trees and limbs and stumps, beating about. Imagine the wharves of the largest city in the world, decayed, and the earth and planking washed away, leaving the spiles standing in loose order, but often of twice the ordinary height, and mingled with and beating against them the wreck of ten thousand navies, all their spars and timbers, while there rises from the water's edge the densest and grimmest wilderness, ready to supply more material when the former fails, and you may get a faint idea of that coast. We could not have landed if we would.

"The Allegash and East Branch" (1864) in *The Maine Woods* (1864), in *The Writings of Henry David Thoreau*, vol. 3, pp. 263–264, Houghton Mifflin (1906).

See also WILDERNESS

Landlords

Who ever thought of the religion of an innkeeper,—whether he was joined to the Church, partook of the sacrament, said his prayers, feared God, or the like? No doubt he has had his experiences, has felt a change, and is a firm believer in the perseverance of the saints. In this last, we suspect, does the peculiarity of his religion consist. But he keeps an inn and not a conscience. How many fragrant charities and sincere social virtues are implied in this daily offering of himself to the public! He cherishes good-will to all, and gives the wayfarer as good and honest advice to direct him on his road as the priest.

"The Landlord" (1843), in *The Writings of Henry David Thoreau*, vol. 5, p. 161, Houghton Mifflin (1906).

See also RELIGION

Language

There are other letters for the child to learn than those which Cadmus invented. The Spaniards have a good term to express this wild and dusky knowledge, *Grammatica parda*, tawny grammar, a kind of mother-wit derived from that same leopard to which I have referred.

"Walking" (1862), in *The Writings of Henry David Thoreau*, vol. 5, p. 239, Houghton Mifflin (1906).

The "leopard to which I have referred" is Nature.

See also KNOWLEDGE

LAW

Law never made men a whit more just; and, by means of their respect for it, even the well-disposed are daily made the agents of injustice.

"Civil Disobedience," originally published as "Resistance to Civil Government" (1849), in *The Writings of Henry David Thoreau*, vol. 4, p. 358, Houghton Mifflin (1906).

See also JUSTICE

I have not read far in the statutes of this Commonwealth. It is not profitable reading. They do not always say what is true; and they do not always mean what they say.

"Slavery in Massachusetts" (1854), in *The Writings of Henry David Thoreau*, vol. 4, p. 391, Houghton Mifflin (1906).

The law will never make a man free; it is men who have got to make the law free.

"Slavery in Massachusetts" (1854), in *The Writings of Henry David Thoreau*, vol. 4, p. 396, Houghton Mifflin (1906).

See also FREEDOM

They are the lovers of law and order who observe the law when the government breaks it.

"Slavery in Massachusetts" (1854), in *The Writings of Henry David Thoreau*, vol. 4, p. 396, Houghton Mifflin (1906).

See also GOVERNMENT

LIBERTY

Is this what all these soldiers, all this *training,* have been for these seventy-nine years past? Have they been trained merely to rob Mexico and carry back fugitive slaves to their masters?

"Slavery in Massachusetts" (1854), in *The Writings of Henry David Thoreau*, vol. 4, p. 392, Houghton Mifflin (1906).

See also SLAVERY

*L*IFE

Every creature is better alive than dead, men and moose and pine trees, and he who understands it aright will rather preserve its life than destroy it.

"Chesuncook" (1858) in *The Maine Woods* (1864), in *The Writings of Henry David Thoreau*, vol. 3, p. 135, Houghton Mifflin (1906).

See also ECOLOGY

Life is so short that it is not wise to take roundabout ways, nor can we spend much time in waiting. . . . We have not got half-way to dawn yet.

Letter, April 10, 1853, to Harrison Blake, in *The Writings of Henry David Thoreau*, vol. 6, p. 220, Houghton Mifflin (1906).

Let us consider the way in which we spend our lives.

"Life Without Principle" (1863), in *The Writings of Henry David Thoreau*, vol. 4, p. 456, Houghton Mifflin (1906).

We do not live by justice, but by grace.

"Thomas Carlyle and His Works" (1847), in *The Writings of Henry David Thoreau*, vol. 4, p. 353, Houghton Mifflin (1906).

See also JUSTICE

I went to the woods because I wished to live deliberately, to front only the essential facts of life, and see if I could not learn what it had to teach, and not, when I came to die, to discover that I had not lived. I did not wish to live what was not life, living is so dear; nor did I wish to practise resignation, unless it was quite necessary. I wanted to live deep and suck out all the marrow of life, to live so sturdily and Spartan-like as to put to rout all that was not life, to cut a broad swath and shave close, to drive life into a corner, and reduce it to its lowest terms, and, if it proved to be mean, why then to get the whole and genuine meanness of it, and publish its meanness to the world; or if it were sublime, to know it by experience, and be able to give a true account of it in my next excursion. For most men, it appears to me, are in a strange uncertainty about it, whether it is of the devil or of God, and have *somewhat hastily* concluded that it is the chief end of man here to "glorify God and enjoy him forever."

Walden (1854), in *The Writings of Henry David Thoreau*, vol. 2, pp. 100–101, Houghton Mifflin (1906).

See also WALDEN POND

One may almost doubt if the wisest man has learned anything of absolute value by living.

> *Walden* (1854), in *The Writings of Henry David Thoreau*, vol. 2, p. 9, Houghton Mifflin (1906).
>
> See also WISDOM

Still we live meanly, like ants; though the fable tells us that we were long ago changed into men; like pygmies we fight with cranes; it is error upon error, and clout upon clout, and our best virtue has for its occasion a superfluous and evitable wretchedness. Our life is frittered away by detail.

> *Walden* (1854), in *The Writings of Henry David Thoreau*, vol. 2, p. 101, Houghton Mifflin (1906).

The mass of men lead lives of quiet desperation.

> *Walden* (1854), in *The Writings of Henry David Thoreau*, vol. 2, p. 8, Houghton Mifflin (1906).

To be awake is to be alive. I have never yet met a man who was quite awake. How could I have looked him in the face?

> *Walden* (1854), in *The Writings of Henry David Thoreau*, vol. 2, p. 100, Houghton Mifflin (1906).
>
> See also INTEGRITY

We are the subjects of an experiment which is not a little interesting to me.

> *Walden* (1854), in *The Writings of Henry David Thoreau*, vol. 2, p. 149, Houghton Mifflin (1906).

LIGHTHOUSES

I thought it a pity that some poor student did not live there, to profit by all that light, since he would not rob the mariner. . . . Think of fifteen Argand lamps to read the newspaper by! Government oil!—light enough, perchance, to read the Constitution by! I thought that he should read nothing less than his Bible by that lamp.

> *Cape Cod* (1855–1865), in *The Writings of Henry David Thoreau*, vol. 4, p. 171, Houghton Mifflin (1906).
>
> See also BIBLE, THE

LITERATURE

That age will be rich indeed when those relics which we call Classics, and the still older and more than classic but even less known Scriptures of the nations, shall have still further accumulated, when the Vaticans shall be filled with Vedas and Zendavestas and Bibles, with Homers and Dantes and Shakespeares, and all the centuries to come shall have successively deposited their trophies in the forum of the world. By such a pile we may hope to scale heaven at last.

> *Walden* (1854), in *The Writings of Henry David Thoreau*, vol. 2, p. 115, Houghton Mifflin (1906).
>
> See also CLASSICS, THE

Where is the literature which gives expression to Nature? He would be a poet who could impress the winds and streams into his service, to speak for him; who nailed words to their primitive senses, as farmers drive down stakes in the spring, which the frost has heaved; who derived his words as often as he used them,—transplanted them to his page with earth adhering to their roots; whose words were so true and fresh and natural that they would appear to expand like the buds at the approach of spring, though they lay half smothered between two musty leaves in a library,— aye, to bloom and bear fruit there, after their kind, annually, for the faithful reader, in sympathy with surrounding Nature. I do not know of any poetry to quote which adequately expresses this yearning for the Wild. Approached from this side, the best poetry is tame.

I do not know where to find in any literature, ancient or modern, any account which contents me of that Nature with which even I am acquainted. You will perceive that I demand something which no Augustan nor Elizabethan age, which no *culture*, in short, can give. Mythology comes nearer it than anything. How much more fertile a Nature, at least, has Grecian mythology its root in than English literature! Mythology is the crop which the Old World bore before its soil was exhausted, before the fancy and imagination were affected with blight; and which it still bears, wherever its pristine vigor is unabated. All other literatures endure only as the elms which overshadow our houses; but this is like the great dragon-tree of the Western Isles, as old as mankind, and, whether that does or not, will endure as long; for the decay of other literatures makes the soil in which it thrives.

> "Walking" (1862), in *The Writings of Henry David Thoreau*, vol. 5, pp. 232–233, Houghton Mifflin (1906).
>
> See also WILDNESS

All men are children, and of one family. The same tale sends them all to bed, and wakes them in the morning.

A Week on the Concord and Merrimack Rivers (1849), in The Writings of Henry David Thoreau, vol. 1, p. 60, Houghton Mifflin (1906).

See also CULTURE

It were vain for me to endeavor to interpret the Silence. She cannot be done into English. For six thousand years men have translated her with what fidelity belonged to each, and still she is little better than a sealed book. A man may run on confidently for a time, thinking he has her under his thumb, and shall one day exhaust her, but he too must at last be silent, and men remark only how brave a beginning he made; for when he at length dives into her, so vast is the disproportion of the told to the untold that the former will seem but the bubble on the surface where he disappeared. Nevertheless, we will go on, like those Chinese cliff swallows, feathering our nests with the froth which may one day be bread of life to such as dwell by the seashore.

A Week on the Concord and Merrimack Rivers (1849), in The Writings of Henry David Thoreau, vol. 1, p. 420, Houghton Mifflin (1906).

See also EXISTENCE

Literature, english

English literature, from the days of the minstrels to the Lake Poets,— Chaucer and Spenser and Milton, and even Shakespeare, included,— breathes no quite fresh and, in this sense, wild strain. It is an essentially tame and civilized literature, reflecting Greece and Rome. Her wildness is a greenwood, her wild man a Robin Hood. There is plenty of genial love of Nature, but not so much of Nature herself. Her chronicles inform us when her wild animals, but not the wild man in her, became extinct.

"Walking" (1862), in The Writings of Henry David Thoreau, vol. 5, p. 231, Houghton Mifflin (1906).

See also WILDNESS

Loons

At length, having come up fifty rods off, he uttered one of those prolonged howls, as if calling on the god of loons to aid him, and immediately there came a wind from the east and rippled the surface, and filled the whole air with misty rain, and I was impressed as if it were the prayer of the loon answered, and his god was angry with me; and so I left him disappearing far away on the tumultuous surface.

Walden (1854), in *The Writings of Henry David Thoreau*, vol. 2, pp. 261–262, Houghton Mifflin (1906).

In the fall the loon (*Colymbus glacialis*) came, as usual, to moult and bathe in the pond, making the woods ring with his wild laughter before I had risen. . . . When I went to get a pail of water early in the morning I frequently saw this stately bird sailing out of my cove within a few rods. If I endeavored to overtake him in a boat, in order to see how he would manœvre, he would dive and be completely lost, so that I did not discover him again, sometimes, till the latter part of the day. But I was more than a match for him on the surface. He commonly went off in a rain.

Walden (1854), in *The Writings of Henry David Thoreau*, vol. 2, pp. 258–259, Houghton Mifflin (1906).

Lost, being

In our most trivial walks, we are constantly, though unconsciously, steering like pilots by certain well-known beacons and headlands, and if we go beyond our usual course we still carry in our minds the bearing of some neighboring cape; and not till we are completely lost, or turned round,— for a man needs only to be turned round once with his eyes shut in this world to be lost,—do we appreciate the vastness and strangeness of nature.

Walden (1854), in *The Writings of Henry David Thoreau*, vol. 2, p. 189, Houghton Mifflin (1906).

See also WALKING

Love

Love is a severe critic.

Essay on "Love" in letter, September 1852, to Harrison Blake, in *The Writings of Henry David Thoreau*, vol. 6, p. 200, Houghton Mifflin (1906).

Do what you love. Know your own bone; gnaw at it, bury it, unearth it, and gnaw it still.

Letter, March 27, 1848, to Harrison Blake, in *The Writings of Henry David Thoreau*, vol. 6, pp. 163–164, Houghton Mifflin (1906).

See also DEEDS

Ignorance and bungling with love are better than wisdom and skill without.

A Week on the Concord and Merrimack Rivers (1849), in *The Writings of Henry David Thoreau*, vol. 1, p. 301, Houghton Mifflin (1906).

Only lovers know the value and magnanimity of truth.

A Week on the Concord and Merrimack Rivers (1849), in *The Writings of Henry David Thoreau*, vol. 1, p. 284, Houghton Mifflin (1906).

See also TRUTH

Our life without love is coke and ashes.

A Week on the Concord and Merrimack Rivers (1849), in *The Writings of Henry David Thoreau*, vol. 1, p. 301, Houghton Mifflin (1906).

See also LIFE

The heart is forever inexperienced.

A Week on the Concord and Merrimack Rivers (1849), in *The Writings of Henry David Thoreau*, vol. 1, p. 278, Houghton Mifflin (1906).

See also FRIENDS AND FRIENDSHIP

The violence of love is as much to be dreaded as that of hate.

A Week on the Concord and Merrimack Rivers (1849), in *The Writings of Henry David Thoreau*, vol. 1, p. 290, Houghton Mifflin (1906).

See also VIOLENCE

To *love* another . . . is, to stand in a true relation to him, so that we give the best to, and receive the best from, him.

A Week on the Concord and Merrimack Rivers (1849), in *The Writings of Henry David Thoreau*, vol. 1, p. 284, Houghton Mifflin (1906).

True love does not quarrel for slight reasons, such mistakes as mutual acquaintances can explain away, but, alas, however slight the apparent cause, only for adequate and fatal and everlasting reasons, which can never be set aside.

A *Week on the Concord and Merrimack Rivers* (1849), in *The Writings of Henry David Thoreau*, vol. 1, p. 300, Houghton Mifflin (1906).

What avails it that another loves you, if he does not understand you? Such love is a curse.

A *Week on the Concord and Merrimack Rivers* (1849), in *The Writings of Henry David Thoreau*, vol. 1, p. 295, Houghton Mifflin (1906).

See also KNOWLEDGE

LUMBERING

This burnt land was an exceedingly wild and desolate region. Judging by the weeds and sprouts, it appeared to have been burnt about two years before. It was covered with charred trunks, either prostrate or standing, which crocked our clothes and hands, and we could not easily have distinguished a bear there by his color. Great shells of trees, sometimes unburnt without, or burnt on one side only, but black within, stood twenty or forty feet high. The fire had run up inside, as in a chimney, leaving the sap-wood. Sometimes we crossed a rocky ravine fifty feet wide, on a fallen trunk; and there were great fields of fire-weed (*Epilobium angustifolium*) on all sides, the most extensive that I ever saw, which presented great masses of pink. Intermixed with these were blueberry and raspberry bushes.

"The Allegash and East Branch" (1864) in *The Maine Woods* (1864), in *The Writings of Henry David Thoreau*, vol. 3, p. 282, Houghton Mifflin (1906).

See also FIRE

It is a war against the pines, the only real Aroostook or Penobscot war.

"Chesuncook" (1858) in *The Maine Woods* (1864), in *The Writings of Henry David Thoreau*, vol. 3, p. 142, Houghton Mifflin (1906).

The mode of clearing and planting is to fell the trees, and burn once what will burn, then cut them up into suitable lengths, roll into heaps, and burn again; then, with a hoe, plant potatoes where you can come at the ground between the stumps and charred logs; for a first crop the ashes suffice for manure, and no hoeing being necessary the first year. In the fall, cut, roll, and burn again, and so on, till the land is cleared; and soon it is ready for grain, and to be laid down.

"Ktaadn" (1848) in *The Maine Woods* (1864), in *The Writings of Henry David Thoreau*, vol. 3, p. 15, Houghton Mifflin (1906).

See also FARMERS AND FARMING

*M*AINE

Let those talk of poverty and hard times who will in the towns and cities; cannot the emigrant who can pay his fare to New York or Boston pay five dollars more to get here ... and be as rich as he pleases, where land virtually costs nothing, and houses only the labor of building, and he may begin life as Adam did? If he will still remember the distinction of poor and rich, let him bespeak him a narrower house forthwith.

"Ktaadn" (1848) in *The Maine Woods* (1864), in *The Writings of Henry David Thoreau*, vol. 3, pp. 15–16, Houghton Mifflin (1906).

This was what you might call a bran-new country; the only roads were of Nature's making, and the few houses were camps. Here, then, one could no longer accuse institutions and society, but must front the true source of evil.

"Ktaadn" (1848) in *The Maine Woods* (1864), in *The Writings of Henry David Thoreau*, vol. 3, p. 18, Houghton Mifflin (1906).

*M*AINE, *LANDSCAPE OF*

I had thought to observe on this carry when we crossed the dividing line between the Penobscot and St. John, but as my feet had hardly been out of water the whole distance, and it was all level and stagnant, I began to despair of finding it. I remembered hearing a good deal about the "highlands" dividing the waters of the Penobscot from those of the St. John, as well as the St. Lawrence, at the time of the northeast boundary dispute. ... I thought that if the commissioners themselves, and the King of Holland with them, had spent a few days here, with their packs upon their backs, looking for that "highland," they would have had an interesting time, and perhaps it would have modified their views of the question somewhat. The King of Holland would have been in his element.

"The Allegash and East Branch" (1864) in *The Maine Woods* (1864), in *The Writings of Henry David Thoreau*, vol. 3, pp. 238–239, Houghton Mifflin (1906).

See also SWAMPS

At sundown, leaving the river road awhile for shortness, we went by way of Enfield, where we stopped for the night. This, like most of the localities bearing names on this road, was a place to name which, in the midst of the unnamed and unincorporated wilderness, was to make a distinction without a difference, it seemed to me.

"Ktaadn" (1848) in *The Maine Woods* (1864), in *The Writings of Henry David Thoreau*, vol. 3, p. 9, Houghton Mifflin (1906).

See also WILDERNESS

It is even more grim and wild than you had anticipated, a damp and intricate wilderness, in the spring everywhere wet and miry. The aspect of the country, indeed, is universally stern and savage, excepting the distant views of the forest from hills, and the lake prospects, which are mild and civilizing in a degree.

"Ktaadn" (1848) in *The Maine Woods* (1864), in *The Writings of Henry David Thoreau*, vol. 3, p. 88, Houghton Mifflin (1906).

See also FORESTS

The country is an archipelago of lakes,—the lake-country of New England.

"Ktaadn" (1848) in *The Maine Woods* (1864), in *The Writings of Henry David Thoreau*, vol. 3, p. 40, Houghton Mifflin (1906).

See also LAKES

*M*ANIFEST DESTINY

The whole enterprise of this nation, which is not an upward, but a westward one, toward Oregon, California, Japan, etc., is totally devoid of interest to me, whether performed on foot, or by a Pacific railroad. . . . It is perfectly heathenish,—a filibustering *toward* heaven by the great western route. No; they may go their way to their manifest destiny, which I trust is not mine. . . . I would rather be a captive knight, and let them all pass by, than be free only to go whither they are bound. What end do they propose to themselves beyond Japan? What aims more lofty have they than the prairie dogs?

Letter, February 27, 1853, to Harrison Blake, in *The Writings of Henry David Thoreau*, vol. 6, p. 210, Houghton Mifflin (1906).

See also WEST, THE (U.S.)

$\mathcal{M}$APLE TREES

Its *virtues*, not its sins, are as scarlet.

"Autumnal Tints" (1862), in *The Writings of Henry David Thoreau*, vol. 5, p. 261, Houghton Mifflin (1906).

$\mathcal{M}$ARRIAGE

There is more of good nature than of good sense at the bottom of most marriages.

Essay on "Love" in letter, September 1852, to Harrison Blake, in *The Writings of Henry David Thoreau*, vol. 6, pp. 199–200, Houghton Mifflin (1906).

See also COMMON SENSE

I have had a tragic correspondence, for the most part all on one side, with Miss _____. She did really wish to—I hesitate to write—marry me. That is the way they spell it. Of course I did not write a deliberate answer. How could I deliberate upon it? I sent back as distinct a *no* as I have learned to pronounce after considerable practice, and I trust that this *no* has succeeded. Indeed, I wished that it might burst, like hollow shot, after it had struck and buried itself and made itself felt there. *There was no other way.* I really had anticipated no such foe as this in my career.

Letter, November 14, 1847, to Ralph Waldo Emerson, in *The Writings of Henry David Thoreau*, vol. 6, pp. 138–139, Houghton Mifflin (1906).

There are only two or three couples in history.

A Week on the Concord and Merrimack Rivers (1849), in *The Writings of Henry David Thoreau*, vol. 1, p. 282, Houghton Mifflin (1906).

See also LOVE

*M*ATHEMATICS

Mathematics should be mixed not only with physics but with ethics.

A Week on the Concord and Merrimack Rivers (1849), in *The Writings of Henry David Thoreau*, vol. 1, p. 387, Houghton Mifflin (1906).

See also MORALITY

*M*EDITATION

Sometimes, in a summer morning, having taken my accustomed bath, I sat in my sunny doorway from sunrise till noon, rapt in a revery, amidst the pines and hickories and sumachs, in undisturbed solitude and stillness, while the birds sang around or flitted noiseless through the house, until by the sun falling in at my west window, or the noise of some traveller's wagon on the distant highway, I was reminded of the lapse of time. I grew in those seasons like corn in the night, and they were far better than any work of the hands would have been. They were not time subtracted from my life, but so much over and above my usual allowance. I realized what the Orientals mean by contemplation and the forsaking of works.

Walden (1854), in *The Writings of Henry David Thoreau*, vol. 2, pp. 123–124, Houghton Mifflin (1906).

See also TIME

*M*ELON-MAN, THE

We had got a loaf of home-made bread, and musk and water melons for dessert. For this farmer, a clever and well-disposed man, cultivated a large patch of melons for the Hooksett and Concord markets. He hospitably entertained us the next day, exhibiting his hop-fields and kiln and melon-patch, warning us to step over the tight rope which surrounded the latter at a foot from the ground, while he pointed to a little bower at one corner, where it connected with the lock of a gun ranging with the line, and where, he informed us, he sometimes sat in pleasant nights to defend his premises against thieves. We stepped high over the line, and sympathized with our host's on the whole quite human, if not humane, interest in the success of his experiment. That night especially thieves were to be expected, from rumors in the atmosphere, and the priming was not wet.

He was a Methodist man, who had his dwelling between the river and Uncannunuc Mountain; who there belonged, and stayed at home there, and by the encouragement of distant political organizations, and by his own tenacity, held a property in his melons, and continued to plant. We suggested melon seeds of new varieties and fruit of foreign flavor to be added to his stock. We had come away up here among the hills to learn the impartial and unbribable influence of Nature. Strawberries and melons grew as well in one man's garden as another's, and the sun lodges as kindly under his hillside,—when we had imagined that she inclined rather to some few earnest and faithful souls whom we know.

> *A Week on the Concord and Merrimack Rivers* (1849), in *The Writings of Henry David Thoreau*, vol. 1, pp. 308–309, Houghton Mifflin (1906).

> Thoreau's reference to "melons" (from the Greek *melon,* or "fruit") suggests that this passage begins a revisionary reenactment of the biblical story of the Fall.

$\mathcal{M}$ENU

Any *moral* philosophy is exceedingly rare. This of Menu addresses our privacy more than most. It is a more private and familiar, and at the same time, a more public and universal word, than is spoken in parlor or pulpit nowadays.

> *A Week on the Concord and Merrimack Rivers* (1849), in *The Writings of Henry David Thoreau*, vol. 1, p. 156, Houghton Mifflin (1906).

> See also PHILOSOPHY AND PHILOSOPHERS

I know of no book which has come down to us with grander pretensions than this, and it is so impersonal and sincere that it is never offensive nor ridiculous. Compare the modes in which modern literature is advertised with the prospectus of this book, and think what a reading public it addresses, what criticism it expects. It seems to have been uttered from some eastern summit, with a sober morning prescience in the dawn of time, and you cannot read a sentence without being elevated as upon the table-land of the Ghauts. It has such a rhythm as the winds of the desert, such a tide as the Ganges, and is as superior to criticism as the Himmaleh Mountains.

> *A Week on the Concord and Merrimack Rivers* (1849), in *The Writings of Henry David Thoreau*, vol. 1, p. 155, Houghton Mifflin (1906).

> Thoreau refers to *The Laws of Menu.*

$\mathcal{M}$ERRIMACK RIVER, MASSACHUSETTS AND NEW HAMPSHIRE

The Concord had rarely been a river, or *rivus*, but barely *fluvius*, or between *fluvius* and *lacus*. This Merrimack was neither *rivus* nor *fluvius* nor *lacus*, but rather *amnis* here, a gently swelling and stately rolling flood approaching the sea. We could even sympathize with its buoyant tide, going to seek its fortune in the ocean, and anticipating the time when "being received within the plain of its freer water," it should "beat the shore for banks."

A Week on the Concord and Merrimack Rivers (1849), in *The Writings of Henry David Thoreau*, vol. 1, p. 113, Houghton Mifflin (1906).

See also CONCORD RIVER, MASSACHUSETTS

$\mathcal{M}$ICE

My only companions were the mice, which came to pick up the crumbs that had been left in those scraps of paper; still, as everywhere, pensioners on man, and not unwisely improving this elevated tract for their habitation. They nibbled what was for them; I nibbled what was for me.

A Week on the Concord and Merrimack Rivers (1849), in *The Writings of Henry David Thoreau*, vol. 1, pp. 196–197, Houghton Mifflin (1906).

$\mathcal{M}$IND, THE

Every man is the lord of a realm beside which the earthly empire of the Czar is but a petty state, a hummock left by the ice.

Walden (1854), in *The Writings of Henry David Thoreau*, vol. 2, p. 353, Houghton Mifflin (1906).

See also THINKING AND THOUGHTS

$\mathcal{M}$ISTAKES

The best way to correct a mistake is to make it right.

Letter, January 24, 1843, to Ralph Waldo Emerson, in *The Writings of Henry David Thoreau*, vol. 6, p. 50, Houghton Mifflin (1906).

See also REFORM AND REFORMERS

$\mathcal{M}$OLES

The moles nested in my cellar, nibbling every third potato, and making a snug bed even there of some hair left after plastering and of brown paper; for even the wildest animals love comfort and warmth as well as man, and they survive the winter only because they are so careful to secure them.

Walden (1854), in *The Writings of Henry David Thoreau*, vol. 2, p. 280, Houghton Mifflin (1906).

See also HUMAN NATURE

$\mathcal{M}$ONADNOCK, MOUNT

From the foundation of a wooden observatory ... we could see Monadnock, in simple grandeur, in the northwest, rising nearly a thousand feet higher, still the "far blue mountain," though with an altered profile. The first day the weather was so hazy that it was in vain we endeavored to unravel the obscurity. It was like looking into the sky again, and the patches of forest here and there seemed to flit like clouds over a lower heaven. As to voyagers of an aerial Polynesia, the earth seemed like a larger island in the ether; on every side, even as low as we, the sky shutting down, like an unfathomable deep, around it, a blue Pacific island, where who knows what islanders inhabit? and as we sail near its shores we see the waving of trees and hear the lowing of kine.

"A Walk to Wachusett" (1843), in *The Writings of Henry David Thoreau*, vol. 5, p. 143, Houghton Mifflin (1906).

See also MOUNTAINS

Money

Absolutely speaking, the more money, the less virtue; for money comes between a man and his objects, and obtains them for him; and it was certainly no great virtue to obtain it.

"Civil Disobedience," originally published as "Resistance to Civil Government" (1849), in *The Writings of Henry David Thoreau*, vol. 4, p. 372, Houghton Mifflin (1906).

See also MORALITY

Moose

The moose is singularly grotesque and awkward to look at. Why should it stand so high at the shoulders? Why have so long a head? Why have no tail to speak of?

"Chesuncook" (1858) in *The Maine Woods* (1864), in *The Writings of Henry David Thoreau*, vol. 3, p. 128, Houghton Mifflin (1906).

These are God's own horses, poor, timid creatures, that will run fast enough as soon as they smell you, though they *are* nine feet high.

"Chesuncook" (1858) in *The Maine Woods* (1864), in *The Writings of Henry David Thoreau*, vol. 3, p. 132, Houghton Mifflin (1906).

We suddenly spied two moose standing just on the edge of the open part of the meadow which we had passed, not more than six or seven rods distant, looking around the alders at us. They made me think of great frightened rabbits, with their long ears and half-inquisitive, half-frightened looks; the true denizens of the forest (I saw at once), filling a vacuum which now first I discovered had not been filled for me,—*moose*-men, *wood-eaters,* the word is said to mean,—clad in a sort of Vermont gray, or homespun.

"Chesuncook" (1858) in *The Maine Woods* (1864), in *The Writings of Henry David Thoreau*, vol. 3, p. 122, Houghton Mifflin (1906).

The track of a full-grown moose is like that of a cow, or larger, and of the young, like that of a calf. . . . Though numerous, they are so wary that the unskillful hunter might range the forest a long time before he could get sight of one. They are sometimes dangerous to encounter, and will not turn out for the hunter, but furiously rush upon him and trample him to death, unless he is lucky enough to avoid them by dodging round a tree.

The largest are nearly as large as a horse, and weigh sometimes one thousand pounds. . . . They are described as exceedingly awkward-looking animals, with their long legs and short bodies, making a ludicrous figure when in full run, but making great headway, nevertheless. It seemed a mystery to us how they could thread these woods, which it required all our suppleness to accomplish,—climbing, stooping, and winding, alternately.

"Ktaadn" (1848) in *The Maine Woods* (1864), in *The Writings of Henry David Thoreau*, vol. 3, pp. 63–64, Houghton Mifflin (1906).

*M*ORALITY

The broadest and most prevalent error requires the most disinterested virtue to sustain it.

"Civil Disobedience," originally published as "Resistance to Civil Government" (1849), in *The Writings of Henry David Thoreau*, vol. 4, p. 366, Houghton Mifflin (1906).

Be not simply good; be good for something.

Letter, March 27, 1848, to Harrison Blake, in *The Writings of Henry David Thoreau*, vol. 6, p. 164, Houghton Mifflin (1906).

See also SPIRITUALITY/PRAYER

Goodness is the only investment that never fails.

Walden (1854), in *The Writings of Henry David Thoreau*, vol. 2, p. 241, Houghton Mifflin (1906).

No man loses ever on a lower level by magnanimity on a higher.

Walden (1854), in *The Writings of Henry David Thoreau*, vol. 2, p. 362, Houghton Mifflin (1906).

Absolutely speaking, Do unto others as you would that they should do unto you is by no means a golden rule, but the best of current silver. An honest man would have but little occasion for it. It is golden not to have any rule at all in such a case.

A Week on the Concord and Merrimack Rivers (1849), in *The Writings of Henry David Thoreau*, vol. 1, p. 74, Houghton Mifflin (1906).

See also LOVE

Men have a singular desire to be good without being good for anything, because, perchance, they think vaguely that so it will be good for them in the end.

> *A Week on the Concord and Merrimack Rivers* (1849), in *The Writings of Henry David Thoreau*, vol. 1, p. 75, Houghton Mifflin (1906).

$\mathcal{M}$ORNING

Little is to be expected of that day, if it can be called a day, to which we are not awakened by our Genius, . . . to a higher life than we fell asleep from.

> *Walden* (1854), in *The Writings of Henry David Thoreau*, vol. 2, p. 99, Houghton Mifflin (1906).

$\mathcal{M}$ORTALITY

Now only a dent in the earth marks the site of these dwellings, with buried cellar stones, and strawberries, raspberries, thimble-berries, hazel-bushes, and sumachs growing in the sunny sward there. . . . These cellar dents, like deserted fox burrows, old holes, are all that is left where once were the stir and bustle of human life, and "fate, free will, foreknowledge absolute," in some form and dialect or other were by turns discussed.

> *Walden* (1854), in *The Writings of Henry David Thoreau*, vol. 2, pp. 289–290, Houghton Mifflin (1906).
>
> See also FATE

Men seem anxious to accomplish an orderly retreat through the centuries, earnestly rebuilding the works behind them, as they are battered down by the encroachments of time; but while they loiter, they and their works both fall prey to the arch enemy.

> *A Week on the Concord and Merrimack Rivers* (1849), in *The Writings of Henry David Thoreau*, vol. 1, pp. 162–163, Houghton Mifflin (1906).
>
> See also TIME

Nature herself has not provided the most graceful end for her creatures. What becomes of all these birds that people the air and forest for our solacement? The sparrow seems always *chipper,* never infirm. We do not see their bodies lie about. Yet there is a tragedy at the end of each one of their lives. They must perish miserably; not one of them is translated.

True, "not a sparrow falleth to the ground without our Heavenly Father's knowledge," but they do fall, nevertheless.

A Week on the Concord and Merrimack Rivers (1849), in *The Writings of Henry David Thoreau*, vol. 1, p. 236, Houghton Mifflin (1906).

See also DEATH

$\mathcal{M}$OUNTAINS

The tops of mountains are among the unfinished parts of the globe, whither it is a slight insult to the gods to climb and pry into their secrets, and try their effect on our humanity. Only daring and insolent men, perchance, go there. Simple races, as savages, do not climb mountains,— their tops are sacred and mysterious tracts never visited by them. Pomola is always angry with those who climb the summit of Ktaadn.

"Ktaadn" (1848) in *The Maine Woods* (1864), in *The Writings of Henry David Thoreau*, vol. 3, pp. 71–72, Houghton Mifflin (1906).

See also KTAADN, MOUNT

And now that we have returned to the desultory life of the plain, let us endeavor to import a little of that mountain grandeur into it. We will remember within what walls we lie, and understand that this level life too has its summit, and why from the mountain-top the deepest valleys have a tinge of blue; that there is elevation in every hour, as no part of the earth is so low that the heavens may not be seen from, and we have only to stand on the summit of our hour to command an uninterrupted horizon.

"A Walk to Wachusett" (1843), in *The Writings of Henry David Thoreau*, vol. 5, p. 151, Houghton Mifflin (1906).

See also LIFE

This observatory was a building of considerable size, erected by the students of Williamstown College, whose buildings might be seen by daylight gleaming far down in the valley. It would be no small advantage if every college were thus located at the base of a mountain, as good at least as one well-endowed professorship. It were as well to be educated in the shadow of a mountain as in more classical shades. Some will remember, no doubt, not only that they went to the college, but that they went to the mountain. Every visit to its summit would, as it were, generalize the particular information gained below, and subject it to more catholic tests.

A Week on the Concord and Merrimack Rivers (1849), in The Writings of Henry David Thoreau, vol. 1, p. 197, Houghton Mifflin (1906).

See also EDUCATION

MOURNING

Why care for these dead bodies? They really have no friends but the worms or fishes. Their owners were coming to the New World, as Columbus and the Pilgrims did; they were within a mile of its shores; but, before they could reach it, they emigrated to a newer world than ever Columbus dreamed of, yet one of whose existence we believe that there is far more universal and convincing evidence—though it has not yet been discovered by science—than Columbus had of this: not merely mariners' tales and some paltry driftwood and seaweed, but a continual drift and instinct to all our shores. I saw their empty hulks that came to land; but they themselves, meanwhile, were cast upon some shore yet further west, toward which we are all tending, and which we shall reach at last, it may be through storm and darkness, as they did. No doubt, we have reason to thank God that they have not been "shipwrecked into life again."

Cape Cod (1855–1865), in The Writings of Henry David Thoreau, vol. 4, pp. 12–13, Houghton Mifflin (1906).

See also DEATH

MYTHOLOGY

The West is preparing to add its fables to those of the East. The valleys of the Ganges, the Nile, and the Rhine having yielded their crop, it remains to be seen what the valleys of the Amazon, the Plate, the Orinoco, the St. Lawrence, and the Mississippi will produce. Perchance, when, in the course of ages, American liberty has become a fiction of the past,—as it is to some extent a fiction of the present,—the poets of the world will be inspired by American mythology.

"Walking" (1862), in *The Writings of Henry David Thoreau*, vol. 5, p. 233, Houghton Mifflin (1906).

Thoreau alludes here to the contemporary belief in a historical *translatio studii* ("transfer of the arts") from East to West.

See also LIBERTY

In my Pantheon, Pan still reigns in his pristine glory, with his ruddy face, his flowing beard, and his shaggy body, his pipe and his crook, his nymph Echo, and his chosen daughter Iambe; for the great god Pan is not dead, as was rumored. No god ever dies. Perhaps of all the gods of New England and of ancient Greece, I am most constant at his shrine.

A Week on the Concord and Merrimack Rivers (1849), in *The Writings of Henry David Thoreau*, vol. 1, p. 65, Houghton Mifflin (1906).

To some extent, mythology is only the most ancient history and biography. So far from being false or fabulous in the common sense, it contains only enduring and essential truth, the I and you, the here and there, the now and then, being omitted. Either time or rare wisdom writes it.

A Week on the Concord and Merrimack Rivers (1849), in *The Writings of Henry David Thoreau*, vol. 1, p. 60, Houghton Mifflin (1906).

See also TRUTH

*N*AMES

At present our only true names are nicknames.

"Walking" (1862), in *The Writings of Henry David Thoreau*, vol. 5, p. 236, Houghton Mifflin (1906).

Methinks it would be some advantage to philosophy if men were named merely in the gross, as they are known. It would be necessary only to know the genus and perhaps the race or variety, to know the individual. We are not prepared to believe that every private soldier in a Roman army had a name of his own,—because we have not supposed that he had a character of his own.

"Walking" (1862), in *The Writings of Henry David Thoreau*, vol. 5, p. 236, Houghton Mifflin (1906).

See also CHARACTER

When looking over a list of men's names in a foreign language, as of military officers, or of authors who have written on a particular subject, I am reminded once more that there is nothing in a name. . . . It is as if they had been named by the child's rigmarole, *Iery wiery ichery van, tittle-tol-tan.* I see in my mind a herd of wild creatures swarming over the earth, and to each the herdsman has affixed some barbarous sound in his own dialect. The names of men are, of course, as cheap and meaningless as *Bose* and *Tray,* the names of dogs.

"Walking" (1862), in *The Writings of Henry David Thoreau,* vol. 5, p. 236, Houghton Mifflin (1906).

See also LANGUAGE

*N*ATIVE *AMERICANS*

I am not sure but all that would tempt me to teach the Indian my religion would be his promise to teach me *his.*

"The Allegash and East Branch" (1864) in *The Maine Woods* (1864), in *The Writings of Henry David Thoreau,* vol. 3, p. 201, Houghton Mifflin (1906).

See also CHRISTIANITY AND CHRISTIANS

I have much to learn of the Indian, nothing of the missionary.

"The Allegash and East Branch" (1864) in *The Maine Woods* (1864), in *The Writings of Henry David Thoreau,* vol. 3, p. 201, Houghton Mifflin (1906).

See also CHRISTIANITY AND CHRISTIANS

These were the sounds that issued from the wigwams of this country before Columbus was born; they have not yet died away; and, with remarkably few exceptions, the language of their forefathers is still copious enough for them. I felt that I stood, or rather lay, as near to the primitive man of America, that night, as any of its discoverers ever did.

"Chesuncook" (1858) in *The Maine Woods* (1864), in *The Writings of Henry David Thoreau,* vol. 3, p. 151, Houghton Mifflin (1906).

See also PRIMITIVISM

Met face to face, these Indians in their native woods looked like the sinister and slouching fellows whom you meet picking up strings and paper in the streets of a city. There is, in fact, a remarkable and unexpected resemblance between the degraded savage and the lowest classes in a great city. The one is no more a child of nature than the other. In the progress of degradation the distinction of races is soon lost.

"Ktaadn" (1848) in *The Maine Woods* (1864), in *The Writings of Henry David Thoreau*, vol. 3, p. 86, Houghton Mifflin (1906).

See also POVERTY AND THE POOR

The island seemed deserted to-day, yet I observed some new houses among the weather-stained ones, as if the tribe still had a design upon life; but generally they have a very shabby, forlorn, and cheerless look, being all back side and woodshed, not homesteads, even Indian homesteads. . . . The church is the only trim-looking building, but that is not Abenaki, that was Rome's doings. Good Canadian it may be, but it is poor Indian. These were once a powerful tribe. Politics are all the rage with them now. I even thought that a row of wigwams, with a dance of pow-wows, and a prisoner tortured at the stake, would be more respectable than this.

"Ktaadn" (1848) in *The Maine Woods* (1864), in *The Writings of Henry David Thoreau*, vol. 3, p. 7, Houghton Mifflin (1906).

See also CATHOLICISM

The Indian's intercourse with Nature is at least such as admits of the greatest independence of each.

A Week on the Concord and Merrimack Rivers (1849), in *The Writings of Henry David Thoreau*, vol. 1, p. 56, Houghton Mifflin (1906).

There are other, savager and more primeval aspects of nature than our poets have sung. It is only white man's poetry. Homer and Ossian even can never revive in London or Boston. And yet, behold how these cities are refreshed by the mere tradition, or the imperfectly transmitted fragrance and flavor of these wild fruits. If we could listen but for an instant to the chant of the Indian muse, we should understand why he will not exchange his savageness for civilization. Nations are not whimsical. Steel and blankets are strong temptations; but the Indian does well to continue Indian.

A Week on the Concord and Merrimack Rivers (1849), in *The Writings of Henry David Thoreau*, vol. 1, p. 56, Houghton Mifflin (1906).

See also NATURE

Natural History

The natural historian is not a fisherman who prays for cloudy days and good luck merely; but as fishing has been styled "a contemplative man's recreation," introducing him profitably to woods and water, so the fruit of the naturalist's observations is not in new genera or species, but in new contemplations still, and science is only a more contemplative man's recreation.

A Week on the Concord and Merrimack Rivers (1849), in *The Writings of Henry David Thoreau,* vol. 1, p. 23, Houghton Mifflin (1906).

See also SCIENTISTS AND SCIENCE

Nature

For one that comes with a pencil to sketch or sing, a thousand come with an axe or rifle. What a coarse and imperfect use Indians and hunters make of nature! No wonder that their race is so soon exterminated.

"Chesuncook" (1858) in *The Maine Woods* (1864), in *The Writings of Henry David Thoreau,* vol. 3, p. 133, Houghton Mifflin (1906).

It is not their bones or hide or tallow that I love most. It is the living spirit of the tree, not its spirit of turpentine, with which I sympathize, and which heals my cuts. It is as immortal as I am, and perchance will go to as high a heaven, there to tower above me still.

"Chesuncook" (1858) in *The Maine Woods* (1864), in *The Writings of Henry David Thoreau,* vol. 3, p. 135, Houghton Mifflin (1906).

See also PINE TREES

There is a higher law affecting our relation to pines as well as to men. A pine cut down, a dead pine, is no more a pine than a dead human carcass is a man.

"Chesuncook" (1858) in *The Maine Woods* (1864), in *The Writings of Henry David Thoreau,* vol. 3, p. 134, Houghton Mifflin (1906).

See also PINE TREES

If a man walk in the woods for love of them half of each day, he is in danger of being regarded as a loafer; but if he spends his whole day as a speculator, shearing off those woods and making earth bald before her time, he is esteemed an industrious and enterprising citizen. As if the town had no interest in its forests but to cut them down!

"Life Without Principle" (1863), in *The Writings of Henry David Thoreau*, vol. 4, p. 457, Houghton Mifflin (1906).

See also ECOLOGY

The universe is not rough-hewn, but perfect in its details. Nature will bear the closest inspection; she invites us to lay our eye level with the smallest leaf, and take an insect view of its plain. She has no interstices; every part is full of life.

"Natural History of Massachusetts" (1842), in *The Writings of Henry David Thoreau*, vol. 5, p. 107, Houghton Mifflin (1906).

Nature has no human inhabitant who appreciates her.

Walden (1854), in *The Writings of Henry David Thoreau*, vol. 2, p. 222, Houghton Mifflin (1906).

For my part, I feel that with regard to Nature I live a sort of border life, on the confines of a world into which I make occasional and transient forays only, and my patriotism and allegiance to the state into whose territories I seem to retreat are those of a moss-trooper.

"Walking" (1862), in *The Writings of Henry David Thoreau*, vol. 5, p. 242, Houghton Mifflin (1906).

See also PATRIOTISM

Her undertakings are secure and never fail.

A Week on the Concord and Merrimack Rivers (1849), in *The Writings of Henry David Thoreau*, vol. 1, p. 340, Houghton Mifflin (1906).

If Nature is our mother, then God is our father.

A Week on the Concord and Merrimack Rivers (1849), in *The Writings of Henry David Thoreau*, vol. 1, pp. 398–399, Houghton Mifflin (1906).

See also GOD

There are moments when all anxiety and stated toil are becalmed in the infinite leisure and repose of nature.

A Week on the Concord and Merrimack Rivers (1849), in *The Writings of Henry David Thoreau*, vol. 1, p. 130, Houghton Mifflin (1906).

There is a slumbering subterranean fire in nature which never goes out, and which no cold can chill.

"A Winter Walk" (1843), in *The Writings of Henry David Thoreau*, vol. 5, p. 167, Houghton Mifflin (1906).

See also WINTER

Nature versus civilization

Here is this vast, savage, howling mother of ours, Nature, lying all around, with such beauty, and such affection for her children, as the leopard; and yet we are so early weaned from her breast to society, to that culture which is exclusively an interaction of man on man,—a sort of breeding in and in, which produces at most a merely English nobility, a civilization destined to have a speedy limit.

"Walking" (1862), in *The Writings of Henry David Thoreau*, vol. 5, p. 237, Houghton Mifflin (1906).

See also NATURE

I wish to speak a word for Nature, for absolute freedom and wildness, as contrasted with a freedom and culture merely civil,—to regard man as an inhabitant, or a part and parcel of Nature, rather than as a member of society. I wish to make an extreme statement, if so I may make an emphatic one, for there are enough champions of civilization: the minister and the school committee and every one of you will take care of that.

"Walking" (1862), in *The Writings of Henry David Thoreau*, vol. 5, p. 205, Houghton Mifflin (1906).

See also FREEDOM

Necessities

It would be some advantage to live a primitive and frontier life, though in the midst of an outward civilization, if only to learn what are the gross necessaries of life and what methods have been taken to obtain them.

Walden (1854), in *The Writings of Henry David Thoreau*, vol. 2, p. 12, Houghton Mifflin (1906).

New England and New Englanders

I would fain say something, not so much concerning the Chinese and Sandwich Islanders as you who read these pages, who are said to live in

New England; something about your condition, especially your outward condition or circumstances in this world, in this town, what it is, whether it is necessary that it be as bad as it is, whether it cannot be improved as well as not.

Walden (1854), in *The Writings of Henry David Thoreau*, vol. 2, p. 4, Houghton Mifflin (1906).

I have not read of any Arcadian life which surpasses the actual luxury and serenity of these New England dwellings. For the outward gilding, at least, the age is golden enough.

A Week on the Concord and Merrimack Rivers (1849), in *The Writings of Henry David Thoreau*, vol. 1, p. 256, Houghton Mifflin (1906).

If men will believe it, *sua si bona norint*, there are no more quiet Tempes, nor more poetic and Arcadian lives, than may be lived in these New England dwellings. We thought that the employment of their inhabitants by day would be to tend the flowers and herds, and at night, like the shepherds of old, to cluster and give names to the stars from the river banks.

A Week on the Concord and Merrimack Rivers (1849), in *The Writings of Henry David Thoreau*, vol. 1, p. 257, Houghton Mifflin (1906).

There were several canal-boats ... passing through the locks, for which we waited. In the forward part of one stood a brawny New Hampshire man, leaning on his pole, bareheaded and in shirt and trousers only, a rude Apollo of a man, coming down from "that vast uplandish country" to the main; of nameless age, with flaxen hair and vigorous, weather-bleached countenance, in whose wrinkles the sun still lodged, as little touched by the heats and frosts and withering cares of life as a maple of the mountain; an undressed, unkempt, uncivil man, with whom we parlayed awhile, and parted not without a sincere interest in one another. His humanity was genuine and instinctive, and his rudeness only a manner. He inquired, just as we were passing out of earshot, if we had killed anything, and we shouted after him that we had shot a *buoy*, and could see him for a long while scratching his head in vain to know if he had heard aright.

A Week on the Concord and Merrimack Rivers (1849), in *The Writings of Henry David Thoreau*, vol. 1, pp. 211–212, Houghton Mifflin (1906).

See also HUMANITY

*N*EW YORK CITY

Give me time enough, and I may like it.

Letter, May 11, 1843, to Thoreau's father and mother, in *The Writings of Henry David Thoreau*, vol. 6, p. 71, Houghton Mifflin (1906).

Thoreau was living on Staten Island at this time.

*N*EWS

Read not the Times. Read the Eternities.

"Life Without Principle" (1863), in *The Writings of Henry David Thoreau*, vol. 4, p. 475, Houghton Mifflin (1906).

In context, Thoreau clearly makes a pun here on *The Times* of London, and "the times" in which he lives.

See also JOURNALISM AND JOURNALISTS

*N*OVELS

I never read a novel, they have so little real life and thought in them.

A Week on the Concord and Merrimack Rivers (1849), in *The Writings of Henry David Thoreau*, vol. 1, p. 72, Houghton Mifflin (1906).

See also READING

*N*OVELTY

Do not trouble yourself much to get new things, whether clothes or friends.

Walden (1854), in *The Writings of Henry David Thoreau*, vol. 2, p. 361, Houghton Mifflin (1906).

See also FRIENDS AND FRIENDSHIP

OBSERVATION

I did not wish to take a cabin passage, but rather to go before the mast and on the deck of the world, for there I could best see the moonlight amid the mountains. I do not wish to go below now.

Walden (1854), in *The Writings of Henry David Thoreau*, vol. 2, p. 356, Houghton Mifflin (1906).

See also TRAVELING AND TRAVELERS

No method nor discipline can supersede the necessity of being forever on the alert. What is a course of history or philosophy, or poetry, no matter how well selected, or the best society, or the most admirable routine of life, compared with the discipline of looking always at what is to be seen? Will you be a reader, a student merely, or a seer? Read your fate, see what is before you, and walk on into futurity.

Walden (1854), in *The Writings of Henry David Thoreau*, vol. 2, p. 123, Houghton Mifflin (1906).

See also EDUCATION

It is a very true and expressive phrase, "He looked daggers at me," for the first pattern and prototype of all daggers must have been a glance of the eye. ... It is wonderful how we get about the streets without being wounded by these delicate and glancing weapons, a man can so nimbly whip out his rapier, or without being noticed carry it unsheathed. Yet it is rare that one gets seriously looked at.

A Week on the Concord and Merrimack Rivers (1849), in *The Writings of Henry David Thoreau*, vol. 1, p. 63, Houghton Mifflin (1906)

See also SOCIETY

OLD AGE

Many old people receive pensions for no other reason, it seems to me, but as a compensation for having lived a long time ago.

"Chesuncook" (1858) in *The Maine Woods* (1864), in *The Writings of Henry David Thoreau*, vol. 3, p. 141, Houghton Mifflin (1906).

Old deeds for old people, and new deeds for new.

Walden (1854), in *The Writings of Henry David Thoreau*, vol. 2, p. 9, Houghton Mifflin (1906).

See also DEEDS

Old versus new

The newest is but the oldest made visible to our senses.

A Week on the Concord and Merrimack Rivers (1849), in *The Writings of Henry David Thoreau*, vol. 1, p. 160, Houghton Mifflin (1906).

Optimism

The still youthful energies of the globe have only to be directed in their proper channel.

"Paradise (To Be) Regained" (1843), in *The Writings of Henry David Thoreau*, vol. 4, p. 282, Houghton Mifflin (1906).

See also REFORM AND REFORMERS

I do not propose to write an ode to dejection, but to brag as lustily as chanticleer in the morning, standing on his roost, if only to wake my neighbors up.

Walden (1854), in *The Writings of Henry David Thoreau*, vol. 2, p. 94, Houghton Mifflin (1906).

Ossian

Ossian reminds us of the most refined and rudest eras, of Homer, Pindar, Isaiah, and the American Indian. In his poetry, as in Homer's, only the simplest and most enduring features of humanity are seen, such essential parts of a man as Stonehenge exhibits of a temple; we see the circles of stone, and the upright shaft alone. The phenomena of life acquire almost an unreal and gigantic size seen through his mists. Like all older and grander poetry, it is distinguished by the few elements in the lives of its heroes. They stand on the heath, between the stars and the earth, shrunk to the bones and sinews. The earth is a boundless plain for their deeds. They lead such a simple, dry, and everlasting life, as hardly needs depart with the flesh, but is transmitted entire from age to age. There are but few objects to distract their sight, and their life is as unencumbered as the course of the stars they gaze at.

A Week on the Concord and Merrimack Rivers (1849), in *The Writings of Henry David Thoreau*, vol. 1, p. 367, Houghton Mifflin (1906).

See also POETRY AND POETS

Owls

I rejoice that there are owls. . . . They represent the stark twilight and unsatisfied thoughts which all have.

Walden (1854), in *The Writings of Henry David Thoreau*, vol. 2, p. 139, Houghton Mifflin (1906).

See also THINKING AND THOUGHTS

Parables

I long ago lost a hound, a bay horse, and a turtle-dove, and am still on their trail. Many are the travellers I have spoken concerning them, describing their tracks and what calls they answered to. I have met one or two who had heard the hound, and the tramp of the horse, and even seen the dove disappear behind a cloud, and they seemed as anxious to recover them as if they had lost them themselves.

Walden (1854), in *The Writings of Henry David Thoreau*, vol. 2, pp. 18–19, Houghton Mifflin (1906).

Parks, National

The kings of England formerly had their forests "to hold the king's game," for sport or food, sometimes destroying villages to create or extend them; and I think that they were impelled by a true instinct. Why should not we, who have renounced the king's authority, have our national preserves, where no villages need be destroyed, in which the bear and panther, and some even of the hunter race, may still exist, and not be "civilized off the face of the earth,"—our forests, not to hold the king's game merely, but to hold and preserve the king himself also, the lord of creation,—not for idle sport or food, but for inspiration and our own true recreation? or shall we, like the villains, grub them all up, poaching on our own national domains?

"Chesuncook" (1858) in *The Maine Woods* (1864), in *The Writings of Henry David Thoreau*, vol. 3, p. 173, Houghton Mifflin (1906).

See also WILDERNESS

$\mathcal{P}$ARTRIDGES

They are not callow like the young of most birds, but more perfectly developed and precocious even than chickens. The remarkably adult yet innocent expression of their open and serene eyes is very memorable. All intelligence seems reflected in them. They suggest not merely the purity of infancy, but a wisdom clarified by experience. Such an eye was not born when the bird was, but is coeval with the sky it reflects. The woods do not yield another such a gem.

Walden (1854), in *The Writings of Henry David Thoreau*, vol. 2, p. 251, Houghton Mifflin (1906).

$\mathcal{P}$AST, THE

The experience of every past moment but belies the faith of each present.

Letter, June 20, 1843, to Lidian Jackson Emerson, in *The Writings of Henry David Thoreau*, vol. 6, p. 88, Houghton Mifflin (1906).

See also EXPERIENCE

We loiter in winter while it is already spring.

Walden (1854), in *The Writings of Henry David Thoreau*, vol. 2, p. 346, Houghton Mifflin (1906).

See also PRESENT, THE

Why look in the dark for light?

A Week on the Concord and Merrimack Rivers (1849), in *The Writings of Henry David Thoreau*, vol. 1, p. 161, Houghton Mifflin (1906).

See also PRESENT, THE

$\mathcal{P}$ATIENCE

Let a man take time enough for the most trivial deed, though it be but the paring of his nails.

A Week on the Concord and Merrimack Rivers (1849), in The Writings of Henry David Thoreau, vol. 1, p. 110, Houghton Mifflin (1906).

$\mathcal{P}$ATRIOTISM

Don't spend your time in drilling soldiers, who may turn out hirelings after all, but give to undrilled peasantry a *country* to fight for.

Letter, September 26, 1855, to Harrison Blake, in The Writings of Henry David Thoreau, vol. 6, p. 260, Houghton Mifflin (1906).

See also SOLDIERS

$\mathcal{P}$ERSPECTIVE

I love a broad margin to my life.

Walden (1854), in The Writings of Henry David Thoreau, vol. 2, p. 123, Houghton Mifflin (1906).

$\mathcal{P}$HILANTHROPY

The best thing a man can do for his culture when he is rich is to endeavor to carry out those schemes which he entertained when he was poor.

"Civil Disobedience," originally published as "Resistance to Civil Government" (1849), in The Writings of Henry David Thoreau, vol. 4, p. 372, Houghton Mifflin (1906).

See also MONEY

A man is not a good *man* to me because he will feed me if I should be starving, or warm me if I should be freezing, or pull me out of a ditch if I should ever fall into one. I can find you a Newfoundland dog that will do as much. Philanthropy is not love for one's fellow-man in the broadest sense. Howard was no doubt an exceedingly kind and worthy man in his way, and has his reward; but, comparatively speaking, what are a hundred

Howards to *us,* if their philanthropy do not help *us* in our best estate, when we are most worthy to be helped? I never heard of a philanthropic meeting in which it was sincerely proposed to do any good to me, or the like of me.

Walden (1854), in *The Writings of Henry David Thoreau,* vol. 2, pp. 82–83, Houghton Mifflin (1906).

Howard is John Howard, an English prison reformer.

See also REFORM AND REFORMERS

I would not subtract anything from the praise that is due to philanthropy, but merely demand justice for all who by their lives and works are a blessing to mankind. I do not value chiefly a man's uprightness and benevolence, which are, as it were, his stem and leaves. . . . I want the flower and fruit of a man; that some fragrance be wafted over from him to me, and some ripeness flavor our intercourse. His goodness must not be a partial and transitory act, but a constant superfluity, which costs him nothing and of which he is unconscious. This is a charity that hides a multitude of sins.

Walden (1854), in *The Writings of Henry David Thoreau,* vol. 2, p. 85, Houghton Mifflin (1906).

If I knew for a certainty that a man was coming to my house with the conscious design of doing me good, I should run for my life . . . for fear that I should get some of his good done to me,—some of its virus mingled with my blood.

Walden (1854), in *The Writings of Henry David Thoreau,* vol. 2, p. 82, Houghton Mifflin (1906).

See also REFORM AND REFORMERS

Philanthropy is almost the only virtue which is sufficiently appreciated by mankind. Nay, it is greatly overrated; and it is our selfishness which overrates it.

Walden (1854), in *The Writings of Henry David Thoreau,* vol. 2, p. 84, Houghton Mifflin (1906).

Probably I should not consciously and deliberately forsake my particular calling to do the good which society demands of me, to save the universe from annihilation; and I believe that a like but infinitely greater stead-fastness elsewhere is all that now preserves it.

Walden (1854), in *The Writings of Henry David Thoreau,* vol. 2, p. 81, Houghton Mifflin (1906).

The kind uncles and aunts of the race are more esteemed than its true spiritual fathers and mothers.

Walden (1854), in *The Writings of Henry David Thoreau,* vol. 2, p. 84, Houghton Mifflin (1906).

$\mathcal{P}$HILLIPS, WENDELL

We must give Mr. Phillips the credit of being a clean, erect, and what was once called a consistent man. He at least is not responsible for slavery, nor for American Independence; for the hypocrisy and superstition of the Church, nor the timidity and selfishness of the State; nor for the indifference and willing ignorance of any. He stands so distinctly, so firmly, and so effectively alone, and one honest man is so much more than a host, that we cannot but feel that he does himself injustice when he reminds us of "the American Society, which he represents."

"Wendell Phillips Before the Concord Lyceum" (1845), in *The Writings of Henry David Thoreau*, vol. 4, p. 312, Houghton Mifflin (1906).

See also INDEPENDENCE

When, said Mr. Phillips, he communicated to a New Bedford audience, the other day, his purpose of writing his life, and telling his name, and the name of his master, and the place he ran from, the murmur ran round the room, and was anxiously whispered by the sons of the Pilgrims, "He had better not!" and it was echoed under the shadow of the Concord monument, "He had better not!"

"Wendell Phillips Before the Concord Lyceum" (1845), in *The Writings of Henry David Thoreau*, vol. 4, p. 313, Houghton Mifflin (1906).

See also SLAVERY

$\mathcal{P}$HILOSOPHY AND PHILOSOPHERS

The philosopher's conception of things will, above all, be truer than other men's, and his philosophy will subordinate all the circumstances of life. To live like a philosopher is to live, not foolishly, like other men, but wisely and according to universal laws.

"Thomas Carlyle and His Works" (1847), in *The Writings of Henry David Thoreau*, vol. 4, pp. 348–349, Houghton Mifflin (1906).

See also CARLYLE, THOMAS

There are nowadays professors of philosophy, but not philosophers. Yet it is admirable to profess because it was once admirable to live. To be a philosopher is not merely to have subtle thoughts, nor even to found a school, but so to love wisdom as to live according to its dictates, a life of simplicity, independence, magnanimity, and trust. It is to solve some of the problems of life, not only theoretically, but practically.

Walden (1854), in *The Writings of Henry David Thoreau*, vol. 2, p. 16, Houghton Mifflin (1906).

See also SCHOLARS AND SCHOLARSHIP

$\mathcal{P}$HOSPHORESCENCE

Getting up some time after midnight to collect the scattered brands together, while my companions were sound asleep, I observed, partly in the fire, which had ceased to blaze, a perfectly regular elliptical ring of light, about five inches in its shortest diameter, six or seven in its longer, and from one eighth to one quarter of an inch wide. It was fully as bright as the fire, but not reddish or scarlet, like a coal, but a white and slumbering light, like the glow-worm's. I could tell it from the fire only by its whiteness. I saw at once that it must be phosphorescent wood, which I had so often heard of, but never chanced to see. Putting my finger on it, with a little hesitation, I found that it was a piece of dead moose-wood (*Acer striatum*). . . . Using my knife, I discovered that the light proceeded from that portion of the sap-wood immediately under the bark, and thus presented a regular ring at the end, which, indeed, appeared raised above the level of the wood, and when I pared off the bark and cut into the sap, it was all aglow along the log.

"The Allegash and East Branch" (1864) in *The Maine Woods* (1864), in *The Writings of Henry David Thoreau*, vol. 3, pp. 198–199, Houghton Mifflin (1906).

$\mathcal{P}$ICKEREL

The swiftest, wariest, and most ravenous of fishes.

A Week on the Concord and Merrimack Rivers (1849), in *The Writings of Henry David Thoreau*, vol. 1, p. 29, Houghton Mifflin (1906).

$\mathcal{P}$ILGRIMS, NEW ENGLAND

It must be confessed that the Pilgrims possessed but few of the qualities of the modern pioneer. They were not the ancestors of the American backwoodsmen. They did not go at once into the woods with their axes. They were a family and church, and were more anxious to keep together, though it were on the sand, than to colonize a New World. . . . It is true they were busy at first about their building, and were hindered in that by much foul weather; but a party of emigrants to California or Oregon, with no less work on their hands,—and more hostile Indians,—would do as much exploring the first afternoon, and the Sieur de Champlain would have sought an interview with the savages, and examined the country as far as the Connecticut, and made a map of it, before Billington had climbed his tree. . . . Nevertheless, the Pilgrims were pioneers, and the ancestors of pioneers, in a far grander enterprise.

> *Cape Cod* (1855–1865), in *The Writings of Henry David Thoreau,* vol. 4, pp. 256–257, Houghton Mifflin (1906).

See also AMERICA AND AMERICANS

$\mathcal{P}$INE TREES

It was the pine alone, chiefly the white pine, that had tempted any but the hunter to precede us on this route.

> "Ktaadn" (1848) in *The Maine Woods* (1864), in *The Writings of Henry David Thoreau,* vol. 3, p. 23, Houghton Mifflin (1906).

$\mathcal{P}$IONEERS

I have no doubt that they lived pretty much the same sort of life in the Homeric age, for men have always thought more of eating than of fighting; then, as now, their minds ran chiefly on the "hot bread and sweet cakes;" and the fur and lumber trade is an old story to Asia and Europe.

> "Chesuncook" (1858) in *The Maine Woods* (1864), in *The Writings of Henry David Thoreau,* vol. 3, p. 142, Houghton Mifflin (1906).

See also HOMER

It is a sort of ranger service. Arnold's expedition is a daily experience with these settlers. They can prove that they were out at almost any time; and I think that all the first generation of them deserve a pension more than any that went to the Mexican war.

> "Chesuncook" (1858) in *The Maine Woods* (1864), in *The Writings of Henry David Thoreau*, vol. 3, p. 145, Houghton Mifflin (1906).

In fact, the deeper you penetrate into the woods, the more intelligent, and, in one sense, less countrified do you find the inhabitants; for always the pioneer has been a traveler, and, to some extent, a man of the world; and, as the distances with which he is familiar are greater, so is his information more general and far reaching than the villager's. If I were to look for a narrow, uninformed, and countrified mind, as opposed to the intelligence and refinement which are thought to emanate from cities, it would be among the rusty inhabitants of an old-settled country, on farms all run out and gone to seed with life-everlasting, in the towns about Boston, even on the high-road in Concord, and not in the back woods of Maine.

> "Ktaadn" (1848) in *The Maine Woods* (1864), in *The Writings of Henry David Thoreau*, vol. 3, p. 24, Houghton Mifflin (1906).
>
> See also CONCORD, MASSACHUSETTS

There is an orientalism in the most restless pioneer, and the farthest west is but the farthest east.

> *A Week on the Concord and Merrimack Rivers* (1849), in *The Writings of Henry David Thoreau*, vol. 1, p. 157, Houghton Mifflin (1906).

*P*OETRY AND POETS

Much of our poetry has the very best manners, but no character.

> *A Week on the Concord and Merrimack Rivers* (1849), in *The Writings of Henry David Thoreau*, vol. 1, p. 400, Houghton Mifflin (1906).
>
> See also CHARACTER

Poetry is the mysticism of mankind.

> *A Week on the Concord and Merrimack Rivers* (1849), in *The Writings of Henry David Thoreau*, vol. 1, p. 350, Houghton Mifflin (1906).

So, too, no doubt, Homer had his Homer, and Orpheus his Orpheus, in the dim antiquity which preceded them. The mythological system of the ancients,—and it is still the mythology of the moderns, the poem of mankind,—interwoven so wonderfully with their astronomy, and matching in grandeur and harmony the architecture of the heavens themselves, seems to point to a time when a mightier genius inhabited the earth. But, after all, man is the great poet, and not Homer nor Shakespeare; and our language itself, and the common arts of life, are his work. Poetry is so universally true and independent of experience that it does not need any particular biography to illustrate it, but we refer it sooner or later to some Orpheus or Linus, and after ages to the genius of humanity and the gods themselves.

> *A Week on the Concord and Merrimack Rivers* (1849), in *The Writings of Henry David Thoreau*, vol. 1, pp. 97–98, Houghton Mifflin (1906).
>
> See also CLASSICS, THE

The poet is he that hath fat enough, like bears and marmots, to suck his claws all winter. He hibernates in this world, and feeds on his own marrow.

> *A Week on the Concord and Merrimack Rivers* (1849), in *The Writings of Henry David Thoreau*, vol. 1, p. 101, Houghton Mifflin (1906).

The poet uses the results of science and philosophy, and generalizes their widest deductions.

> *A Week on the Concord and Merrimack Rivers* (1849), in *The Writings of Henry David Thoreau*, vol. 1, p. 387, Houghton Mifflin (1906).
>
> See also SCIENTISTS AND SCIENCE

The wisest definition of poetry the poet will instantly prove false by setting aside its requisitions.

> *A Week on the Concord and Merrimack Rivers* (1849), in *The Writings of Henry David Thoreau*, vol. 1, p. 93, Houghton Mifflin (1906).
>
> See also POETRY AND POETS

We love to think in winter, as we walk over the snowy pastures, of those happy dreamers that lie under the sod, of dormice and all that race of dormant creatures, which have such a superfluity of life enveloped in thick folds of fur, impervious to cold. Alas, the poet too is in one sense a sort of dormouse gone into winter quarters of deep and serene thoughts, insensible to surrounding circumstances; his words are the relation of his oldest and finest memory, a wisdom drawn from the remotest experience. Other men lead a starved existence, meanwhile, like hawks, that would fain keep on the wing, and trust to pick up a sparrow now and then.

A Week on the Concord and Merrimack Rivers (1849), in *The Writings of Henry David Thoreau*, vol. 1, pp. 101–102, Houghton Mifflin (1906).

See also WINTER

POLIS, JOE

I was surprised to hear him say that he liked to go to Boston, New York, Philadelphia, etc., etc.; that he would like to live there. But then, as if relenting a little, when he thought what a poor figure he would make there, he added, "I suppose, I live in New York, I be poorest hunter, I expect." He understood very well both his superiority and his inferiority to the whites. He criticized the people of the United States as compared with other nations, but the only distinct idea with which he labored was, that they were "very strong," but, like some individuals, "too fast." He must have the credit of saying this just before the general breakdown of railroads and banks.

"The Allegash and East Branch" (1864) in *The Maine Woods* (1864), in *The Writings of Henry David Thoreau*, vol. 3, p. 218, Houghton Mifflin (1906).

So quickly we changed the civilizing sky of Chesuncook for the dark wood of the Caucomgomoc. On reaching the Indian's camping-ground, on the south side, where the bank was about a dozen feet high, I read on the trunk of a fir tree, blazed by an axe, an inscription in charcoal which had been left by him. It was surmounted by a drawing of a bear paddling a canoe, which he said was the sign which had been used by his family always. The drawing, though rude, could not be mistaken for anything but a bear, and he doubted my ability to copy it.

"The Allegash and East Branch" (1864) in *The Maine Woods* (1864), in *The Writings of Henry David Thoreau*, vol. 3, pp. 219–220, Houghton Mifflin (1906).

See also WILDERNESS

The first man we saw on the island was an Indian named Joseph Polis, whom my relative had known from a boy, and now addressed familiarly as "Joe." He was dressing a deer-skin in his yard. The skin was spread over a slanting log, and he was scraping it with a stick held by both hands. He was stoutly built, perhaps a little above the middle height, with a broad face, and, as others said, perfect Indian features and complexion. His house was a two-story white one, with blinds, the best-looking that I noticed there, and as good as an average one on a New England village street. It was surrounded by a garden and fruit-trees, single cornstalks standing thinly amid the beans.

"The Allegash and East Branch" (1864) in *The Maine Woods* (1864), in *The Writings of Henry David Thoreau*, vol. 3, pp. 174–175, Houghton Mifflin (1906).

See also NATIVE AMERICANS

You would not have thought, if you had seen him lying about thus, that he was the proprietor of so many acres in that neighborhood, was worth six thousand dollars, and had been to Washington. It seemed to me that, like the Irish, he made a greater ado about his sickness than a Yankee does, and was more alarmed about himself.

"The Allegash and East Branch" (1864) in *The Maine Woods* (1864), in *The Writings of Henry David Thoreau*, vol. 3, p. 320, Houghton Mifflin (1906).

See also IRELAND AND THE IRISH

$\mathcal{P}$OLITICS AND POLITICIANS

No man with a genius for legislation has appeared in America. They are rare in the history of the world. There are orators, politicians, and eloquent men, by the thousand; but the speaker has not yet opened his mouth to speak who is capable of settling the much-vexed questions of the day. We love eloquence for its own sake, and not for any truth which it may utter, or any heroism it may inspire. Our legislators have not yet learned the comparative value of free trade and of freedom, of union, and of rectitude, to a nation.

"Civil Disobedience," originally published as "Resistance to Civil Government" (1849), in *The Writings of Henry David Thoreau*, vol. 4, p. 386, Houghton Mifflin (1906).

See also GOVERNMENT

Statesmen and legislators, standing so completely within the institution, never distinctly and nakedly behold it. They speak of moving society, but they have no resting-place without it. They may be men of a certain experience and discrimination, and have no doubt invented ingenious and even useful systems, for which we sincerely thank them; but all their wit and usefulness lie within certain not very wide limits. They are wont to forget that the world is not governed by policy and expediency.

"Civil Disobedience," originally published as "Resistance to Civil Government" (1849), in *The Writings of Henry David Thoreau*, vol. 4, p. 384, Houghton Mifflin (1906).

The "institution" to which Thoreau refers is government.

See also GOVERNMENT

We are a nation of politicians, concerned about the outmost defenses only of freedom. It is our children's children who may perchance be really free.

"Life Without Principle" (1863), in *The Writings of Henry David Thoreau*, vol. 4, p. 477, Houghton Mifflin (1906).

See also LIBERTY

What is called politics is comparatively something so superficial and inhuman, that practically I have never fairly recognized that it concerns me at all.

"Life Without Principle" (1863), in *The Writings of Henry David Thoreau*, vol. 4, p. 480, Houghton Mifflin (1906).

ℙOVERTY AND THE POOR

Cultivate poverty like a garden herb, like sage.

Walden (1854), in *The Writings of Henry David Thoreau*, vol. 2, p. 361, Houghton Mifflin (1906).

See also SIMPLICITY

It is a mistake to suppose that, in a country where the usual evidences of civilization exist, the condition of a very large body of inhabitants may not be as degraded as that of savages. I refer to the degraded poor, not now to the degraded rich. To know this I should not need to look farther than to the shanties which everywhere border our railroads, that last improvement in civilization; where I see in my daily walks human beings living in sties, and all winter with an open door, for the sake of light, without any visible, often imaginable, wood-pile, and the forms of both old and young are permanently contracted by the long habit of shrinking from cold and misery, and the development of all their limbs and faculties is checked. . . . Such too, to a greater or less extent, is the condition of the operatives of every denomination in England, which is the great work-

house of the world. Or I could refer you to Ireland, which is marked as
one of the white or enlightened spots on the map. Contrast the physical
condition of the Irish with that of the North American Indian, or the
South Sea Islander, or any other savage race before it was degraded by
contact with the civilized man. Yet I have no doubt that that people's
rulers are as wise as the average of civilized rulers. Their condition only
proves what squalidness may consist with civilization.

Walden (1854), in The Writings of Henry David Thoreau, vol. 2, pp. 38–39, Houghton Mifflin (1906).

See also CIVILIZATION

Often the poor man is not so cold and hungry as he is dirty and ragged
and gross. It is partly his taste, and not merely his misfortune. If you give
him money, he will perhaps buy more rags with it.

Walden (1854), in The Writings of Henry David Thoreau, vol. 2, p. 83, Houghton Mifflin (1906).

See also PHILANTHROPY

The setting sun is reflected from the windows of the alms-house as
brightly as from the rich man's abode; the snow melts before its door as
early in the spring. I do not see but a quiet mind may live as contentedly
there, and have as cheering thoughts, as in a palace.

Walden (1854), in The Writings of Henry David Thoreau, vol. 2, p. 361, Houghton Mifflin (1906).

See also WEALTH AND THE WEALTHY

$\mathcal{P}$RAYER

Great God! I ask thee for no meaner pelf
Than that I may not disappoint myself;
That in my action I may soar as high
As I can now discern with this clear eye;
And next in value, which thy kindness lends,
That I may greatly disappoint my friends,
Howe'er they think or hope that it may be,
They may not dream how thou'st distinguished me;
That my weak hand may equal my firm faith,
And my life practice more than my tongue saith;

That my low conduct may not show,
Nor my relenting lines,
That I thy purpose did not know,
Or overrated thy designs.

"Prayer," l. 1–14 (1842), in *The Writings of Henry David Thoreau*, vol. 5, pp. 418–419, Houghton Mifflin (1906).

See also GOD

$\mathcal{P}$RESENT, THE

We should be blessed if we lived in the present always, and took advantage of every accident that befell us, like the grass which confesses the influence of the slightest dew that falls on it; and did not spend our time in atoning for the neglect of past opportunities, which we call doing our duty.

Walden (1854), in *The Writings of Henry David Thoreau*, vol. 2, p. 346, Houghton Mifflin (1906).

$\mathcal{P}$RIMITIVISM

Thus a man shall lead his life away here on the edge of the wilderness, on Indian Millinocket Stream, in a new world, far in the dark of a continent, and have a flute to play at evening here, while his strains echo to the stars, amid the howling of wolves; shall live, as it were, in the primitive age of the world, a primitive man. Yet he shall spend a sunny day, and in this century be my contemporary; perchance shall read some scattered leaves of literature, and sometimes talk with me. Why read history, then, if the ages and the generations are now? He lives three thousand years deep into time, an age not yet described by poets. Can you well go further back in history than this? Ay! ay!—for there turns up but now into the mouth of Millinocket Stream a still more ancient and primitive man, whose history is not brought down even to the former. In a bark vessel sewn with the roots of the spruce, with hornbeam paddles, he dips his way along. He is but dim and misty to me, obscured by the æons that lie between the bark canoe and the batteau. He builds no house of logs, but a wigwam of skins. He eats no hot bread and sweet cake, but musquash and moose meat and the fat of bears. He glides up the Millinocket and is lost to my sight, as a more distant and misty cloud is seen flitting by behind a nearer, and is lost in space. So he goes about his destiny, the red face of man.

"Ktaadn" (1848) in *The Maine Woods* (1864), in *The Writings of Henry David Thoreau*, vol. 3, pp. 87–88, Houghton Mifflin (1906).

See also NATIVE AMERICANS

PRINTING

Before printing was discovered, a century was equal to a thousand years.

A Week on the Concord and Merrimack Rivers (1849), in *The Writings of Henry David Thoreau*, vol. 1, p. 60, Houghton Mifflin (1906).

PRISON

I have paid no poll-tax for six years. I was put into a jail once on this account, for one night; and, as I stood considering the walls of solid stone, two or three feet thick, the door of wood and iron, a foot thick, and the iron grating which strained the light, I could not help being struck with the foolishness of that institution which treated me as if I were mere flesh and blood and bones, to be locked up. I wondered that it should have concluded at length that this was the best use it could put me to, and had never thought to avail itself of my services in some way. I saw that, if there was a wall of stone between me and my townsmen, there was a still more difficult one to climb or break through before they could get to be as free as I was. I did not for a moment feel confined, and the walls seemed a great waste of stone and mortar. I felt as if I alone of all my townsmen had paid my tax.

"Civil Disobedience," originally published as "Resistance to Civil Government" (1849), in *The Writings of Henry David Thoreau*, vol. 4, p. 375, Houghton Mifflin (1906).

See also CIVIL DISOBEDIENCE

I was put into jail as I was going to the shoemaker's to get a shoe which was mended. When I was let out the next morning, I proceeded to finish

my errand, and, having put on my mended shoe, joined a huckleberry party, who were impatient to put themselves under my conduct;
and in half an hour ... was in the midst of a huckleberry field, on one
of our highest hills, two miles off, and then the State was nowhere to
be seen.

"Civil Disobedience," originally published as "Resistance to Civil Government" (1849), in *The Writings
of Henry David Thoreau,* vol. 4, p. 380, Houghton Mifflin (1906).

When I came out of prison,—for some one interfered, and paid that tax,—
I did not perceive that great changes had taken place on the common ...
and yet a change had to my eyes come over the scene,—the town, and
State, and country,—greater than any that mere time could effect. I saw
yet more distinctly the State in which I lived. I saw to what extent the
people among whom I lived could be trusted as good neighbors and
friends; that their friendship was for summer weather only; that they did
not greatly propose to do right; that they were a distinct race from me by
their prejudices and superstitions, as the Chinamen and Malays are; that
in their sacrifices to humanity they ran no risks, not even to their property; that after all they were not so noble but they treated the thief as he
had treated them, and hoped, by a certain outward observance and a few
prayers, and by walking in a particular straight though useless path from
time to time, to save their souls. This may be to judge my neighbors
harshly; for I believe that many of them are not aware that they have such
an institution as the jail in their village.

"Civil Disobedience," originally published as "Resistance to Civil Government" (1849), in *The Writings
of Henry David Thoreau,* vol. 4, pp. 379–380, Houghton Mifflin (1906).

See also GOVERNMENT

*P*ROGRESS

The life in us is like the water in the river. It may rise this year higher than
man has ever known it, and flood the parched uplands; even this may be
the eventful year, which will drown out all our muskrats. It was not always
dry land where we dwell. I see far inland the banks which the stream
anciently washed, before science began to record its freshets. Every one
has heard the story which has gone the rounds of New England, of a
strong and beautiful bug which came out of the dry leaf of an old table of

apple-tree wood, which had stood in a farmer's kitchen for sixty years, first in Connecticut, and afterward in Massachusetts,—from an egg deposited in the living tree many years earlier still, as appeared by counting the annual layers beyond it; which was heard gnawing out for several weeks, hatched perchance by the heat of an urn. Who does not feel his faith in a resurrection and immortality strengthened by hearing of this? Who knows what beautiful and winged life, whose egg has been buried for ages under many concentric layers of woodenness in the dead dry life of society, deposited at first in the alburnum of the green and living tree, which has been gradually converted into the semblance of its well-seasoned tomb,— heard perchance gnawing out now for years by the astonished family of man, as they sat round the festal board,—may unexpectedly come forth from amidst society's most trivial and handselled furniture, to enjoy its perfect summer life at last!

I do not say that John or Jonathan will realize all this; but such is the character of that morrow which mere lapse of time can never make to dawn. The light which puts out our eyes is darkness to us. Only that day dawns to which we are awake. There is more day to dawn. The sun is but a morning star.

<small>*Walden* (1854), in *The Writings of Henry David Thoreau,* vol. 2, pp. 366–367, Houghton Mifflin (1906).</small>

<small>"John or Jonathan" refer to the two stereotypes of England and America during Thoreau's day: John Bull and his wayward son, "Jonathan" (the predecessor of "Uncle Sam").</small>

<small>See also HISTORY</small>

We do not ride on the railroad; it rides upon us. Did you ever think what those sleepers are that underlie the railroad? Each one is a man, an Irishman, or a Yankee man. The rails are laid on them, and they are covered with sand, and the cars run smoothly over them. They are sound sleepers, I assure you. And every few years a new lot is laid down and run over; so that, if some have the pleasure of riding on a rail, others have the misfortune to be ridden upon. And when they run over a man that is walking in his sleep, a supernumerary sleeper in the wrong position, and wake him up, they suddenly stop the cars, and make a hue and cry about it, as if this were an exception. I am glad to know that it takes a gang of men for every five miles to keep the sleepers down and level in their beds as it is, for this is a sign that they may sometime get up again.

<small>*Walden* (1854), in *The Writings of Henry David Thoreau,* vol. 2, pp. 102–103, Houghton Mifflin (1906).</small>

<small>Thoreau's pun rests upon his use of the British term, "sleepers," instead of the American, "railroad ties."</small>

<small>See also LABOR</small>

Property

It would surpass the powers of a well man nowadays to take up his bed and walk, and I should certainly advise a sick one to lay down his bed and run.

Walden (1854), in *The Writings of Henry David Thoreau*, vol. 2, p. 74, Houghton Mifflin (1906).

The customs of some savage nations might, perchance, be profitably imitated by us, for they at least go through the semblance of casting their slough annually; they have the idea of the thing, whether they have the reality or not.

Walden (1854), in *The Writings of Henry David Thoreau*, vol. 2, p. 75, Houghton Mifflin (1906).

To enjoy a thing exclusively is commonly to exclude yourself from the true enjoyment of it.

"Walking" (1862), in *The Writings of Henry David Thoreau*, vol. 5, p. 216, Houghton Mifflin (1906).

Provincialism

I aspire to be acquainted with wiser men than this our Concord soil has produced, whose names are hardly known here.

Walden (1854), in *The Writings of Henry David Thoreau*, vol. 2, p. 119, Houghton Mifflin (1906).

See also FAME

Instead of noblemen, let us have noble villages of men.

Walden (1854), in *The Writings of Henry David Thoreau*, vol. 2, p. 122, Houghton Mifflin (1906).

See also EUROPE VERSUS AMERICA

While England endeavors to cure the potato-rot, will not any endeavor to cure the brain-rot, which prevails so much more widely and fatally?

Walden (1854), in *The Writings of Henry David Thoreau*, vol. 2, p. 358, Houghton Mifflin (1906).

Thoreau comments here on American provinciality and conformity, as well as on more general ignorance. He also refers specifically to the Irish Potato Famine.

See also CONFORMITY

PUBLISHERS AND PUBLISHING

Time & Co. are, after all, the only quite honest and trustworthy publishers that we know.

Letter, March 8, 1848, to Elliot Cabot, in *The Writings of Henry David Thoreau*, vol. 6, p. 156, Houghton Mifflin (1906).

See also FAME

Much is published, but little printed.

Walden (1854), in *The Writings of Henry David Thoreau*, vol. 2, p. 123, Houghton Mifflin (1906).

See also WRITERS AND WRITING

QUEBEC CITY

At the ramparts on the cliff near the old Parliament House I counted twenty-four thirty-two-pounders in a row, pointed over the harbor, with their balls piled pyramid-wise between them,—there are said to be in all about one hundred and eighty guns mounted at Quebec,—all which were faithfully kept dusted by officials, in accordance with the motto, "In time of peace prepare for war"; but I saw no preparations for peace: she was plainly an uninvited guest.

"A Yankee in Canada" (1853), in *The Writings of Henry David Thoreau*, vol. 5, p. 76, Houghton Mifflin (1906).

See also WAR

Separating ourselves from the crowd, we walked up a narrow street, thence ascended by some wooden steps, called the Break-neck Stairs, into another steep, narrow, and zigzag street, blasted through the rock, which last led through a low, massive stone portal, called Prescott Gate, the principal thoroughfare into the Upper Town. This passage was defended by cannon, with a guard-house over it, a sentinel at his post, and other soldiers at hand ready to relieve him. I rubbed my eyes to be sure that I was in the Nineteenth Century, and was not entering one of those portals which sometimes adorn the frontispieces of new editions of old black-letter volumes. I thought it would be a good place to read Froissart's Chronicles. It was such a reminiscence of the Middle Ages as Scott's novels. Men apparently dwelt there for security! Peace be unto them! As if the inhabitants of New York were to go over to Castle William to live! What a place it must be to bring up children!

> "A Yankee in Canada" (1853), in *The Writings of Henry David Thoreau*, vol. 5, p. 23, Houghton Mifflin (1906).

QUEBEC PROVINCE

To a traveler from the Old World, Canada East may appear like a new country, and its inhabitants like colonists, but to me, coming from New England and being a very green traveler withal, . . . it appeared as old as Normandy itself, and realized much that I had heard of Europe and the Middle Ages. Even the names of humble Canadian villages affected me as if they had been those of the renowned cities of antiquity. To be told by a habitan, when I asked the name of a village in sight, that it is *St. Féreol* or *St. Anne*, the *Guardian Angel* or the *Holy Joseph's*; or of a mountain, that it was *Bélange* or *St. Hyacinthe!* As soon as you leave the States, these saintly names begin . . . and thenceforward, the names of mountains, and streams, and villages reel, if I may so speak, with the intoxication of poetry,—*Chambly, Longueuil, Pointe aux Trembles, Bartholomy*, etc., etc.; as if it needed only a little foreign accent, a few more liquids and vowels perchance in the language, to make us locate our ideals at once. I began to dream of Provence and the Troubadours, and of places and things which have no existence on the earth. They veiled the Indian and the primitive forest, and the woods towards Hudson's Bay were only as the forests of Germany. I could not at once bring myself to believe that the inhabitants who pronounced daily those beautiful and, to me, significant names lead as prosaic lives as we of New England. In short, the Canada which I saw was not merely a place for railroads to terminate in and for criminals to run to.

> "A Yankee in Canada" (1853), in *The Writings of Henry David Thoreau*, vol. 5, pp. 56–57, Houghton Mifflin (1906).

> "Canada East" and "Lower Canada" were early nineteenth-century political designations including much of what is now the Province of Quebec.

See also LANGUAGE

RAILROAD CUT, THE

Few phenomena gave me more delight than to observe the forms which thawing sand and clay assume in flowing down the sides of a deep cut on the railroad through which I passed on my way to the village, a phenomenon not very common on so large a scale. . . . When the frost comes out in the spring, and even in a thawing day in the winter, the sand begins to flow down the slopes like lava, sometimes bursting out through the snow and overflowing it where no sand was to be seen before. Innumerable little streams overlap and interlace one with another, exhibiting a sort of hybrid product, which obeys half way the law of currents, and half way that of vegetation. As it flows it takes the forms of sappy leaves or vines, making heaps of pulpy sprays a foot or more in depth, and resembling, as you look down on them, the lacinated, lobed, and imbricated thalluses of some lichens; or you are reminded of coral, of leopard's paws or birds' feet, of brains or lungs or bowels, and excrements of all kinds. It is a truly *grotesque* vegetation.

Walden (1854), in *The Writings of Henry David Thoreau,* vol. 2, pp. 336–337, Houghton Mifflin (1906).

The whole bank, which is from twenty to forty feet high, is sometimes overlaid with a mass of this kind of foliage, or sandy rupture, for a quarter of a mile on one or both sides, the produce of one spring day. What makes this sand foliage remarkable is its springing into existence thus suddenly. When I see on the one side the inert bank,—for the sun acts on one side first,—and on the other this luxuriant foliage, the creation of an hour, I am affected as if in a peculiar sense I stood in the laboratory of the Artist who made the world and me,—had come to where he was still at work, sporting on this bank, and with excess of energy strewing his fresh designs about. I feel as if I were nearer to the vitals of the globe, for this sandy overflow is something such a foliaceous mass as the vitals of the animal body. You find thus in the very sands an anticipation of the vegetable leaf. No wonder that the earth expresses itself outwardly in leaves, it labors with the idea inwardly. The atoms have already learned this law, and are pregnant by it. The overhanging leaf sees here its prototype. *Internally,* whether in the globe or animal body, it is a moist thick *lobe,* a word especially applicable to the liver and lungs and the *leaves* of fat (*leibo, labor, lapsus,* to flow or slip downward, a lapsing; *lobos, globus,* lobe, globe; also lap, flap, and many other words); *externally,* a dry thin *leaf,* even as the *f* and *v* are a pressed and dried *b.* The radicals of *lobe* are *lb,* the soft mass of the *b* (single-lobed, or *B*, double-lobed), with the liquid *l* behind it pressing it forward. In globe, *glb*, the gutteral *g* adds to the meaning the capacity of the throat. The feather and wings of birds are still drier and thinner leaves. Thus, also, you pass from the lumpish grub in the earth to the airy and fluttering butterfly. The very globe continually transcends and translates itself, and becomes winged in its orbit.

Walden (1854), in *The Writings of Henry David Thoreau*, vol. 2, pp. 337–338, Houghton Mifflin (1906).

See also GOD

RALEIGH, SIR WALTER

Sir Walter Raleigh might well be studied, if only for the excellence of his style, for he is remarkable in the midst of so many masters. There is a natural emphasis in his style, like a man's tread, and a breathing space between the sentences, which the best of modern writing does not furnish. His chapters are like English parks, or say rather like a Western forest, where the larger growth keeps down the underwood, and one may ride on horseback through the openings.

A Week on the Concord and Merrimack Rivers (1849), in *The Writings of Henry David Thoreau*, vol. 1, pp. 106–107, Houghton Mifflin (1906).

Thoreau uses the traditional spelling, "Raleigh," rather than the spelling used by the author himself as well as by modern scholars: "Ralegh."

See also STYLE

READING

My residence was more favorable, not only to thought, but to serious reading, than a university; and though I was beyond the range of the ordinary circulating library, I had more than ever come within the influence of those books which circulate round the world, whose sentences were first written on bark, and are now merely copied from time to time on to linen paper.

Walden (1854), in *The Writings of Henry David Thoreau*, vol. 2, p. 110, Houghton Mifflin (1906).

See also WALDEN POND

The works of the great poets have never yet been read by mankind, for only great poets can read them. They have only been read as the multitude read the stars, at most astrologically, not astronomically.

Walden (1854), in *The Writings of Henry David Thoreau*, vol. 2, pp. 115–116, Houghton Mifflin (1906).

See also POETRY AND POETS

Read the best books first, or you may not have a chance to read them at all.

A Week on the Concord and Merrimack Rivers (1849), in *The Writings of Henry David Thoreau*, vol. 1, p. 98, Houghton Mifflin (1906).

See also BOOKS

Some hard and dry book in a dead language, which you have found it impossible to read at home, but for which you still have a lingering regard, is the best to carry with you on a journey.

A Week on the Concord and Merrimack Rivers (1849), in *The Writings of Henry David Thoreau*, vol. 1, p. 327, Houghton Mifflin (1906).

See also BOOKS

REFORM AND REFORMERS

There are a thousand hacking at the branches of evil to one who is striking at the root, and it may be that he who bestows the largest amount of time and money on the needy is doing the most by his mode of life to produce that misery which he strives in vain to relieve.

Walden (1854), in *The Writings of Henry David Thoreau*, vol. 2, p. 84, Houghton Mifflin (1906).

See also PHILANTHROPY

It is a great pleasure to escape sometimes from the restless class of Reformers. What if these grievances exist? So do you and I.

A Week on the Concord and Merrimack Rivers (1849), in *The Writings of Henry David Thoreau*, vol. 1, p. 130, Houghton Mifflin (1906).

RELIGION

One revelation has been made to the Indian, another to the white man.

"The Allegash and East Branch" (1864) in *The Maine Woods* (1864), in *The Writings of Henry David Thoreau*, vol. 3, p. 201, Houghton Mifflin (1906).

See also CHRISTIANITY AND CHRISTIANS

Our manners have been corrupted by communication with the saints. Our hymn-books resound with a melodious cursing of God and enduring Him forever. One would say that even the prophets and redeemers had rather consoled the fears than confirmed the hopes of man. There is nowhere recorded a simple and irrepressible satisfaction with the gift of life, any memorable praise of God.

> *Walden* (1854), in *The Writings of Henry David Thoreau*, vol. 2, p. 87, Houghton Mifflin (1906).

Bribed with a little sunlight and a few prismatic tints, we bless our Maker, and stave off his wrath with hymns.

> *A Week on the Concord and Merrimack Rivers* (1849), in *The Writings of Henry David Thoreau*, vol. 1, p. 69, Houghton Mifflin (1906).
>
> See also GOD

Every people have gods to suit their circumstances.

> *A Week on the Concord and Merrimack Rivers* (1849), in *The Writings of Henry David Thoreau*, vol. 1, p. 66, Houghton Mifflin (1906).

In respect to religion and the healing art, all nations are still in a state of barbarism. In the most civilized countries the priest is still but a Powwow, and the physician a Great Medicine.

> *A Week on the Concord and Merrimack Rivers* (1849), in *The Writings of Henry David Thoreau*, vol. 1, p. 272, Houghton Mifflin (1906).

It would be worthy of the age to print together the collected Scriptures or Sacred Writings of the several nations, the Chinese, the Hindoos, the Persians, the Hebrews, and others, as the Scripture of mankind. The New Testament is still, perhaps, too much on the lips and in the hearts of men to be called a Scripture in this sense. Such a juxtaposition and comparison might help to liberalize the faith of men. . . . This would be the Bible, or Book of Books, which let the missionaries carry to the uttermost parts of the earth.

> *A Week on the Concord and Merrimack Rivers* (1849), in *The Writings of Henry David Thoreau*, vol. 1, p. 150, Houghton Mifflin (1906).
>
> See also BIBLE, THE

Really, there is no infidelity, nowadays, so great as that which prays, and keeps the Sabbath, and rebuilds the churches. The sealer of the South Pacific preaches a truer doctrine.

> *A Week on the Concord and Merrimack Rivers* (1849), in *The Writings of Henry David Thoreau*, vol. 1, p. 77, Houghton Mifflin (1906).
>
> See also HYPOCRISY

The church is a sort of hospital for men's souls, and as full of quackery as the hospital for their bodies. Those who are taken into it live like pensioners in their Retreat or Sailor's Snug Harbor, where you may see a row of religious cripples sitting outside in sunny weather.

> *A Week on the Concord and Merrimack Rivers* (1849), in *The Writings of Henry David Thoreau*, vol. 1, pp. 77–78, Houghton Mifflin (1906).

The reading which I love best is the scriptures of the several nations, though it happens that I am better acquainted with those of the Hindoos, the Chinese, and the Persians, than of the Hebrews, which I have come to last. Give me one of these bibles, and you have silenced me for a while. When I recover the use of my tongue, I am wont to worry my neighbors with the new sentences; but commonly they cannot see that there is any wit in them. Such has been my experience with the New Testament. I have not yet got to the crucifixion, I have read it over so many times. I should love dearly to read it aloud to my friends, some of whom are seriously inclined; it is so good, and I am sure that they have never heard it, it fits their case exactly, and we should enjoy it so much together,—but I instinctively despair of getting their ears. They soon show, by signs not to be mistaken, that it is inexpressibly wearisome to them. I do not mean to imply that I am any better than my neighbors; for, alas! I know that I am only as good, though I love better books than they.

> *A Week on the Concord and Merrimack Rivers* (1849), in *The Writings of Henry David Thoreau*, vol. 1, pp. 72–73, Houghton Mifflin (1906).
>
> See also READING

There is more religion in men's science than there is science in their religion.

> *A Week on the Concord and Merrimack Rivers* (1849), in *The Writings of Henry David Thoreau*, vol. 1, p. 79, Houghton Mifflin (1906).
>
> See also SCIENTISTS AND SCIENCE

REPUTATIONS

You need not rest your reputation on the dinners you give.

> *Walden* (1854), in *The Writings of Henry David Thoreau*, vol. 2, pp. 157–158, Houghton Mifflin (1906).
>
> See also INTEGRITY

RIVERS

They are the natural highways of all nations.

A Week on the Concord and Merrimack Rivers (1849), in The Writings of Henry David Thoreau, vol. 1, p. 11, Houghton Mifflin (1906).

ROOSTERS

All climates agree with brave Chanticleer. He is more indigenous even than the natives. His health is ever good, his lungs are sound, his spirits never flag.

Walden (1854), in The Writings of Henry David Thoreau, vol. 2, p. 141, Houghton Mifflin (1906).

SAILING

Two men in a skiff, whom we passed hereabouts, floating buoyantly amid the reflections of the trees, like a feather in mid-air, or a leaf which is wafted gently from its twig to the water without turning over, seemed still in their element, and to have very delicately availed themselves of the natural laws. Their floating there was a beautiful and successful experiment in natural philosophy, and it served to ennoble in our eyes the art of navigation; for as birds fly and fishes swim, so these men sailed. It reminded us how much fairer and nobler all the actions of man might be, and that our life in its whole economy might be as beautiful as the fairest works of art or nature.

A Week on the Concord and Merrimack Rivers (1849), in The Writings of Henry David Thoreau, vol. 1, p. 48, Houghton Mifflin (1906).

See also BOATMEN

SAILORS

All sailors pause to watch a steamer, and shout in welcome or derision. In one a large Newfoundland dog put his paws on the rail and stood up as high as any of them, and looked as wise. But the skipper, who did not

wish to be seen no better employed than a dog, rapped him on the nose
and sent him below. Such is human justice!

Cape Cod (1855–1865), in *The Writings of Henry David Thoreau*, vol. 4, p. 261, Houghton Mifflin
(1906).

Sand

The sand is the great enemy here. . . . The sand drifts like snow, and
sometimes the lower story of a house is concealed by it, though it is kept
off by a wall. The houses were formerly built on piles, in order that the
driving sand might pass under them. . . . There was a schoolhouse, just
under the hill on which we sat, filled with sand up to the tops of the
desks, and of course the master and scholars had fled. Perhaps they had
imprudently left the windows open one day, or neglected to mend a
broken pane.

Cape Cod (1855–1865), in *The Writings of Henry David Thoreau*, vol. 4, pp. 220–221, Houghton Mifflin
(1906).

See also SEASHORE

Sauntering

To tell the truth, I saw an advertisement for able-bodied seamen, when I
was a boy, sauntering in my native port, and as soon as I came of age I
embarked.

"Life Without Principle" (1863), in *The Writings of Henry David Thoreau*, vol. 4, p. 460, Houghton
Mifflin (1906).

I have met with but one or two persons in the course of my life who
understood the art of Walking, that is, of taking walks,—who had a
genius, so to speak, for *sauntering*, which word is beautifully derived
"from idle people who roved about the country, in the Middle Ages, and
asked charity, under the pretense of going *à la Sainte Terre*," to the Holy
Land, till the children exclaimed, "There goes a *Sainte-Terrer*," a Saunterer,
a Holy-Lander. They who never go to the Holy Land in their walks, as
they pretend, are indeed mere idlers and vagabonds; but they who do go
there are saunterers in the good sense, such as I mean. Some, however,
would derive the word from *sans terre*, without land or a home, which,

therefore, in the good sense, will mean, having no particular home, but equally at home everywhere. For this is the secret of successful sauntering. He who sits still in a house all the time may be the greatest vagrant of all; but the saunterer, in the good sense, is no more vagrant than the meandering river, which is all the while sedulously seeking the shortest course to the sea. But I prefer the first, which, indeed, is the most probable derivation. For every walk is a sort of crusade, preached by some Peter the Hermit in us, to go forth and reconquer this Holy Land from the hands of the Infidels.

"Walking" (1862), in *The Writings of Henry David Thoreau,* vol. 5, pp. 205–206, Houghton Mifflin (1906).

Scholars and Scholarship

Men have a respect for scholarship and learning greatly out of proportion to the use they commonly serve.

A Week on the Concord and Merrimack Rivers (1849), in *The Writings of Henry David Thoreau,* vol. 1, p. 108, Houghton Mifflin (1906).

Scholars are wont to sell their birthright for a mess of learning.

A Week on the Concord and Merrimack Rivers (1849), in *The Writings of Henry David Thoreau,* vol. 1, p. 98, Houghton Mifflin (1906).

See also KNOWLEDGE

Some creatures are made to see in the dark.

A Week on the Concord and Merrimack Rivers (1849), in *The Writings of Henry David Thoreau,* vol. 1, p. 164, Houghton Mifflin (1906).

See also HISTORY

Science

I exulted like "a pagan suckled in a creed" that had never been worn at all, but was bran-new, and adequate to the occasion. I let science slide, and rejoiced in that light as if it had been a fellow creature. I saw that it was excellent, and was very glad to know that it was so cheap. A scientific *explanation,* as it is called, would have been altogether out of place there. That is for pale daylight.

"The Allegash and East Branch" (1864) in *The Maine Woods* (1864), in *The Writings of Henry David Thoreau,* vol. 3, p. 200, Houghton Mifflin (1906).

See also PHOSPHORESCENCE

Linnæus, setting out for Lapland, surveys his "comb" and "spare shirt," "leathern breeches" and "gauze cap to keep off gnats," with as much complacency as Bonaparte a park of artillery for the Russian campaign. The quiet bravery of the man is admirable.

"Natural History of Massachusetts" (1842), in *The Writings of Henry David Thoreau,* vol. 5, p. 107, Houghton Mifflin (1906).

What an admirable training is science for the more active warfare of life! Indeed, the unchallenged bravery which these studies imply, is far more impressive than the trumpeted valor of the warrior.

"Natural History of Massachusetts" (1842), in *The Writings of Henry David Thoreau,* vol. 5, p. 105, Houghton Mifflin (1906).

See also LIFE

The true man of science will know nature better by his finer organization; he will smell, taste, see, hear, feel, better than other men. His will be a deeper and finer experience. We do not learn by inference and deduction and the application of mathematics to philosophy, but by direct inter-course and sympathy. It is with science as with ethics,—we cannot know truth by contrivance and method; the Baconian is as false as any other, and with all the helps of machinery and the arts, the most scientific will still be the healthiest and friendliest man, and possess a more perfect Indian wisdom.

"Natural History of Massachusetts" (1842), in *The Writings of Henry David Thoreau,* vol. 5, p. 131, Houghton Mifflin (1906).

See also DEATH

Let us consider under what disadvantages Science has hitherto labored before we pronounce thus confidently on her progress.

"Paradise (To Be) Regained" (1843), in *The Writings of Henry David Thoreau,* vol. 4, p. 301, Houghton Mifflin (1906).

See also PROGRESS

There is a chasm between knowledge and ignorance which the arches of science can never span.

A Week on the Concord and Merrimack Rivers (1849), in *The Writings of Henry David Thoreau*, vol. 1, p. 100, Houghton Mifflin (1906).

See also KNOWLEDGE

SEA, THE

Sometimes we met a wrecker with his cart and dog,—and his dog's faint bark at us wayfarers, heard through the roaring of the surf, sounded ridiculously faint. To see a little trembling dainty-footed cur stand on the margin of the ocean, and ineffectually bark at a beach-bird, amid the roar of the Atlantic! Come with design to bark at a whale, perchance! That sound will do for farmyards. All the dogs looked out of place there, naked and as if shuddering at the vastness; and I thought that they would not have been there had it not been for the countenance of their masters. Still less could you think of a cat bending her steps that way, and shaking her wet foot over the Atlantic; yet even this happens sometimes, they tell me.

Cape Cod (1855–1865), in *The Writings of Henry David Thoreau*, vol. 4, p. 185, Houghton Mifflin (1906).

The ocean is but a larger lake. At midsummer you may sometimes see a strip of glassy smoothness on it, a few rods in width and many miles long, as if the surface were covered with a thin pellicle of oil, just as on a country pond. . . . Yet this same placid ocean, as civil now as a city's harbor, a place for ships and commerce, will ere long be lashed into sudden fury, and all its caves and cliffs will resound with tumult. It will ruthlessly heave these vessels to and fro, break them in pieces in its sandy or stony jaws, and deliver their crews to sea-monsters. It will play with them like seaweed, distend them like dead frogs, and carry them about, now high, now low, to show to the fishes, giving them a nibble. This gentle ocean will toss and tear the rag of a man's body like the father of mad bulls, and his relatives may be seen seeking the remnants for weeks along the strand. From some quiet inland hamlet they have rushed weeping to the unheard-of shore, and now stand uncertain where a sailor has recently been buried amid the sand-hills.

Cape Cod (1855–1865), in *The Writings of Henry David Thoreau*, vol. 4, pp. 124–126, Houghton Mifflin (1906).

See also DEATH

The sea, vast and wild as it is, bears thus the waste and wrecks of human art to its remotest shore. There is no telling what it may not vomit up.

Cape Cod (1855–1865), in *The Writings of Henry David Thoreau*, vol. 4, p. 115, Houghton Mifflin (1906).

There was nothing but that savage ocean between us and Europe.

Cape Cod (1855–1865), in *The Writings of Henry David Thoreau*, vol. 4, p. 57, Houghton Mifflin (1906).

See also CAPE COD

Though for some time I have not spoken of the roaring of the breakers, and the ceaseless flux and reflux of the waves, yet they did not for a moment cease to dash and roar, with such a tumult that, if you had been there, you could scarcely have heard my voice the while; and they are dashing and roaring this very moment,—though it may be with less din and violence,—for there the sea never rests. We were wholly absorbed by this spectacle and tumult, and like Chryses, though in a different mood from him, we walked silent along the shore of the resounding sea ... — though I doubt if Homer's *Mediterranean* Sea ever sounded so loud as this.

Cape Cod (1855–1865), in *The Writings of Henry David Thoreau*, vol. 4, pp. 66–67, Houghton Mifflin (1906).

We do not associate the idea of antiquity with the ocean, nor wonder how it looked a thousand years ago, as we do of the land, for it was equally wild and unfathomable always. The Indians have left no traces on its surface, but it is the same to the civilized man and the savage. The aspect of the shore only has changed.

Cape Cod (1855–1865), in *The Writings of Henry David Thoreau*, vol. 4, p. 188, Houghton Mifflin (1906).

See also WILDNESS

*S*EASHORE

Before the land rose out of the ocean, and became *dry* land, chaos reigned; and between high and low water mark, where she is partially disrobed and rising, a sort of chaos reigns still, which only anomalous creatures can inhabit.

Cape Cod (1855–1865), in *The Writings of Henry David Thoreau*, vol. 4, p. 71, Houghton Mifflin (1906).

It is a wild, rank place, and there is no flattery in it. Strewn with crabs, horseshoes, and razor clams, and whatever the sea casts up,—a vast *morgue,* where famished dogs may range in packs, and crows come daily to glean the pittance which the tide leaves them. The carcasses of men and beasts together lie stately up upon its shelf, rotting and bleaching in the sun and waves, and each tide turns them in their beds, and tucks fresh sand under them. There is naked Nature,—inhumanly sincere, wasting no thought on man, nibbling at the cliffy shore where gulls wheel amid the spray.

Cape Cod (1855–1865), in *The Writings of Henry David Thoreau*, vol. 4, pp. 186–187, Houghton Mifflin (1906).

See also DEATH

SELF-ESTEEM

Public opinion is a weak tyrant compared with our own private opinion. What a man thinks of himself, that it is which determines, or rather indicates, his fate.

Walden (1854), in *The Writings of Henry David Thoreau*, vol. 2, p. 8, Houghton Mifflin (1906).

See also FATE

SELF-KNOWLEDGE

What was the meaning of that South-Sea Exploring Expedition, with all its parade and expense, but an indirect recognition of the fact that there are continents and seas in the moral world to which every man is an isthmus or an inlet, yet unexplored by him, but that it is easier to sail many thousand miles through cold and storm and cannibals, in a government ship, with five hundred men and boys to assist one, than it is to explore the private sea, the Atlantic and Pacific Ocean of one's being alone.

Walden (1854), in *The Writings of Henry David Thoreau,* vol. 2, p. 354, Houghton Mifflin (1906).

See also SEA

SHIPS AND BOATS

There were many vessels, like gulls, skimming over the surface of the sea, now half concealed in its troughs, their dolphin-strikers plowing the water, now tossed on the top of the billows. . . . Some of these vessels lagged behind, while others steadily went ahead. We narrowly watched their rig and the cut of their jibs, and how they walked the water, for there was all the difference between them that there is between living creatures. But we wondered that they should be remembering Boston and New York and Liverpool, steering for them, out there; as if the sailor might forget his peddling business on such a grand highway. They had perchance brought oranges from the Western Isles; and were they carrying back the peel? We might as well transport our old traps across the ocean of eternity. Is *that* but another "trading flood," with its blessed isles? Is Heaven such a harbor as the Liverpool docks?

Cape Cod (1855–1865), in *The Writings of Henry David Thoreau,* vol. 4, pp. 105–106, Houghton Mifflin (1906).

If rightly made, a boat would be a sort of amphibious animal, a creature of two elements, related by one half its structure to some swift and shapely fish, and by the other to some strong-winged and graceful bird.

A Week on the Concord and Merrimack Rivers (1849), in *The Writings of Henry David Thoreau,* vol. 1, p. 13, Houghton Mifflin (1906).

SIGHT

What I see is mine.

A Week on the Concord and Merrimack Rivers (1849), in *The Writings of Henry David Thoreau,* vol. 1, p. 373, Houghton Mifflin (1906).

See also MIND, THE

SILENCE

In human intercourse the tragedy begins, not when there is misunder-standing about words, but when silence is not understood. Then there can never be an explanation.

> *A Week on the Concord and Merrimack Rivers* (1849), in *The Writings of Henry David Thoreau*, vol. 1, p. 295, Houghton Mifflin (1906).

Silence is the universal refuge, the sequel to all dull discourses and all foolish acts, a balm to our every chagrin, as welcome after satiety as after disappointment.

> *A Week on the Concord and Merrimack Rivers* (1849), in *The Writings of Henry David Thoreau*, vol. 1, p. 418, Houghton Mifflin (1906).

There are some things which a man never speaks of, which are much finer kept silent about. To the highest communications we only lend a silent ear.

> *A Week on the Concord and Merrimack Rivers* (1849), in *The Writings of Henry David Thoreau*, vol. 1, p. 295, Houghton Mifflin (1906).

SIMPLICITY

Every morning was a cheerful invitation to make my life of equal simplic-ity, and I may say innocence, with Nature herself.

> *Walden* (1854), in *The Writings of Henry David Thoreau*, vol. 2, p. 98, Houghton Mifflin (1906).
>
> See also INNOCENCE

In short, I am convinced, both by faith and experience, that to maintain one's self on this earth is not a hardship but a pastime, if we will live simply and wisely; as the pursuits of the simpler nations are still the sports of the more artificial. It is not necessary that a man should earn his living by the sweat of his brow, unless he sweats easier than I do.

> *Walden* (1854), in *The Writings of Henry David Thoreau*, vol. 2, p. 78, Houghton Mifflin (1906).
>
> See also LABOR

It is desirable that a man be clad so simply that he can lay his hands on himself in the dark, and that he live in all respects so compactly and preparedly that, if an enemy take the town, he can, like the old philosopher, walk out the gate empty-handed without anxiety.

Walden (1854), in *The Writings of Henry David Thoreau,* vol. 2, pp. 26–27, Houghton Mifflin (1906).

See also CLOTHING

It is life near the bone where it is sweetest. You are defended from being a trifler.

Walden (1854), in *The Writings of Henry David Thoreau,* vol. 2, p. 362, Houghton Mifflin (1906).

See also INTEGRITY

Most of the luxuries, and many of the so-called comforts of life, are not only not indispensable, but positive hindrances to the elevation of mankind. With respect to luxuries and comforts, the wisest have ever lived a more simple and meagre life than the poor. The ancient philosophers, Chinese, Hindoo, Persian, and Greek, were a class than which none has been poorer in outward riches, none so rich in inward. . . . The same is true of the more modern reformers and benefactors of their race. None can be an impartial or wise observer of human life but from the vantage ground of what *we* should call voluntary poverty.

Walden (1854), in *The Writings of Henry David Thoreau,* vol. 2, pp. 15–16, Houghton Mifflin (1906).

See also NECESSITIES

Simplify, simplify.

Walden (1854), in *The Writings of Henry David Thoreau,* vol. 2, p. 102, Houghton Mifflin (1906).

SINCERITY

I, on my side, require of every writer, first or last, a simple and sincere account of his own life, and not merely what he has heard of other men's lives; some such account as he would send to his kindred from a distant land; for if he has lived sincerely, it must have been in a distant land to me.

Walden (1854), in *The Writings of Henry David Thoreau,* vol. 2, p. 4, Houghton Mifflin (1906).

See also WRITERS AND WRITING

Any sincere thought is irresistible.

A Week on the Concord and Merrimack Rivers (1849), in *The Writings of Henry David Thoreau*, vol. 1, p. 159, Houghton Mifflin (1906).

See also THINKING AND THOUGHTS

SLAVERY

This people must cease to hold slaves, and to make war on Mexico, though it cost them their existence as a people.

"Civil Disobedience," originally published as "Resistance to Civil Government" (1849), in *The Writings of Henry David Thoreau*, vol. 4, p. 362, Houghton Mifflin (1906).

Again it happens that the Boston Court-House is full of armed men, holding prisoner and trying a MAN, to find out if he is not really a SLAVE. Does anyone think that justice or God awaits Mr. Loring's decision? For him to sit there deciding still, when this question is already decided from eternity to eternity, and the unlettered slave himself and the multitude around have long since heard and assented to the decision, is simply to make himself ridiculous.... Such an arbiter's very existence is an impertinence. We do not ask him to make up his mind, but to make up his pack.

"Slavery in Massachusetts" (1854), in *The Writings of Henry David Thoreau*, vol. 4, p. 389, Houghton Mifflin (1906).

Thoreau refers to the return of the fugitive slave, Anthony Burns, from Massachusetts to the South.

See also JUSTICE

The judges and lawyers ... consider, not whether the Fugitive Slave Law is right, but whether it is what they call *constitutional.* Is virtue constitutional, or vice? Is equity constitutional, or inequity? In important moral and vital questions, like this, it is just as impertinent to ask whether a law is constitutional or not, as to ask whether it is profitable or not.... The question is, not whether you or your grandfather, seventy years ago, did not enter into an agreement to serve the devil, and that service is not accordingly now due; but whether you will not now, for once and at last, serve God,—in spite of your own past recreancy, or that of your ances-tor,—by obeying that eternal and only just CONSTITUTION, which He, and not any Jefferson or Adams, has written in your being.

"Slavery in Massachusetts" (1854), in *The Writings of Henry David Thoreau*, vol. 4, pp. 401–402, Houghton Mifflin (1906).

Three years ago, also, when the Sims tragedy was acted, I said to myself, There is such an officer, if not such a man, as the Governor of Massachusetts,—what has he been about the last fortnight? Has he had as much as he could do to keep on the fence during this moral earthquake? . . . He could at least have *resigned* himself into fame.

"Slavery in Massachusetts" (1854), in *The Writings of Henry David Thoreau*, vol. 4, p. 390, Houghton Mifflin (1906).

Thoreau refers here to the return of the fugitive slave, Thomas Sims, to the South from Massachusetts.

I sometimes wonder that we can be so frivolous . . . as to attend to the gross but somewhat foreign form of servitude called Negro Slavery, there are so many keen and subtle masters that enslave both north and south. It is hard to have a southern overseer; it is worse to have a northern one; but worst of all when you are the slave-driver of yourself.

Walden (1854), in *The Writings of Henry David Thoreau*, vol. 2, p. 8, Houghton Mifflin (1906).

See also LABOR

Society

In society you will not find health, but in nature. Unless our feet at least stood in the midst of nature, all our faces would be pale and livid. Society is always diseased, and the best is the most so.

"Natural History of Massachusetts" (1842), in *The Writings of Henry David Thoreau*, vol. 5, p. 105, Houghton Mifflin (1906).

See also NATURE

As I walked in the woods to see the birds and squirrels, so I walked in the village to see the men and boys; instead of the wind among the pines I heard the carts rattle. In one direction from my house there was a colony of muskrats in the river meadows; under the grove of elms and buttonwoods in the other horizon was a village of busy men, as curious to me as if they had been prarie-dogs, each sitting at the mouth of its burrow, or running over to a neighbor's to gossip. I went there frequently to observe their habits.

Walden (1854), in *The Writings of Henry David Thoreau*, vol. 2, p. 185, Houghton Mifflin (1906).

See also CONCORD, MASSACHUSETTS

I observed that the vitals of the village were the grocery, the bar-room, the post-office, and the bank; and, as a necessary part of the machinery, they kept a bell, a big gun, and a fire-engine, at convenient places; and the houses were so arranged as to make the most of mankind, in lanes and fronting one another, so that every traveller had to run the gauntlet, and every man, woman, and child might get a lick at him.... For the most part I escaped wonderfully from these dangers, either by proceeding at once boldly and without deliberation to the goal, as is recommended to those who run the gauntlet, or by keeping my thoughts on high things, like Orpheus, who, "loudly singing the praises of the gods to his lyre, drowned the voices of the Sirens, and kept out of danger." Sometimes I bolted suddenly, and nobody could tell my whereabouts, for I did not stand much about gracefulness, and never hesitated at a gap in a fence. I was even accustomed to make an irruption into some houses, where I was well entertained, and after learning the kernels and the very last sieveful of news,—what had subsided, the prospects of war and peace, and whether the world was likely to hold together much longer,—I was let out through the rear avenues, and so escaped to the woods again.

> *Walden* (1854), in *The Writings of Henry David Thoreau*, vol. 2, pp. 186–187, Houghton Mifflin (1906).
>
> See also CONCORD, MASSACHUSETTS

It is surprising how many great men and women a small house will contain. I have had twenty-five or thirty souls, with their bodies, at once under my roof, and yet we often parted without being aware that we had come very near to one another.

> *Walden* (1854), in *The Writings of Henry David Thoreau*, vol. 2, p. 155, Houghton Mifflin (1906).
>
> See also SOLITUDE

SOLDIERS

Visit the Navy-Yard, and behold a marine, such a man as an American government can make, or such as it can make a man with its black arts,— a mere shadow and reminiscence of humanity, a man laid out alive and standing, and already, as one may say, buried under arms with funeral accompaniments.

> "Civil Disobedience," originally published as "Resistance to Civil Government" (1849), in *The Writings of Henry David Thoreau*, vol. 4, p. 359, Houghton Mifflin (1906).
>
> See also GOVERNMENT

Far up in the country,—for we would be faithful to our experience,—in Thornton, perhaps, we met a soldier lad in the woods, going to muster in full regimentals, and holding the middle of the road; deep in the forest, with shouldered musket and military step, and thoughts of war and glory all to himself. It was a sore trial to the youth, tougher than many a battle, to get by us creditably and with soldier-like bearing. Poor man! He actually shivered like a reed in his thin military pants, and by the time we had got up with him, all the sternness that becomes the soldier had forsaken his face, and he skulked past as if he were driving his father's sheep under a sword-proof helmet. It was too much for him to carry any extra armor then, who could not easily dispose of his natural arms. And for his legs, they were like heavy artillery in boggy places; better to cut the traces and forsake them. His greaves chafed and wrestled one with another for want of other foes. But he did get by and get off with all his munitions, and lived to fight another day; and I do not record this as casting any suspicion on his honor and real bravery in the field.

A Week on the Concord and Merrimack Rivers (1849), in The Writings of Henry David Thoreau, vol. 1, pp. 333–334, Houghton Mifflin (1906).

I have no doubt that soldiers well drilled are, as a class, peculiarly destitute of originality and independence. . . . It is impossible to give the soldier a good education without making him a deserter. His natural foe is the government that drills him.

"A Yankee in Canada" (1853), in The Writings of Henry David Thoreau, vol. 5, p. 27, Houghton Mifflin (1906).

See also GOVERNMENT

SOLITUDE

A man thinking or working is always alone, let him be where he will.

Walden (1854), in The Writings of Henry David Thoreau, vol. 2, p. 150, Houghton Mifflin (1906).

See also LABOR

For what reason have I this vast range and circuit, some square miles of unfrequented forest, for my privacy, abandoned to me by men? My nearest neighbor is a mile distant, and no house is visible from any place but the hill-tops within half a mile of my own. I have my horizon bounded by woods all to myself; a distant view of the railroad where it touches the pond on the one hand, and of the fence which skirts the woodland road on the other. But for the most part it is as solitary where I live as on the prairies. It is as much Asia or Africa as New England. I have, as it were, my own sun and moon and stars, and a little world all to myself.

Walden (1854), in *The Writings of Henry David Thoreau,* vol. 2, p. 144, Houghton Mifflin (1906).

See also WALDEN POND

I find it wholesome to be alone the greater part of the time. To be in company, even with the best, is soon wearisome and dissipating. I love to be alone. I never found the companion that was so companionable as solitude.

Walden (1854), in *The Writings of Henry David Thoreau,* vol. 2, p. 150, Houghton Mifflin (1906).

See also FRIENDS AND FRIENDSHIP

We are for the most part more lonely when we go abroad among men than when we stay in our chambers.

Walden (1854), in *The Writings of Henry David Thoreau,* vol. 2, p. 150, Houghton Mifflin (1906).

Sounds

There is something singularly grand and impressive in the sound of a tree falling in a perfectly calm night like this, as if the agencies which over-throw it did not need to be excited, but worked with a subtle, deliberate, and conscious force, like a boa-constrictor, and more effectively then than even in a windy day.

"Chesuncook" (1858) in *The Maine Woods* (1864), in *The Writings of Henry David Thoreau,* vol. 3, p. 115, Houghton Mifflin (1906).

See also TREES

Space Travel

Perchance, coming generations will not abide the dissolution of the globe, but, availing themselves of future inventions in aerial locomotion, and the navigation of space, the entire race may migrate from the earth, to settle some vacant and more western planet. . . . It took but little art, a simple application of natural laws, a canoe, a paddle, and a sail of matting, to people the isles of the Pacific, and a little more will people the shining isles of space. Do we not see in the firmament the lights carried along the shore by night, as Columbus did? Let us not despair or mutiny.

> "Paradise (To Be) Regained" (1843), in *The Writings of Henry David Thoreau*, vol. 4, p. 292, Houghton Mifflin (1906).
>
> See also PROGRESS

SPIRITUALITY

He who eats the fruit should at least plant the seed; ay, if possible, a better seed than that whose fruit he has enjoyed.

> *A Week on the Concord and Merrimack Rivers* (1849), in *The Writings of Henry David Thoreau*, vol. 1, p. 129, Houghton Mifflin (1906).
>
> See also ECOLOGY

We have need to be earth-born as well as heaven-born, *gegeneis*, as was said of the Titans of old, or in a better sense than they.

> *A Week on the Concord and Merrimack Rivers* (1849), in *The Writings of Henry David Thoreau*, vol. 1, p. 406, Houghton Mifflin (1906).

SPRING

As every season seems best to us in its turn, so the coming in of spring is like the creation of Cosmos out of Chaos and the realization of the Golden Age.

> *Walden* (1854), in *The Writings of Henry David Thoreau*, vol. 2, p. 346, Houghton Mifflin (1906).

As it grew darker, I was startled by the honking of geese flying low over the woods, like weary travellers getting in late from Southern lakes, and indulging at last in unrestrained complaint and mutual consolation. Standing at my door, I could hear the rush of their wings; when, driving toward my house, they suddenly spied my light, and with hushed clamor wheeled and settled in the pond. So I came in, and shut the door, and passed my first spring night in the woods.

> *Walden* (1854), in *The Writings of Henry David Thoreau*, vol. 2, p. 345, Houghton Mifflin (1906).

In a pleasant spring morning all men's sins are forgiven. Such a day is a truce to vice. While such a sun holds out to burn, the vilest sinner may return.

Walden (1854), in *The Writings of Henry David Thoreau*, vol. 2, p. 346, Houghton Mifflin (1906).

One attraction in coming to the woods to live was that I should have leisure and opportunity to see the spring come in. The ice in the pond at length begins to be honeycombed, and I can set my heel in it as I walk. Fogs and rains and warmer suns are gradually melting the snow; the days have grown sensibly longer; and I see how I shall get through the winter without adding to my wood-pile, for large fires are no longer necessary. I am on the alert for the first signs of spring, to hear the chance note of some arriving bird, or the striped squirrel's chirp, for his stores must be now nearly exhausted, or see the woodchuck venture out of his winter quarters.

Walden (1854), in *The Writings of Henry David Thoreau*, vol. 2, p. 333, Houghton Mifflin (1906).

See also WALDEN POND

The first sparrow of spring! The year beginning with younger hope than ever! . . . What at such a time are histories, chronologies, traditions, and all written revelations? The brooks sing carols and glees to the spring.

Walden (1854), in *The Writings of Henry David Thoreau*, vol. 2, p. 342, Houghton Mifflin (1906).

See also BIRDS

Walden is melting apace. There is a canal two rods wide along the northerly and westerly sides, and wider still the east end. A great field of ice has cracked off from the main body. I hear a song sparrow singing from the bushes on the shore,—*olit, olit, olit,*—*chip, chip, chip, che char,*— *che wiss, wiss, wiss.* He too is helping to crack it. How handsome the great sweeping curves in the edge of the ice, answering somewhat to those of the shore, but more regular! It is unusually hard, owing to the recent severe but transient cold, and all watered or waved like a palace floor. But the wind slides eastward over its opaque surface in vain, till it reaches the living surface beyond. It is glorious to behold this ribbon of water spar- kling in the sun, the bare face of the pond full of glee and youth, as if it spoke the joy of the fishes within it, and of the sands on its shore,—a silvery sheen as from the scales of a *leuciscus,* as it were all one active fish.

Such is the contrast between winter and spring. Walden is dead and is alive again. But this spring it broke up more steadily, as I have said.

Walden (1854), in *The Writings of Henry David Thoreau*, vol. 2, pp. 343–344, Houghton Mifflin (1906).

See also WALDEN POND

*S*QUIRRELS

At the approach of spring the red squirrels got under my house, two at a time, directly under my feet as I sat reading or writing, and kept up the queerest chuckling and chirruping and vocal pirouetting and gurgling sounds that ever were heard; and when I stamped they only chirruped the louder, as if past all fear and respect in their mad pranks, defying humanity to stop them. No, you don't—chickaree—chickaree. They were wholly deaf to my arguments, or failed to perceive their force, and fell into a strain of invective that was irresistible.

Walden (1854), in *The Writings of Henry David Thoreau*, vol. 2, p. 342, Houghton Mifflin (1906).

See also SPRING

*S*TARS

Truly the stars were given for a consolation to man.

"A Walk to Wachusett" (1843), in *The Writings of Henry David Thoreau*, vol. 5, p. 146, Houghton Mifflin (1906).

*S*TRANGERS

A stranger may easily detect what is strange to the oldest inhabitant, for the strange is his province.

Cape Cod (1855–1865), in *The Writings of Henry David Thoreau*, vol. 4, p. 192, Houghton Mifflin (1906).

STYLE

We think it is the richest prose style we know of.

"Thomas Carlyle and His Works" (1847), in *The Writings of Henry David Thoreau*, vol. 4, p. 330, Houghton Mifflin (1906).

See also CARLYLE, THOMAS

Who cares what a man's style is, so it is intelligible,—as intelligible as his thought. Literally and really, the style is no more than the *stylus*, the pen he writes with; and it is not worth scraping and polishing, and gilding, unless it will write his thoughts the better for it. It is something for use, and not to look at. The question for us is, not whether Pope had a fine style, wrote with a peacock's feather, but whether he uttered useful thoughts.

"Thomas Carlyle and His Works" (1847), in *The Writings of Henry David Thoreau*, vol. 4, p. 330, Houghton Mifflin (1906).

See also CARLYLE, THOMAS

A sentence should read as if its author, had he held a plow instead of a pen, could have drawn a furrow deep and straight to the end.

A Week on the Concord and Merrimack Rivers (1849), in *The Writings of Henry David Thoreau*, vol. 1, p. 110, Houghton Mifflin (1906).

Every sentence is the result of a long probation.

A Week on the Concord and Merrimack Rivers (1849), in *The Writings of Henry David Thoreau*, vol. 1, p. 107, Houghton Mifflin (1906).

We are often struck by the force and precision of style to which hard-working men, unpracticed in writing, easily attain when required to make the effort. As if plainness and vigor and sincerity, the ornaments of style, were better learned on the farm and in the workshop than in the schools. The sentences written by such rude hands are nervous and tough, like hardened thongs, the sinews of the deer, or the roots of the pine.

A Week on the Concord and Merrimack Rivers (1849), in *The Writings of Henry David Thoreau*, vol. 1, p. 109, Houghton Mifflin (1906).

See also LABOR

*S*UCCESS

Yet we must try the harder, the less the prospect of success.

"The Allegash and East Branch" (1864) in *The Maine Woods* (1864), in *The Writings of Henry David Thoreau*, vol. 3, p. 286, Houghton Mifflin (1906).

*S*UNDAYS

I was once reproved by a minister who was driving a poor beast to some meeting-house horse-sheds among the hills of New Hampshire, because I was bending my steps to a mountain-top on the Sabbath, instead of a church, when I would have gone farther than he to hear a true word spoken on that or any day. He declared that I was "breaking the Lord's fourth commandment," and proceeded to enumerate, in a sepulchral tone, the disasters which had befallen him whenever he had done any ordinary work on the Sabbath. He really thought that a god was on the watch to trip up those men who followed any secular work on this day, and did not see that it was the evil conscience of the workers that did it. The country is full of this superstition, so that when one enters a village, the church, not only really but from association, is the ugliest looking building in it, because it is the one in which human nature stoops the lowest and is most disgraced. Certainly, such temples as these shall ere long cease to deform the landscape. There are few things more disheartening and disgusting than when you are walking the streets of a strange village on the Sabbath, to hear a preacher shouting like a boatswain in a gale of wind, and thus harshly profaning the quiet atmosphere of the day. You fancy him to have taken off his coat, as when men are about to do hot and dirty work.

A Week on the Concord and Merrimack Rivers (1849), in *The Writings of Henry David Thoreau*, vol. 1, pp. 76–77, Houghton Mifflin (1906).

See also CLERGY

It was a quiet Sunday morning, with more of the auroral rosy and white than of the yellow light in it, as if it dated from earlier than the fall of man, and still preserved a heathenish integrity.

A Week on the Concord and Merrimack Rivers (1849), in *The Writings of Henry David Thoreau*, vol. 1, p. 42, Houghton Mifflin (1906).

Surveying

Taking a surveyor's and a naturalist's liberty, I have been in the habit of going across your lots much oftener than is usual, as many of you, perhaps to your sorrow, are aware. Yet many of you, to my relief, have seemed not to be aware of it; and, when I came across you in some out-of-the-way nook of your farms, have inquired, with an air of surprise, if I were not lost, since you had never seen me in that part of the town or county before; when, if the truth were known, and it had not been for betraying my secret, I might with more propriety have inquired if *you* were not lost, since I have never seen *you* there before. I have several times shown the proprietor the shortest way out of his wood-lot.

"The Succession of Forest Trees" (1860), in *The Writings of Henry David Thoreau*, vol. 5, p. 185, Houghton Mifflin (1906).

See also NATURAL HISTORY

Suspicion

There is no rule more invariable than that we are paid for our suspicions by finding what we suspected.

A Week on the Concord and Merrimack Rivers (1849), in *The Writings of Henry David Thoreau*, vol. 1, p. 294, Houghton Mifflin (1906).

Swamps

It was a mossy swamp, which it required the long legs of a moose to traverse, and it is very likely that we scared some of them in our transit, though we saw none. It was ready to echo the growl of a bear, the howl of a wolf, or the scream of a panther; but when you get fairly into the middle of one of these grim forests, you are surprised to find that the larger inhabitants are not at home commonly, but have left only a puny red squirrel to bark at you. ... I did, however, see one dead porcupine;

perhaps he had succumbed to the difficulties of the way. These bristly fellows are a very suitable small fruit of such unkempt wildernesses.

"The Allegash and East Branch" (1864) in *The Maine Woods* (1864), in *The Writings of Henry David Thoreau*, vol. 3, p. 242, Houghton Mifflin (1906).

See also SQUIRRELS

When I would recreate myself, I seek the darkest wood, the thickest and most interminable and, to the citizen, most dismal, swamp. I enter a swamp as a sacred place, a *sanctum sanctorum*. There is the strength, the marrow, of Nature.

"Walking" (1862), in *The Writings of Henry David Thoreau*, vol. 5, p. 228, Houghton Mifflin (1906).

*T*AVERNS

The tavern will compare favorably with the church. The church is the place where prayers and sermons are delivered, but the tavern is where they are to take effect, and if the former are good, the latter cannot be bad.

"The Landlord" (1843), in *The Writings of Henry David Thoreau*, vol. 5, pp. 161–162, Houghton Mifflin (1906).

See also CHURCHES

*T*EMPERANCE

If you would be chaste, you must be temperate.

Walden (1854), in *The Writings of Henry David Thoreau*, vol. 2, p. 244, Houghton Mifflin (1906).

See also CHASTITY

*T*HEATER

The world is a strange place for a playhouse to stand within it.

A Week on the Concord and Merrimack Rivers (1849), in *The Writings of Henry David Thoreau*, vol. 1, pp. 68–69, Houghton Mifflin (1906).

See also WORLD, THE

THEORY

The theories and speculations of men concern us more than their puny accomplishment. It is with a certain coldness and languor that we loiter about the actual and so-called practical.

"Paradise (To Be) Regained" (1843), in *The Writings of Henry David Thoreau*, vol. 4, p. 302, Houghton Mifflin (1906).

See also ACTION

THERIEN, ALEX

A more simple and natural man it would be hard to find. Vice and disease, which cast such a sombre moral hue over the world, seemed to have hardly any existence for him.

Walden (1854), in *The Writings of Henry David Thoreau*, vol. 2, p. 160, Houghton Mifflin (1906).

See also PRIMITIVISM

He suggested that there might be men of genius in the lowest grades of life, however permanently humble and illiterate, who take their own view always, or do not pretend to see at all; who are as bottomless even as Walden Pond was thought to be, though they may be dark and muddy.

Walden (1854), in *The Writings of Henry David Thoreau*, vol. 2, p. 166, Houghton Mifflin (1906).

See also GENIUS

He was so genuine and unsophisticated that no introduction would serve to introduce him, more than if you introduced a woodchuck to your neighbor. He had got to find him out as you did. He would not play any part. Men paid him wages for work, and so helped to feed and clothe him; but he never exchanged opinions with them. He was so simply and naturally humble—if he can be called humble who never aspires—that humility was no distinct quality in him, nor could he conceive of it. Wiser men were demigods to him. . . . He particularly reverenced the writer and the preacher. Their performances were miracles.

Walden (1854), in *The Writings of Henry David Thoreau*, vol. 2, p. 163, Houghton Mifflin (1906).

See also PRIMITIVISM

I heard that a distinguished wise man and reformer asked him if he did not want the world to be changed; but he answered with a chuckle of surprise in his Canadian accent, not knowing that the question had ever been entertained before, "No, I like it well enough." It would have suggested many things to a philosopher to have dealings with him. To a stranger he appeared to know nothing of things in general; yet I sometimes saw in him a man whom I had not seen before, and I did not know whether he was as wise as Shakespeare or as simply ignorant as a child, whether to suspect him of a fine poetic consciousness or of stupidity. A townsman told me that when he met him sauntering through the village in his small close-fitting cap, and whistling to himself, he reminded him of a prince in disguise.

Walden (1854), in *The Writings of Henry David Thoreau*, vol. 2, p. 164, Houghton Mifflin (1906).

See also PRIMITIVISM

In him the animal man chiefly was developed. In physical endurance and contentment he was cousin to the pine and the rock. . . . But the intellectual and what is called spiritual man in him were slumbering as in an infant. He had been instructed only in that innocent and ineffectual way in which the Catholic priests teach the aborigines, by which the pupil is never educated to the degree of consciousness, but only to the degree of trust and reverence, and a child is not made a man, but kept a child.

Walden (1854), in *The Writings of Henry David Thoreau*, vol. 2, pp. 162–163, Houghton Mifflin (1906).

See also PRIMITIVISM

Who should come to my lodge this morning but a true Homeric or Paphlagonian man,—he had so suitable and poetic a name that I am sorry I cannot print it here,—a Canadian, a woodchopper and post-maker, who can hole fifty posts in a day, who made his last supper on a woodchuck which his dog caught.

Walden (1854), in *The Writings of Henry David Thoreau*, vol. 2, pp. 159–160, Houghton Mifflin (1906).

The surname of Alex Therien, Thoreau's eponymous French Canadian woodchopper here, roughly translates as "wild man."

See also PRIMITIVISM

*T*HINKING AND THOUGHTS

A single gentle rain makes the grass many shades greener. So our prospects brighten on the influx of better thoughts.

Walden (1854), in *The Writings of Henry David Thoreau*, vol. 2, p. 346, Houghton Mifflin (1906).

Nothing was ever so unfamiliar and startling to a man as his own thoughts.

A Week on the Concord and Merrimack Rivers (1849), in *The Writings of Henry David Thoreau*, vol. 1, p. 362, Houghton Mifflin (1906).

THOREAU, JOHN

We, too, were but dwellers on the shore, like the bittern of the morning; and our pursuit, the wrecks of snails and cockles. Nevertheless, we were contented to know the better one fair particular shore.

A Week on the Concord and Merrimack Rivers (1849), in *The Writings of Henry David Thoreau*, vol. 1, p. 255, Houghton Mifflin (1906).

Thoreau's reference to John Milton's "Lycidas" ("dwellers on the shore") suggests that this passage is an elegaic allusion to the subsequent death of his own brother, John.

THOREAU'S JOURNAL

For a long time I was reporter to a journal, of no very wide circulation, whose editor has never yet seen fit to print the bulk of my contributions, and, as is too common with writers, I got only my labor for my pains. However, in this case my pains were their own reward.

Walden (1854), in *The Writings of Henry David Thoreau*, vol. 2, p. 19, Houghton Mifflin (1906).

TIME

In any weather, at any hour of the day or night, I have been anxious to improve the nick of time, and notch it on my stick too; to stand on the meeting of two eternities, the past and the future, which is precisely the present moment; to toe that line.

Walden (1854), in *The Writings of Henry David Thoreau*, vol. 2, p. 18, Houghton Mifflin (1906).

See also LIFE

Time is but the stream I go a-fishing in.

Walden (1854), in *The Writings of Henry David Thoreau,* vol. 2, p. 109, Houghton Mifflin (1906).

See also EXPERIENCE

There is something even in the lapse of time by which time recovers itself.

A Week on the Concord and Merrimack Rivers (1849), in *The Writings of Henry David Thoreau,* vol. 1, p. 374, Houghton Mifflin (1906).

Time hides no treasures; we want not its *then,* but its *now.*

A Week on the Concord and Merrimack Rivers (1849), in *The Writings of Henry David Thoreau,* vol. 1, p. 161, Houghton Mifflin (1906).

See also PRESENT, THE

*T*OWNS (*COUNTRY*)

A town is saved, not more by the righteous men in it than by the woods and swamps that surround it.

"Walking" (1862), in *The Writings of Henry David Thoreau,* vol. 5, p. 229, Houghton Mifflin (1906).

See also NATURE VERSES CIVILIZATION

*T*RADITION

Why put up with the almshouse when you may go to heaven?

Letter, March 27, 1848, to Harrison Blake, in *The Writings of Henry David Thoreau,* vol. 6, p. 161, Houghton Mifflin (1906).

See also CHANGE

*T*RANSCENDENTALISM

It would seem from this and various indications beside, that there is a transcendentalism in mechanics as well as in ethics. While the whole field of the one reformer lies beyond the boundaries of space, the other is pushing his schemes for the elevation of the race to its utmost limits. While one scours the heavens, the other sweeps the earth. One says he will reform himself, and then nature and circumstances will be right. . . . The other will reform nature and circumstances, and then man will be right.

"Paradise (To Be) Regained" (1843), in *The Writings of Henry David Thoreau*, vol. 4, p. 281, Houghton Mifflin (1906).

See also REFORM AND REFORMERS

When one man has reduced a fact of the imagination to be a fact to his understanding, I foresee that all men will at length establish their lives on that basis.

Walden (1854), in *The Writings of Henry David Thoreau*, vol. 2, p. 12, Houghton Mifflin (1906).

See also IMAGINATION

The anecdotes of modern astronomy affect me in the same way as do those faint revelations of the Real which are vouchsafed to men from time to time, or rather from eternity to eternity. When I remember the history of that faint light in our firmament which we call Venus, which ancient men regarded, and which most modern men still regard, as a bright spark attached to a hollow sphere revolving about our earth, but which we have discovered to be *another world*, in itself,—how Copernicus, reasoning long and patiently about the matter, predicted confidently concerning it, before yet the telescope had been invented, . . . and that within a century after his death the telescope was invented, and that prediction verified, by Galileo,—I am not without hope that we may, even here and now, obtain some accurate information concerning that OTHER WORLD which the instinct of mankind has so long predicted.

A Week on the Concord and Merrimack Rivers (1849), in *The Writings of Henry David Thoreau*, vol. 1, pp. 411–412, Houghton Mifflin (1906).

We need pray for no higher heaven than the pure senses can furnish, a *purely* sensuous life. Our present senses are but the rudiments of what they are destined to become. We are comparatively deaf and dumb and blind, and without smell or taste or feeling. Every generation makes the discovery that its divine vigor has been dissipated, and each sense and faculty misapplied and debauched. The ears were made, not for such trivial uses as men are wont to suppose, but to hear celestial sounds. The eyes were not made for such groveling uses as they are now put to and worn out by, but to behold beauty now invisible. May we not *see* God? Are we to be put off and amused in this life, as it were with a mere allegory? Is not Nature, rightly read, that of which she is commonly taken to be the symbol merely? . . . But where is the instructed teacher? Where are the *normal* schools?

A Week on the Concord and Merrimack Rivers (1849), in *The Writings of Henry David Thoreau*, vol. 1, pp. 408–409, Houghton Mifflin (1906).

*T*RANSLATION

Translate a book a dozen times from one language to another, and what becomes of its style? Most books would be worn out and disappear in this ordeal. The pen which wrote it is soon destroyed, but the poem survives.

"Thomas Carlyle and His Works" (1847), in *The Writings of Henry David Thoreau*, vol. 4, p. 330, Houghton Mifflin (1906).

See also STYLE

*T*RAVELING AND TRAVELERS

I suspect that, if you should go to the end of the world, you would find somebody there going farther, as if just starting for home at sundown, and having a last word before he drove off.

"Ktaadn" (1848) in *The Maine Woods* (1864), in *The Writings of Henry David Thoreau*, vol. 3, p. 14, Houghton Mifflin (1906).

I never voyaged so far in all my life.

A Week on the Concord and Merrimack Rivers (1849), in *The Writings of Henry David Thoreau*, vol. 1, p. 6, Houghton Mifflin (1906).

These men had no need to travel to be as wise as Solomon in all his glory, so similar are the lives of men in all countries, and fraught with the same homely experiences. One half the world *knows* how the other half lives.

A Week on the Concord and Merrimack Rivers (1849), in *The Writings of Henry David Thoreau*, vol. 1, p. 227, Houghton Mifflin (1906).

See also HUMAN NATURE

We styled ourselves the Knights of the Umbrella and the Bundle; for, wherever we went . . . the umbrella and the bundle went with us; for we wished to be ready to digress at any moment. We made it our home nowhere in particular, but everywhere where our umbrella and bundle were.

"A Yankee in Canada" (1853), in *The Writings of Henry David Thoreau*, vol. 5, p. 33, Houghton Mifflin (1906).

TREES

For beauty, give me trees with the fur on.

"Chesuncook" (1858) in *The Maine Woods* (1864), in *The Writings of Henry David Thoreau*, vol. 3, p. 139, Houghton Mifflin (1906).

TRUTH

They who know of no purer sources of truth, who have traced up its stream no higher, stand, and wisely stand, by the Bible and the Constitution, and drink at it there with reverence and humility; but they who behold where it comes trickling into this lake or that pool, gird up their loins once more, and continue their pilgrimage toward its fountain-head.

"Civil Disobedience," originally published as "Resistance to Civil Government" (1849), in *The Writings of Henry David Thoreau*, vol. 4, pp. 385–386, Houghton Mifflin (1906).

How sweet it would be to treat men and things, for an hour, for just what they are!

Letter, April 3, 1850, to Harrison Blake, in *The Writings of Henry David Thoreau*, vol. 6, p. 177, Houghton Mifflin (1906).

See also INTEGRITY

In short, as a snow-drift is formed where there is a lull in the wind, so, one would say, where there is a lull of truth, an institution springs up. But the truth blows right on over it, nevertheless, and at length blows it down.

"Life Without Principle" (1863), in *The Writings of Henry David Thoreau*, vol. 4, p. 480, Houghton Mifflin (1906).

See also INSTITUTIONS

I am resolved that I will not through humility become the devil's attorney. I will endeavor to speak a good word for the truth.

Walden (1854), in *The Writings of Henry David Thoreau*, vol. 2, p. 55, Houghton Mifflin (1906).

Rather than love, than money, than fame, give me truth.

Walden (1854), in *The Writings of Henry David Thoreau*, vol. 2, p. 364, Houghton Mifflin (1906).

See also LOVE

Say what you have to say, not what you ought. Any truth is better than make-believe.

Walden (1854), in *The Writings of Henry David Thoreau*, vol. 2, p. 360, Houghton Mifflin (1906).

See also HYPOCRISY

The greatest gains and values are farthest from being appreciated. We easily come to doubt if they exist. We soon forget them. They are the highest reality.

Walden (1854), in *The Writings of Henry David Thoreau*, vol. 2, p. 239, Houghton Mifflin (1906).

See also PROGRESS

A true account of the actual is the rarest poetry, for common sense always takes a hasty and superficial view.

A Week on the Concord and Merrimack Rivers (1849), in *The Writings of Henry David Thoreau*, vol. 1, p. 347, Houghton Mifflin (1906).

See also COMMON SENSE

If we dealt only with the false and dishonest, we should at last forget how to speak truth.

A Week on the Concord and Merrimack Rivers (1849), in *The Writings of Henry David Thoreau*, vol. 1, p. 284, Houghton Mifflin (1906).

See also HYPOCRISY

It takes two to speak the truth,—one to speak, and another to hear.

A Week on the Concord and Merrimack Rivers (1849), in *The Writings of Henry David Thoreau*, vol. 1, p. 283, Houghton Mifflin (1906).

See also COMMUNICATION

Truth never turns to rebuke falsehood; her own straightforwardness is the severest correction.

A Week on the Concord and Merrimack Rivers (1849), in *The Writings of Henry David Thoreau*, vol. 1, p. 328, Houghton Mifflin (1906).

Underground railroad

The only *free* road, the Underground Railroad, is owned and managed by the Vigilant Committee. *They* have tunneled under the whole breadth of the land.

"A Plea for Captain John Brown" (1859), in *The Writings of Henry David Thoreau*, vol. 4, pp. 431–432, Houghton Mifflin (1906).

United states

Some are dinning in our ears that we Americans, and moderns generally, are intellectual dwarfs compared with the ancients, or even the Elizabethan men. But what is that to the purpose? A living dog is better than a dead lion. Shall a man go and hang himself because he belongs to the race of pygmies, and not be the biggest pygmy that he can? Let every one mind his own business, and endeavor to be what he was made.

Walden (1854), in *The Writings of Henry David Thoreau*, vol. 2, p. 358, Houghton Mifflin (1906).

See also EUROPE VERSES AMERICA

Universe, the

The universe is wider than our views of it.

Walden (1854), in *The Writings of Henry David Thoreau*, vol. 2, p. 352, Houghton Mifflin (1906).

See also PERSPECTIVE

Vices

Our vices always lie in the direction of our virtues, and in their best estate are but plausible imitations of the latter.

A Week on the Concord and Merrimack Rivers (1849), in *The Writings of Henry David Thoreau*, vol. 1, p. 331, Houghton Mifflin (1906).

See also CHARACTER

*V*ICTIMS

He who receives an injury is to some extent an accomplice of the wrong-doer.

A Week on the Concord and Merrimack Rivers (1849), in *The Writings of Henry David Thoreau*, vol. 1, p. 329, Houghton Mifflin (1906).

*V*IOLENCE

I do not wish to kill nor to be killed, but I can foresee circumstances in which both these things would be by me unavoidable.

"A Plea for Captain John Brown" (1859), in *The Writings of Henry David Thoreau*, vol. 4, pp. 433–434, Houghton Mifflin (1906).

See also BROWN, JOHN

The same indignation that is said to have cleared the temple once will clear it again. The question is not about the weapon, but the spirit in which you use it. No man has appeared in America, as yet, who loved his fellow-man so well, and treated him so tenderly He lived for him. He took up his life and he laid it down for him.

"A Plea for Captain John Brown" (1859), in *The Writings of Henry David Thoreau*, vol. 4, p. 434, Houghton Mifflin (1906).

See also BROWN, JOHN

*V*IRGIL

We could get no further into the Æneid than

—atque altae moenia Romae,
—and the wall of high Rome,

before we were constrained to reflect by what myriad tests a work of genius has to be tried; that Virgil, away in Rome, two thousand years off, should have to unfold his meaning, the inspiration of Italian vales, to the pilgrim on New England hills. This life so raw and modern, that so civil and ancient; and yet we read Virgil mainly to be reminded of the identity of human nature in all ages, and, by the poet's own account, we are both the children of a late age, and live equally under the reign of Jupiter.

"A Walk to Wachusett" (1843), in *The Writings of Henry David Thoreau*, vol. 5, p. 138, Houghton Mifflin (1906).

See also CLASSICS, THE

$\mathcal{V}$OTING

All voting is a sort of gaming, like checkers or backgammon, with a slight moral tinge to it, a playing with right and wrong, with moral questions; and betting naturally accompanies it. The character of the voters is not staked. I cast my vote, perchance, as I think right; but I am not vitally concerned that the right should prevail. I am willing to leave it to the majority.

"Civil Disobedience," originally published as "Resistance to Civil Government" (1849), in *The Writings of Henry David Thoreau*, vol. 4, p. 363, Houghton Mifflin (1906).

$\mathcal{W}$ACHUSETT, MOUNT

Who knows but this hill may one day be a Helvellyn, or even a Parnassus, and the Muses haunt here, and other Homers frequent the neighboring plains? . . . It was a place where gods might wander, so solemn and solitary, and removed from all contagion with the plain.

"A Walk to Wachusett" (1843), in *The Writings of Henry David Thoreau*, vol. 5, p. 144, Houghton Mifflin (1906).

See also MOUNTAINS

$\mathcal{W}$ALDEN POND

A lake is the landscape's most beautiful and expressive feature. It is earth's eye; looking into which the beholder measures the depth of his own nature. The fluviatile trees next the shore are the slender eyelashes which fringe it, and the wooded hills and cliffs around are its overhanging brows.

Walden (1854), in *The Writings of Henry David Thoreau*, vol. 2, pp. 206–207, Houghton Mifflin (1906).

See also LAKES

All our Concord waters have two colors at least; one when viewed at a distance, and another, more proper, close at hand. . . . Walden is blue at one time and green at another, even from the same point of view. Lying between the earth and the heavens, it partakes of the color of both.

Walden (1854), in *The Writings of Henry David Thoreau*, vol. 2, pp. 195–196, Houghton Mifflin (1906).

But I can assure my readers that Walden has a reasonably tight bottom at a not unreasonable, though at an unusual, depth. I fathomed it easily with a cod-line and a stone weighing about a pound and a half, and could tell accurately when the stone left the bottom, by having to pull so much harder before the water got underneath to help me. The greatest depth was exactly one hundred and two feet; to which may be added the five feet which it has risen since, making one hundred and seven. This is a remarkable depth for so small an area; yet not an inch of it can be spared by the imagination.

Walden (1854), in *The Writings of Henry David Thoreau*, vol. 2, p. 316, Houghton Mifflin (1906).

I had but three chairs in my house; one for solitude, two for friendship; three for society. When visitors came in larger and unexpected numbers there was but the third chair for them all, but they generally economized the room by standing up.

Walden (1854), in *The Writings of Henry David Thoreau*, vol. 2, p. 155, Houghton Mifflin (1906).

See also SOLITUDE

I had this advantage, at least, in my mode of life, over those who were obliged to look abroad for amusement, to society and the theatre, that my life itself was become my amusement and never ceased to be novel. It was a drama of many scenes and without an end.

Walden (1854), in *The Writings of Henry David Thoreau*, vol. 2, p. 125, Houghton Mifflin (1906).

I left the woods for as good a reason as I went there. Perhaps it seemed to me that I had several more lives to live, and could not spare any more time for that one.

Walden (1854), in *The Writings of Henry David Thoreau*, vol. 2, p. 355, Houghton Mifflin (1906).

See also LIFE

I was more independent than any farmer in Concord, for I was not anchored to a house or farm, but could follow the bent of my genius, which is a very crooked one, every moment.

Walden (1854), in *The Writings of Henry David Thoreau*, vol. 2, p. 62, Houghton Mifflin (1906).

See also INDEPENDENCE

In such a day, in September or October, Walden is a perfect forest mirror, set round with stones as precious to my eye as if fewer or rarer. Nothing so fair, so pure, and at the same time so large, as a lake, perchance, lies on the surface of the earth. Sky water. It needs no fence. Nations come and go without defiling it. It is a mirror which no stone can crack, whose quicksilver will never wear off, whose gilding Nature continually repairs; no storms, no dust, can dim its surface ever fresh;—a mirror in which all impurity presented to it sinks, swept and dusted by the sun's hazy brush,— this the light-dust cloth,—which retains no breath that is breathed on it, but sends its own to float as clouds high above its surface, and be reflected in its bosom still.

Walden (1854), in *The Writings of Henry David Thoreau*, vol. 2, p. 209, Houghton Mifflin (1906).

Many have believed that Walden reached quite through to the other side of the globe.

Walden (1854), in *The Writings of Henry David Thoreau*, vol. 2, p. 315, Houghton Mifflin (1906).

Some think it is bottomless.

Walden (1854), in *The Writings of Henry David Thoreau*, vol. 2, p. 198, Houghton Mifflin (1906).

The Fitchburg Railroad touches the pond about a hundred rods south of where I dwell. I usually go to the village along its causeway, and am, as it were, related to society by this link. The men on the freight trains, who go over the whole length of the road, bow to me as to an old acquaintance, they pass me so often, and apparently they take me for an employee; and so I am. I too would fain be a track-repairer somewhere in the orbit of the earth.

Walden (1854), in *The Writings of Henry David Thoreau*, vol. 2, pp. 127–128, Houghton Mifflin (1906).

The scenery of Walden is on a humble scale, and, though very beautiful, does not approach to grandeur, nor can it much concern one who has not long frequented it or lived by its shore; yet this pond is so remarkable for its depth and purity as to merit a particular description. It is a clear and deep green well, half a mile long and a mile and three quarters in circumference, and contains about sixty-one and a half acres; a perennial spring in the midst of pine and oak woods, without any visible inlet or outlet except by the clouds and evaporation. The surrounding hills rise abruptly from the water to the height of forty to eighty feet, though on the southeast and east they attain to about one hundred and one hundred

and fifty feet respectively, within a quarter and a third of a mile. They are
exclusively woodland.

Walden (1854), in *The Writings of Henry David Thoreau,* vol. 2, p. 195, Houghton Mifflin (1906).

There have been many stories told about the bottom, or rather no bottom,
of this pond, which certainly had no foundation for themselves. It is
remarkable how long men will believe in the bottomlessness of a pond
without taking the trouble to sound it.

Walden (1854), in *The Writings of Henry David Thoreau,* vol. 2, p. 315, Houghton Mifflin (1906).

This pond never breaks up so soon as the others in this neighborhood, on
account both of its greater depth and its having no stream passing through
it to melt or wear away the ice. . . . It indicates better than any water
hereabouts the absolute progress of the season, being least affected by
transient changes of temperature. A severe cold of a few days' duration in
March may very much retard the opening of the former ponds, while the
temperature of Walden increases almost uninterruptedly.

Walden (1854), in *The Writings of Henry David Thoreau,* vol. 2, p. 330, Houghton Mifflin (1906).

See also ICE

When I first took up my abode in the woods, that is, began to spend my
nights as well as days there, which, by accident, was on Independence Day,
or the Fourth of July, 1845, my house was not finished for winter, but was
merely a defence against the rain, without plastering or chimney, the walls
being of rough, weather-stained boards, with wide chinks, which made it
cool at night. The upright white hewn studs and freshly planed door and
window casings gave it a clean and airy look, especially in the morning,
when its timbers were saturated with dew, so that I fancied that by noon
some sweet gum would exude from them. To my imagination it retained
throughout the day more or less of this auroral character, reminding me
of a certain house on a mountain which I had visited a year before. This
was an airy and unplastered cabin, fit to entertain a travelling god, and
where a goddess might trail her garments. The winds which passed over
my dwelling were such as sweep over the ridges of mountains, bearing the
broken strains, or celestial parts only, of terrestrial music. The morning
wind forever blows, the poem of creation is uninterrupted; but few are the
ears that hear it. Olympus is but the outside of the earth everywhere.

Walden (1854), in *The Writings of Henry David Thoreau,* vol. 2, p. 94, Houghton Mifflin (1906).

See also HOUSES AND HOMES

When I had mapped the pond ... I laid a rule on the map lengthwise, and then breadthwise, and found, to my surprise, that the line of greatest length intersected the line of greatest breadth *exactly* at the point of greatest depth.

Walden (1854), in *The Writings of Henry David Thoreau*, vol. 2, pp. 318–319, Houghton Mifflin (1906).

See also SURVEYING

WALDEN, WRITING OF

Perhaps these pages are more particularly addressed to poor students. As for the rest of my readers, they will accept such portions as apply to them.

Walden (1854), in *The Writings of Henry David Thoreau*, vol. 2, p. 4, Houghton Mifflin (1906).

When I wrote the following pages, or rather the bulk of them, I lived alone, in the woods, a mile from any neighbor, in a house which I had built myself, on the shore of Walden Pond, in Concord, Massachusetts, and earned my living by the labor of my hands only. I lived there two years and two months. At present I am a sojourner in civilized life again.

Walden (1854), in *The Writings of Henry David Thoreau*, vol. 2, p. 3, Houghton Mifflin (1906).

See also LABOR

WALKING

I have learned that the swiftest traveller is he that goes afoot.

Walden (1854), in *The Writings of Henry David Thoreau*, vol. 2, p. 58, Houghton Mifflin (1906).

See also TRAVELING AND TRAVELERS

If you are ready to leave father and mother, and brother and sister, and wife and child and friends, and never see them again,—if you have paid your debts and made your will, and settled all your affairs, and are a free man, then you are ready for a walk.

"Walking" (1862), in *The Writings of Henry David Thoreau*, vol. 5, p. 206, Houghton Mifflin (1906).

*W*AR

When the soldier is hit by a cannon-ball, rags are as becoming as purple.

Walden (1854), in *The Writings of Henry David Thoreau*, vol. 2, pp. 28–29, Houghton Mifflin (1906).

See also CLOTHING

*W*EALTH AND THE WEALTHY

Superfluous wealth can buy superfluities only.

Walden (1854), in *The Writings of Henry David Thoreau*, vol. 2, p. 362, Houghton Mifflin (1906).

*W*EBSTER, DANIEL

As we thus swept along, our Indian repeated in a deliberate and drawling tone the words "Daniel Webster, great lawyer," apparently reminded of him by the name of the stream, and he described his calling on him once in Boston, at what he supposed was his boarding-house. He had no business with him, but merely went to pay his respects, as we should say. In answer to our questions, he described his person well enough. It was on the day after Webster delivered his Bunker Hill oration, which I believe Polis heard. The first time he called he waited till he was tired without seeing him, and then went away. The next time, he saw him go by the door of the room in which he was waiting several times, in his shirt-sleeves, without noticing him. He thought that if he had come to see Indians, they would not have treated him so. At length, after very long delay, he came in, walked toward him, and asked in a loud voice, gruffly, "What do you want?" and he, thinking at first, by the motion of his hand, that he was going to strike him, said to himself, "You'd better take care; if you try that I shall know what to do." He did not like him, and declared that all he said "was not worth talk about a musquash." We suggested that probably Mr. Webster was very busy, and had a great many visitors just then.

"The Allegash and East Branch" (1864) in *The Maine Woods* (1864), in *The Writings of Henry David Thoreau*, vol. 3, p., Houghton Mifflin (1906).

"Musquash" is the Indian word for "muskrat."

See also POLIS, JOE

WEBSTER STREAM, MAINE

It was the most wild and desolate region we had camped in, where, if anywhere, one might expect to meet with befitting inhabitants, but I heard only the squeak of a nighthawk flitting over. The moon in her first quarter, in the fore part of the night, setting over the bare rocky hills garnished with tall, charred, and hollow stumps or shells of trees, served to reveal the desolation.

"The Allegash and East Branch" (1864) in *The Maine Woods* (1864), in *The Writings of Henry David Thoreau*, vol. 3, p. 288, Houghton Mifflin (1906).

See also LUMBERING

"THE WELLFLEET OYSTERMAN"

This was the merriest old man that we had ever seen, and one of the best preserved. His style of conversation was coarse and plain enough to have suited Rabelais. He would have made a good Panurge. Or rather he was a sober Silenus, and we were the boys Chromis and Mnasilus, who listened to his story. . . . There was a strange mingling of past and present in his conversation, for he had lived under King George, and might have remembered when Napoleon and the moderns generally were born.

Cape Cod (1855–1865), in *The Writings of Henry David Thoreau*, vol. 4, pp. 91–92, Houghton Mifflin (1906).

See also HISTORY

*W*EST, THE (U.S.)

To Americans I hardly need to say,—
"Westward the star of empire takes its way."

"Walking" (1862), in *The Writings of Henry David Thoreau*, vol. 5, p. 223, Houghton Mifflin (1906).

Thoreau here evokes the contemporary belief in a historical *translatio imperii* ("transfer of empire") and *translatio studii* ("transfer of the arts") by slightly misquoting the eighteenth-century Anglo-Irish philosopher, Bishop Berkeley, who had written "Westward the star of empire takes its sway."

*W*HITMAN, WALT

We visited Whitman the next morning . . . and were much interested and provoked. He is apparently the greatest democrat the world has seen. Kings and aristocracy go by the board at once, as they have long deserved to. A remarkably strong though coarse nature, of a sweet disposition, and much prized by his friends. Though peculiar and rough in his exterior, his skin . . . red, he is essentially a gentleman. I am still somewhat in a quandry about him,—feel that he is essentially strange to me, at any rate; but I am surprised by the sight of him. He is very broad, but, as I have said, not fine. He said that I misapprehended him. I am not quite sure that I do. He told us that he loved to ride up and down Broadway all day on an omnibus, sitting beside the driver, listening to the roar of the carts, and sometimes gesticulating and declaiming Homer at the top of his voice. He has long been an editor and writer for the newspapers, . . . but now has no employment but to read and write in the forenoon, and walk in the afternoon, like the rest of the scribbling gentry.

Letter, November 19, 1856, to Harrison Blake, in *The Writings of Henry David Thoreau*, vol. 6, p. 291, Houghton Mifflin (1906).

That Walt Whitman, of whom I wrote to you, is the most interesting fact to me at present. I have just read his second edition (which he gave me), and it has done me more good than any reading for a long time. Perhaps I remember best the poem of Walt Whitman, an American, and the Sun-Down Poem. There are two or three pieces in the book which are disagreeable, to say the least; simply sensual. He does not celebrate love at all. It is as if the beasts spoke. I think that men have not been ashamed of themselves without reason. No doubt there have always been dens where such deeds were unblushingly recited, and it is no merit to compete with their inhabitants. But even on this side he has spoken more truth than any American or modern that I know. I have found his poem exhilarating, encouraging. As for its sensuality,—and it may turn out to be less sensual than it appears,—I do not so much wish that those parts were not written, as that men and women were so pure that they could read them without harm, that is, without understanding them. One woman told me that no woman could read it,—as if a man could read what a woman could not. Of course Walt Whitman can communicate to us no experience, and if we are shocked, whose experience is it that we are reminded of?

On the whole, it sounds to me very brave and American, after whatever deductions. I do not believe that all the sermons, so called, that have been preached in this land put together are equal to it for preaching.

Letter, December 7, 1856, to Harrison Blake, in *The Writings of Henry David Thoreau*, vol. 6, pp. 295–296, Houghton Mifflin (1906).

Thoreau here refers to Whitman's *Leaves of Grass,* including "Song of Myself."

We ought to rejoice greatly in him. He occasionally suggests something a little more than human. You can't confound him with the other inhabitants of Brooklyn or New York. How they must shudder when they read him! He is awfully good.

To be sure I sometimes feel a little imposed on. By his heartiness and broad generalities he puts me into a liberal frame of mind prepared to see wonders,—as it were, sets me upon a hill or in the midst of a plain,—stirs me well up, and then—throws in a thousand of brick. Though rude, and sometimes ineffectual, it is a great primitive poem,—an alarum or trumpet-note ringing through the American camp. Wonderfully like the Orientals, too. . . .

Since I have seen him, I find that I am not disturbed by any brag or egoism in his book. He may turn out the least of a braggart of all, having a better right to be confident.

He is a great fellow.

Letter, December 7, 1856, to Harrison Blake, in *The Writings of Henry David Thoreau*, vol. 6, p. 296, Houghton Mifflin (1906).

Thoreau refers to Whitman's *Leaves of Grass,* including "Song of Myself."

See also NEW YORK CITY

*W*ILDERNESS

Places where he might live and die and never hear of the United States, which make such a noise in the world,—never hear of America, so called from the name of a European gentleman.

"The Allegash and East Branch" (1864) in *The Maine Woods* (1864), in *The Writings of Henry David Thoreau*, vol. 3, pp. 260–261, Houghton Mifflin (1906).

See also UNITED STATES

What a glorious time they must have in that wilderness, far from mankind and election day!

"The Allegash and East Branch" (1864) in *The Maine Woods* (1864), in *The Writings of Henry David Thoreau*, vol. 3, p. 214, Houghton Mifflin (1906).

"They" refers to sparrows.

See also BIRDS

*W*ILDNESS

We need the tonic of wildness,—to wade sometimes in marshes where the bittern and the meadow-hen lurk, and hear the booming of the snipe; to smell the whispering sedge where only some wilder and more solitary fowl builds her nest, and the mink crawls with its belly close to the ground.

Walden (1854), in *The Writings of Henry David Thoreau*, vol. 2, p. 350, Houghton Mifflin (1906).

See also BIRDS

Every tree sends its fibres forth in search of the Wild. The cities import it at any price. Men plow and sail for it. From the forest and wilderness come the tonics and barks which brace mankind.

"Walking" (1862), in *The Writings of Henry David Thoreau*, vol. 5, p. 224, Houghton Mifflin (1906).

See also WILDERNESS

In short, all good things are wild and free. There is something in a strain of music, whether produced by an instrument or by the human voice,—take the sound of a bugle in a summer night, for instance,—which by its wildness, to speak without satire, reminds me of the cries emitted by wild beasts in their native forests. It is so much of their wildness as I can understand. Give me for my friends and neighbors wild men, not tame ones. The wildness of the savage is but a faint symbol of the awful ferity with which good men and lovers meet.

"Walking" (1862), in *The Writings of Henry David Thoreau,* vol. 5, p. 234, Houghton Mifflin (1906).

See also PRIMITIVISM

The West of which I speak is but another name for the Wild; and what I have been preparing to say is, that in Wildness is the preservation of the World.

"Walking" (1862), in *The Writings of Henry David Thoreau,* vol. 5, p. 224, Houghton Mifflin (1906).

See also WEST, THE (U.S.)

*W*INDMILLS

The most foreign and picturesque structures on the Cape, to an inlander, not excepting the salt-works, are the windmills,—gray-looking, octagonal towers, with long timbers slanting to the ground in the rear, and there resting on a cart-wheel, by which their fans are turned round to face the wind. . . . They looked loose and slightly locomotive, like huge wounded birds, trailing a wing or a leg, and reminded one of pictures of the Netherlands. Being on elevated ground, and high in themselves, they serve as landmarks,—for there are no tall trees, or other objects commonly, which can be seen at a distance in the horizon; though the outline of the land itself is so firm and distinct, that an insignificant cone, or even a precipice of sand, is visible at a great distance from over the sea. Sailors making the land commonly steer either by the windmills, or the meeting-houses. In the country, we are obliged to steer by the meeting-houses alone. Yet the meeting-house is a kind of windmill, which runs one day in seven, turned either by the winds of doctrine or public opinion, or more rarely by the winds of Heaven, where another sort of grist is ground, of which, if it be not all bran or musty, if it be not *plaster,* we trust to make the bread of life.

Cape Cod (1855–1865), in *The Writings of Henry David Thoreau,* vol. 4, pp. 34–35, Houghton Mifflin (1906).

See also CHURCHES

*W*INTER

At this season I seldom had a visitor. When the snow lay deepest no wanderer ventured near my house for a week or fortnight at a time, but there I lived as snug as a meadow mouse.

Walden (1854), in *The Writings of Henry David Thoreau*, vol. 2, pp. 291–292, Houghton Mifflin (1906).

See also MICE

In winter we lead a more inward life. Our hearts are warm and cheery, like cottages under drifts, whose windows and doors are half concealed, but from whose chimneys the smoke cheerfully ascends.... We enjoy now, not an Oriental, but a Boreal leisure, around warm stoves and fireplaces, and watch the shadow of motes in the sunbeams.

"A Winter Walk" (1843), in *The Writings of Henry David Thoreau*, vol. 5, pp. 182–183, Houghton Mifflin (1906).

*W*ISDOM

The community has no bribe that will tempt a wise man.

"Life Without Principle" (1863), in *The Writings of Henry David Thoreau*, vol. 4, p. 460, Houghton Mifflin (1906).

See also MONEY

I have always been regretting that I was not as wise as the day I was born.

Walden (1854), in *The Writings of Henry David Thoreau*, vol. 2, p. 109, Houghton Mifflin (1906).

The life of a wise man is most of all extemporaneous, for he lives out of an eternity which includes all time.

A Week on the Concord and Merrimack Rivers (1849), in *The Writings of Henry David Thoreau*, vol. 1, p. 332, Houghton Mifflin (1906).

The wise are not so much wiser than others as respecters of their own wisdom.

A Week on the Concord and Merrimack Rivers (1849), in *The Writings of Henry David Thoreau*, vol. 1, p. 348, Houghton Mifflin (1906).

Women

I at length reached the last house but one, where the path to the summit diverged to the right, while the summit itself rose directly in front. But I determined to follow up the valley to its head, and then find my own route up the steep as the shorter and more adventurous way. I had thoughts of returning to this house, which was well kept and so nobly placed, the next day, and perhaps remaining a week there, if I could have entertainment. Its mistress was a frank and hospitable young woman, who stood before me in a dishabille, busily and unconcernedly combing her long black hair while she talked, giving her head the necessary toss with each sweep of the comb, with lively, sparkling eyes, and full of interest in that lower world from which I had come, talking all the while as familiarly as if she had known me for years, and reminding me of a cousin of mine. She at first had taken me for a student from Williamstown, for they went by in parties, she said, either riding or walking, almost every pleasant day, and were a pretty wild set of fellows; but they never went by the way I was going.

A *Week on the Concord and Merrimack Rivers* (1849), in *The Writings of Henry David Thoreau*, vol. 1, pp. 191–192, Houghton Mifflin (1906).

Workers

For myself I found that the occupation of a day-laborer was the most independent of any, especially as it required only thirty or forty days in a year to support one. The laborer's day ends with the going down of the sun, and he is then free to devote himself to his chosen pursuit, independent of his labor; but his employer, who speculates from month to month, has no respite from one end of the year to the other.

Walden (1854), in *The Writings of Henry David Thoreau*, vol. 2, p. 78, Houghton Mifflin (1906).

See also LABOR

There are many skillful apprentices, but few master workmen.

A *Week on the Concord and Merrimack Rivers* (1849), in *The Writings of Henry David Thoreau*, vol. 1, p. 129, Houghton Mifflin (1906).

See also LABOR

*W*ORLD, *THE*

I have seen how the foundations of the world are laid, and I have not the least doubt that it will stand a good while.

A Week on the Concord and Merrimack Rivers (1849), in *The Writings of Henry David Thoreau*, vol. 1, p. 182, Houghton Mifflin (1906).

This world is but canvas to our imaginations.

A Week on the Concord and Merrimack Rivers (1849), in *The Writings of Henry David Thoreau*, vol. 1, p. 310, Houghton Mifflin (1906).

See also IMAGINATION

*W*RITERS AND WRITING

This unlettered man's speaking and writing are standard English. Some words and phrases deemed vulgarisms and Americanisms before, he has made standard American; such as *"It will pay."* It suggests that the one great rule of composition—and if I were a professor of rhetoric I should insist on this—is, to *speak the truth*. This first, this second, this third; pebbles in your mouth or not. This demands earnestness and manhood chiefly.

"The Last Days of John Brown" (1860), in *The Writings of Henry David Thoreau*, vol. 4, pp. 447–448, Houghton Mifflin (1906).

See also LANGUAGE

A written word is the choicest of relics. It is something at once more intimate with us and more universal than any other work of art. It is the work of art nearest to life itself. It may be translated into every language, and not only be read but actually breathed from all human lips;—not be represented on canvas or in marble only, but be carved out of the breath of life itself. The symbol of an ancient man's thought becomes a modern man's speech.

Walden (1854), in *The Writings of Henry David Thoreau*, vol. 2, p. 114, Houghton Mifflin (1906).

See also LANGUAGE

However much we admire the orator's occasional bursts of eloquence, the noblest written words are commonly as far behind or above the fleeting spoken language as the firmament with its stars is behind the clouds.

Walden (1854), in *The Writings of Henry David Thoreau*, vol. 2, p. 113, Houghton Mifflin (1906).

I fear chiefly lest my expression may not be *extra-vagant* enough, may not wander far enough beyond the narrow limits of my daily experience, so as to be adequate to the truth of which I have been convinced.

Walden (1854), in *The Writings of Henry David Thoreau*, vol. 2, p. 357, Houghton Mifflin (1906).

See also EXPERIENCE

I feel as if my life had grown more outward when I can express it.

A Week on the Concord and Merrimack Rivers (1849), in *The Writings of Henry David Thoreau*, vol. 1, p. 351, Houghton Mifflin (1906).

The scholar may be sure that he writes the tougher truth for the calluses on his palms. They give firmness to the sentence. Indeed, the mind never makes a great and successful effort, without a corresponding energy of the body.

A Week on the Concord and Merrimack Rivers (1849), in *The Writings of Henry David Thoreau*, vol. 1, p. 109, Houghton Mifflin (1906).

See also LABOR